George Eliot

a reference guide
1972-1987

*A
Reference
Guide
to
Literature*

Alan D. Perlis
Editor

George Eliot

a reference guide
1972-1987

KAREN L. PANGALLO

G.K. HALL &CO.
70 LINCOLN STREET, BOSTON, MASS.

Library of Congress Cataloging-in-Publication Data

Pangallo, Karen L.
     George Eliot: a reference guide, 1972-1987/ Karen L. Pangallo.
        p. cm.-- (A Reference guide to literature)
     ISBN 0-8161-8973-0
     1. Eliot, George, 1819-1880--Bibliography. I. Title. II. Series.
Z8259.P36 1989
[PR4681]
016.823'8--dc20   89-35908
                                           CIP

This publication is printed on permanent/durable acid-free paper
MANUFACTURED IN THE UNITED STATES OF AMERICA

to

Salvatore, Dominick, and Matteo

with love and affection

Contents

The Author

Karen L. Pangallo is a reference librarian at the North Shore Community College – Lynn Campus, as well as a freelance indexer and bibliographer. She received her MLS from Simmons College and her BS from Salem State College. She resides in Salem, Massachusetts, with her husband, a teacher, and their two sons.

Preface

Arranged chronologically, the entries in this bibliography cover material concerning George Eliot – criticisms, analyses, reviews, biographies, and bibliographies – published between 1972 and 1987. The scope of this compilation is to trace modern response to Eliot's writing, particularly in regard to the growing body of literature that considers issues of feminism and women writers. One book that bears special mention, but was omitted from the bibliography due to conflicts concerning publishing dates, is Alan D. Perlis's *A Return to the Primal Self: Identity in the Fiction of George Eliot* (American University Studies, English Language and Literature Series 4, vol. 71. New York: Peter Lang, 1989). I read this book in manuscript form and its footnotes and bibliography were the springboard for my delve into George Eliot.

Sources of items in this bibliography were the standard indexes to literature, biography, social sciences, and humanities, and *Dissertations Abstracts International*. The *Bulletin of Bibliography*, *MLA International Bibliography of Books and Articles on the Modern Languages and Literatures*, *Abstracts of English Studies*, *The Annual Bibliography of English Language and Literature*, and bibliographies following journal articles and monographs were other avenues that led to this compilation. Foreign-language publications have been cited, but not always annotated. I have attempted to compile a complete bibliography of references to George Eliot and apologize for inadvertent omissions. I hope any omissions will spur further research.

I would like to acknowledge the enthusiastic support, guidance, and encouragement given me by Alan Perlis of the University of Alabama – Birmingham. I would also like to extend my appreciation to the librarians of North Shore Community College, Boston University, Salem State College, Gordon College, the University of Massachusetts – Amherst, Smith College, Amherst College, and the University of California at Los

Preface

Angeles. A most special thank you goes to all of my family for bearing with me through this project.

Introduction

The need for a bibliography that covers the last two decades of Eliot criticism is indeed great. Nearly all the dramatic changes occurring in literary criticism and theory have found their way into interpretations of Eliot's work, and to such a degree that it often seems as if a heretofore undiscovered author had stimulated the critical imagination. In the appropriate format one could use Eliot criticsm as the focal point for the lengthy examination of trends in post-new critical literary interpretation. She is simply not the same author that four generations of scholarly readers made her out to be.

Perhaps the culminating work of these earlier generations is F. R. Leavis's *The Great Tradition* (1948), which establishes once and for all Eliot's importance in the pantheon of Victorian fiction. Depicted by Leavis as the exemplar of Victorian moral values, Eliot became the subject of several significant moral inquiries in the fifties and sixties. Notable among these are Reva Stump's *Movement and Vision in George Eliot's Novels* (1959), Barbara Hardy's *The Novels of George Eliot: A Study in Form* (1959), Bernard J. Paris's *Experiments in Life: George Eliot's Quest for Values* (1965), U. C. Knoepflmacher's *Religious Humanism in the Victorian Novel*, and Hardy's collection of seminal essays in *Critical Essays on George Eliot* (1970). Two issues pervade these studies and define the character of Eliot criticism in general during the twenty-year period preceding the seventies: the destructive behavior of Eliot's egotistical characters – how they destroy their own lives and severely restrict the lives of others – and the necessary burden of moral vision and action in a world where every event has consequences, a burden that these egoists deny. The critical emphasis behind these issues is on Eliot's insistence on "fellow feeling" as the only appropriate human response to a world depicted as an "intricate web" of destructive circumstances.

The voice of the compassionate and insightful Mr. Irwine, the liberal clergyman in *Adam Bede*, seems to permeate the important studies of the fifties and sixties. When the would-be egoist Adam sets out to destroy Arthur Donnithorne for seducing Hetty Sorrel, Mr. Irwine argues that "Men's lives are as thoroughly blended with each other as the air they breathe; evil spreads as necessarily as disease." He urges Adam to restrain his desire for vengeance; in a world where every action contributes to an affective web of circumstance, understanding and self-control are the only moral responses. Our responsibility is to regard our fellow beings' actions with disinterest and equanimity, to see them in the broad context of a universal struggle against daunting circumstance. Mr. Irwine's richly developed ethical sensibility becomes the starting point for many scholarly examinations of Eliot's values.

Among the important Eliot critics and scholars of the seventies and eighties, Felicia Bonaparte has done the most to keep our attention on these moral issues. Her *Will and Destiny* (1975) explores the nature of Eliot's determinism and places it in the context of the tragic tradition. She examines those elements innate to character that conspire to shape an individual's destiny. Arguing, for example, that Arthur Donnithorne "is a remarkable study of the principle that determinism is self-created," she introduces him as "a man conspiring in his own moral corruption." Similarly, George Levine examines the web of circumstance as "George Eliot's hypothesis of reality" and investigates the ways in which character creates the seemingly external "reality" that later swallows it up. But while during the seventies Bonaparte, Levine, and others continued to map out the moral arena in which Eliot's fiction takes place, the preponderance of criticism takes on a rather different nature.

Perhaps the seeds of change can be found in Gordon Haight's (still definitive) biography of George Eliot (1968), or perhaps in his publication of the first of what would be nine volumes of Eliot's letters in 1954, a project Haight completed in 1978. Haight's biography differs from its forerunners principally in the intimacy he has for his subject. Eliot's "marriage" to George Henry Lewes receives its most thorough treatment, and is especially well developed in relation to the author's strained relationship with her demanding father. The biography, and the publication of a new volume of letters every three years, coincided with the rise of feminism and, in the seventies and eighties, contributed greatly to a new interest in Eliot's life as a remarkably independent woman. Her work ethic as a writer and thinker, her attitudes toward women, her anxieties over her own independence, her strained and ambivalent response to being a member of a community of writers, and her continual conflict with the values and character of her father and brother, become subjects for a great and commanding variety of books and articles.

Of special significance among these are Ruby Redinger's *The Emergent Self* (1975) and Laura Emery's *George Eliot's Creative Conflict* (1976).

Redinger views Eliot's novels as her means of re-evaluating her role in the confrontation with her father over religious issues, while Emery, and later Diane Sadoff in *Monsters of Affection* (1982), treat the novels as Eliot's principal means for fantasizing a healing of childhood wounds opened by loss and separation, which occur after Eliot's renunciation of the religious faith of her father. These books coincide not only with the rising feminist critical perspective and the new outpouring of gender studies, but also with the coming of age of psychobiography. The publication of Hélène Cixous's brilliant psychobiography, *The Exile of James Joyce* (1972), seems to have enabled biographers to reopen inquiry into authors' writings as expressions of personal events and the constellation of anxieties and neuroses the events produce. This chapter of literary history, begun by Freudian critics in the twenties and thirties, had been cut short by the overwhelming presence of New Criticism, and its emphasis on the formal aspects of literary works themselves. But the poststructuralist critical approaches of the seventies have enabled many important scholars to expand psychological inquiry to an unprecedented degree.

One work seems to stand out as the psychobiographic prototype of recent Eliot criticism: Sandra M. Gilbert and Susan Gubar's *The Madwoman in the Attic* (1979). Their chapter entitled "George Eliot as the Angel of Destruction" evaluates the "contradiction between feminine renunciation countenanced by the narrator [and a] female (even feminist) vengeance exacted by the author." Arguing that Eliot's alienation from the human community as a result of her denial of her father's religion and her relationship with George Henry Lewes left her in the position of a "fallen female," Gilbert and Gubar demonstrate how Eliot attacks from that perspective conventional male attitudes toward women's roles in society. They see Eliot's novels in part as the dramatization of "a struggle between the transcendent male and the immanent female." Jenni Calder, on the other hand, has argued in *Women and Marriage in Victorian Fiction* (1976) that Eliot essentially capitulated to male expectations that a woman's life must be one of limited aspiration. "Sadly," Calder writes, Eliot "does not commit herself fully to the energies and aspirations she let loose in [her female protagonists]. Does she not cheat them, and cheat us, ultimately, in allowing them so little? Does she not excite our interest through the breadth and challenge of the implications of her fiction, and then deftly dam up and fence round the momentum she has so powerfully created?" Similarly, Sadoff suggests that the daughter figure in Eliot's fiction "may become mired in the father's meaning and so herself never banish his shadow from her life." Within the context of feminist criticism, it would seem, a very creative conflict has emerged between those scholars such as Gilbert, Gubar, and Nina Auerbach (whose seven articles annotated in this bibliography comprise a confident and extensive treatment of Eliot's emergence from her father's influence) who see Eliot enjoying success in overcoming male dominance in her life and fiction, and Sadoff and Calder, who are less optimistic about the outcome of the author's struggle.

If in fact this conflict can be resolved, the point of resolution has yet to be found. Meanwhile, still other new critical methodologies have provided a richer understanding of Eliot's creative accomplishment. Studies in the fifties and sixties often concerned themselves with Eliot's perception of the moral responsibility the individual must have in order to play a role in social development. Paris sees this responsibility as the principal source of Eliot's creation of her characters: they evolve as individuated beings precisely as a result of their growing social consciousness. Calvin Bedient, on the other hand, in *Architects of the Self* (1972), sees Eliot's vision of a "social ideal of the self" as a critical flaw in her work: a kind of escape hatch that allows the author not to penetrate her characters through psychological observation. But the critical consensus in the seventies and eighties is that the social context of Eliot's work is so rich and complicated that historical, sociological, philosophical, and, perhaps most important, scientific events and discoveries, are intricately bound in the lives of Eliot's characters, and that society and individual are inextricably convolved into something larger than character itself: character as history. The idea lying beneath this seeming hyperbole is that, among English novelists of her age, Eliot possessed the deepest understanding of social and scientific trends and that her genius as a witness of contemporary life speaks powerfully in her fiction.

The books and articles that consider this understanding comprise a significant example of new historicism, which is another element of the revolt against the formalist limitations of New Criticism. One of the most compelling of these studies is Mary Wilson Carpenter's "The Apocalypse of the Old Testament: *Daniel Deronda* and the Interpretation of Interpretation," *PMLA* (1984), which attempts to unite the seemingly disparate narratives of Daniel and Gwendolen Harleth by arguing that this double aspect resembles the "prophetic structure of Jewish History. Gwendolen's narrative represents the English, or Christian, stream of history, Daniel's the Jewish...." Carpenter's argument is based on what she feels is Eliot's expansive and subtle understanding of an emerging Zionist movement and implies that among non-Jewish authors, she had the fullest grasp of the Anglo-Jewish sensibility. Moreover, "The Apocalypse of the Old Testament" demonstrates the usefulness of deconstructive criticism for breaking down previously assumed polarities in the narrative structure of Eliot's fiction by employing Derridean "differance" to account for the subtle interplay of Christian and Jewish versions of revelation. Set against *The Great Tradition*, with its confident claim that narrative structures are fully purposive and, in the case of *Daniel Deronda*, are not only divided but aesthetically divisive, Carpenter's work establishes an entirely new reading of the novel, based on recent theories of intertextuality.

In other studies, Eliot is found to have had heretofore unrevealed knowledge of several areas of contemporary study. While books and articles in the fifties and sixties tended on the whole to assume that the author had an intimate relation to and knowledge of Comtean positivism, more recent studies (probably following Haight's lead) downplay this connection and instead focus on her apparently subtle awareness of trends in contemporary science, especially Darwinian theory and cell physiology. In *George Eliot and Nineteenth-Century Science* (1984), for example, Sally Shuttleworth contends that Eliot carefully studied theories of organicism that grew out of the Darwinian revolution and was able to integrate those theories into the plots of her novels. Gillian Beer, in *Darwin's Plots* (1983), examines with even greater specificity the extent of Eliot's scientific background and argues that Eliot's plots recapitulate Darwinian evolution both in terms of how characters develop and how the author's often labyrinthine fictional circumstances resemble the phylogenic development of biological species. In her treatment of *Daniel Deronda*, she contends that the novelist's "vision of the future" is based on a scientific model of biological evolution and has Huxley and Darwin as its principal sources. My own recently published *In Search of the Primal Self: Identity in the Fiction of George Eliot* (1989) argues that Tertius Lydgate's search for the primitive tissue that unites all of organic life's forms in *Middlemarch* stems from Eliot's own research into early experiments in cell physiology and from her study of the speeches and essays of Thomas Henry Huxley.

What each of these studies has in common is the assumption that Eliot, who knew most of England's intellectual luminaries of her time, was committed to developing a rich knowledge of the climate in which she lived. One could argue, I think, that most studies of Eliot's work prior to the seventies focused on establishing her position as a great writer by pointing to the universality and the profoundly moral character of her themes. If there is a single dramatic change in the direction of the scholarship, it has been toward establishing the social and the personal context in which the novels were written. Twenty years ago we may have known nearly as much as we do today about the writer's aesthetic and the themes she hoped to convey; but the past twenty years of scholarship have vastly increased our awareness both of how Eliot was a product and a shaper of her times and how she used her characters to work out the traumatic elements both in the psychodrama of her own life and in the sadly constrained lives of Victorian women.

Alan D. Perlis

Writings by George Eliot

Novels

Scenes of Clerical Life (Edinburgh, 1858)
Adam Bede (Edinburgh, 1859)
The Mill on the Floss (Edinburgh, 1860)
Silas Marner, The Waever of Raveloe (Edinburgh, 1861)
Romola (London, 1863)
Felix Holt, the Radical (Edinburgh, 1866)
Middlemarch: A Study of Provincial Life (Edinburgh, 1871-1872)
Daniel Deronda (Edinburgh, 1876)

Novellas

"The Lifted Veil" (1859)
"Brother Jacob" (1864)

Poetry

The Spanish Gypsy: A Poem (Edinburgh, 1868)
Brother and Sister (1869)
How Lisa Loved the King (Boston, 1869)
The Legend of Jubal and Other Poems (Edinburgh, 1874)
Complete Poems (1889)

Essays

Impressions of Theophrastus Such (Edinburgh, 1879)
Essays and Leaves From a Notebook (Edinburgh, 1884)
Early Essays (London, 1919)

Translations

The Life of Jesus Critically Examined, by David Friedrich Strauss (London, 1846)
The Essence of Christianity, by Ludwig Feuerbach (London, 1854)
Ethics, by Benedict de Spinoza (London, 1855)
Tractatus Theologico-Politicus, by Benedict de Spinoza (Hamburg, 1670)

Collections

The Novels. 6 vols. (Edinburgh, 1867-78)
The Works. Cabinet Edition. 20 vols. (Edinburgh, 1878-80)
The Complete Poetical Works (New York, 1888)
The Complete Poems, ed. M. Brown (Boston, 1888)
The Works. Warwick Edition. 12 vols. (Edinburgh, 1901-3)
The Works. 21 vols. (London, 1908-11)

Writings about George Eliot, 1972-1987

1972

1 ALLEY, HENRY MELTON. "*Middlemarch* and *Daniel Deronda*: Heroes of Erudition and Experience." Ph.D dissertation, Cornell University, 239 pp.

Examines Eliot's method of manipulating the reader's memory and creating an atmosphere of recollection between the characters of *Middlemarch* and *Daniel Deronda* and the reader. See *Dissertations Abstracts International* 32, no. 8 (1972):4552A.

2 BAKER, WILLIAM. "George Eliot's Readings in Nineteenth-Century Jewish Historians: A Note on the Background of *Daniel Deronda*." *Victorian Studies*, no. 4 (June):463-73.

Surveys Eliot's use of her readings of nineteenth-century Jewish historians – Abraham Geiger, Zunz, Jost, Sachs, Munk, Heinrich Graetz, Delitzsch, and Steinschneider – in the novel *Daniel Deronda*.

3 BAROLINI, HELEN. "George Eliot as Mary Ann Cross." *South Atlantic Quarterly* 71, no. 3 (Summer):292-306.

Examines the elements of ambiguity and respectability in Eliot's marriage and relationship to John Cross. Considers her motives for marrying a man twenty years her junior.

4 BEDIENT, CALVIN. *Architects of the Self: George Eliot, D.H. Lawrence, and E.M. Forster*. Berkeley: University of California Press, 275 pp.

1972

Presents the problems Eliot, Forster, and Lawrence faced in presenting a new ideal of the self. Analyzes Eliot's ideal of the social self and how it conflicts with the demands of egoism.

5 _____. "George Eliot and D.H. Lawrence: Either/Or." In *Architects of the Self: George Eliot, D.H. Lawrence, and E.M. Forster*. Berkeley: University of California Press, pp. 98-111.

Compares and contrasts Eliot with D.H. Lawrence. Finds that "Eliot belongs to an ethical but not to a religious tradition, and Lawrence belongs to a religious but not to an ethical tradition."

6 _____. "*Middlemarch*: Touching Down." In *Architects of the Self: George Eliot, D.H. Lawrence and E.M. Forster*. Berkeley: University of California Press, pp. 80-97.

Examines the literary realism of *Middlemarch* and why it is an essential element of what is considered Eliot's greatest work. Analyzes the novel's commitment to truth and doomed idealism.

7 _____. "The Radicalism of Virtue." In *Architects of the Self: George Eliot, D.H. Lawrence, and E.M. Forster*. Berkeley: University of California Press, pp. 70-79.

Analyzes the theme of the varying degrees of virtue in *Felix Holt, the Radical*. Argues that Eliot fails to convey compassion and moral recognition.

8 _____. "The Social Self." In *Architects of the Self: George Eliot, D.H. Lawrence, and E.M. Forster*. Berkeley: University of California Press, pp. 33-69.

"George Eliot's characteristic subject is the necessary submission of individuals to their own society . . . and this submission is to be made not so much in the interest of this or that society as in the general interest of the socialization of the self. For her, any society is preferable to the explosive egoism of the individual. Society's function is to contain man. . . . The essence of George Eliot's fiction is a mixture of moral caution and a strong sentiment of sociality."

9 BELL, SRILEKHA. "George Eliot: A Study in the Intellectual Development of Her Novels." Ph.D. dissertation, University of Wisconsin, 232 pp.

Discusses the differences in thematic purpose and content of Eliot's novels written before 1861 and those written after 1861. This division at this time period reflects changes in ideas in biology and evolution as well as a result of Darwin's *Origin of Species*. Eliot's novels written before 1861 express her belief in an inner force that directs people to their predestined goals. Novels written after 1861 deal with changes in the inabilities of individuals to provide solutions to problems caused by society and forces those individuals to become aware of the limitations of social models of ideal behavior. See *Dissertations Abstracts International* 32, no. 12 (1972):6918A.

10   BERLE, LINA WRIGHT. *George Eliot and Thomas Hardy: A Contrast*. Folcroft, Penn.: Folcroft Library Editions, 174 pp. Orig. pub. New York: Mitchell Kennerley, 1917.
        Contrasts the humanitarianism of Thomas Hardy with the rational idealism of Eliot. Portrays Hardy as the romantic decadent in his attitude toward life and literature. Portrays Eliot as a humanitarian willing to take a "radical position in a crisis rather than abandon a principle to convention."

11   BOLSTAD, R. MONTELLE. "The Myth of Sensibility in George Eliot." *Recovering Literature* 1, no. 2 (Fall):26-39.
        Criticizes Eliot's themes of duty, self-sacrifice and self-transcendence in *Daniel Deronda* and *Middlemarch*.

12   BRADLEY, ANTHONY GERARD. "Pastoral in the Novels of George Eliot." Ph.D. dissertation, State University of New York at Buffalo, 140 pp.
        Demonstrates Eliot's distinct version of pastoral in the novels *Adam Bede, The Mill on the Floss, Silas Marner*, and *Middlemarch*. Eliot's affinities to the realism and ethical elements of Virgil's *Georgics*. "The structure of pastoral involves putting relatively complex ideas into an apparently simple representation of the rustic." Considers Eliot's ethical idealism and the inspiration of Comte and Feuerbach in her perceptions of the secular religion of humanity. See *Dissertations Abstracts International* 33, no. 8 (1973): 4334A.

13   BREWSTER, JACK. "The Virtuous Heroes of the English Novel." Ph.D. dissertation, Indiana University, 388 pp.
        Analyzes Daniel Deronda and Adam Bede as heroic and virtuous characters. These characters adhere to the value system of Eliot and exhibit a "high degree of internal equilibrium." See *Dissertations Abstracts International* 32, no. 8 (1972):4601A.

1972

14 BROWNING, OSCAR. *The Life of George Eliot*. Port Washington, N.Y., and London: Kennikat Press, 188 pp. Orig. pub. London: Walter Scott, 1890.
   Biography and account of Eliot's undertaking the role of novelist. Takes many references from Cross's *Life and Letters of George Eliot*, as well as the author's personal relationship with Eliot.

15 BUCKLER, WILLIAM E. "Memory, Morality, and the Tragic Vision in the Early Novels of George Eliot." In *The English Novel in the Nineteenth-Century: Essays on the Literary Mediation of Human Values*. Edited by George Goodin. Urbana: University of Illinois Press, pp. 145-63.
   Examines Eliot's use of memory in *Silas Marner, Adam Bede*, and *The Mill on the Floss*, as a device for characterization and for illustration of the conflicts in the values of love, belief, and loyalty. Memory was Eliot's means for making the moralist relevant and for arbitrating between the idea of tragedy of character and tragedy of circumstance. The use of memory allows Eliot's characters to measure their lives against history.

16 BYRD, SCOTT. "The Fractured Crystal in *Middlemarch* and *The Golden Bowl*." *Modern Fiction Studies* 18, no. 4 (Winter):551-54.
   Cites Eliot's influence on Henry James's *The Golden Bowl*. The image of fractured crystal from *Middlemarch* is used by James as a central symbol in his novel. In both instances, the flawed crystal is representative of a flawed marriage.

17 COVENEY, PETER. Introduction to *Felix Holt, the Radical*. Harmondsworth, Eng.: Penguin Books, pp. 7-65.
   Treats the struggle Eliot underwent in writing *Felix Holt, the Radical* - "as with all novels written *a these*, too much derives from the idea and too little from the awareness of a novelist." Examines Eliot's sometimes successful fusion of social and psychological interests and elements of tragedy in the novel.

18 DAVIS, NORMA JEAN. "Pictorialism in George Eliot's Art." Ph.D. dissertation, Northwestern University, 284 pp.
   Discusses Eliot's use of literary pictorialism and how it was influenced by Dutch, English, and Italian architecture as well as landscape- and portrait-painting. Analyzes the heroic-mythic landscape painting in *Adam Bede* and the picturesque landscapes in *The Mill on*

the Floss and *Romola*. George Eliot's verbal paintings express the narrator's moral vision. See *Dissertations Abstracts International* 33, no. 10 (1973):5673A.

19 DEEGAN, THOMAS. "George Eliot's Novels of the Historical Imagination." *CLIO* 1, no. 3 (June):21-33.

Eliot's novels of the historical imagination–*Scenes of Clerical Life*, *Adam Bede*, *The Mill on the Floss*, *Felix Holt, the Radical*, *Middlemarch*, and *Romola*–demonstrate the relation between historical public events and the private lives of the characters. Eliot embodies her theory of the historical novel in *Middlemarch*, where she combines the idea of reform in history and fiction.

20 DeGROOT, ELIZABETH M. "*Middlemarch* and Dorothea Brooke: The Saints Go Marching Out." *Christianity and Literature* 22, no. 1 (Fall):13-18.

Examines the impossibility of Dorothea's attainment of sainthood. Finds that Eliot could not develop this theme adequately and thus put women in the throes of spiritual mediocrity.

21 DUNHAM, ROBERT HANCOCK. "Wordsworthian Themes and Attitudes in George Eliot's Novels." Ph.D. dissertation, Stanford University, 252 pp.

Describes Wordsworthian precepts in Eliot's fiction. In discussing Wordsworth's poetry, Dunham draws parallels to *The Mill on the Floss*, *Adam Bede*, and *Silas Marner*. Both authors attempt to present a fuller picture of the every day world and to stimulate personal memory and natural moral impulses. See *Dissertations Abstracts International* 32, no. 10 (1972): 5734A.

22 EDWARDS, LEE R. "Women, Energy, and *Middlemarch*." *Massachusetts Review* 13, nos. 1-2 (Winter-Spring): 223-38. Reprint. *Woman: An Issue*, edited by Lee R. Edwards, Mary Heath, and Lisa Baskin (Boston: Little, Brown & Co., 1972), pp. 223-38.

Examines the motives of a woman critic moved by life's experiences to analyze women and energy in *Middlemarch*. Examines the structure of the book as well as its tragic/comic modes and characters. Considers how Dorothea and Rosamond handle internal energy in combination with society's conventions.

1972

23   EDWARDS, MICHAEL. "A Reading of *Adam Bede*." *Critical Quarterly* 14, no. 3 (Autumn):205-18.
Considers *Adam Bede* with an emphasis on the characterization of Dinah Morris. Studies Dinah's language, poetry within the novel, use of imagery, and the tragic structure.

24   ELSBREE, LANGDON. "The Purest and Most Perfect Form of Play: Some Novelists and the Dance." *Criticism* 14, no. 4 (Fall):361-72.
Analyzes and compares the function of the dance in the novels of Eliot, Jane Austen, Thomas Hardy, and D.H. Lawrence. Gives particular attention to the English country-dance. In Eliot, "the dance is a synecdoche of the pattern of relationships that constitute a society and the degree of freedom an individual thinks he has."

25   EVANS, C.F.H. "George Eliot's Maternal Ancestry." *Notes & Queries* 19 (November):409-16.
Traces the ancestry of Christiana Pearson Evans, the mother of George Eliot.

26   FERNANDO, LLOYD. "Special Pleading and Art in *Middlemarch*: The Relations between the Sexes." *Modern Language Review* 67, no. 1 (January):44-49.
Examines the relations of the sexes in *Middlemarch*; in particular, sees Dorothea and Lydgate as a pair instead of as contrasted individuals. The gap in their relationship is the "locus of a creatively balanced inter-play of character and of an organic extension of theme."

27   FRIEDBERG, JOAN BREST. "Tragedy in George Eliot and Thomas Hardy." Ph.D. dissertation, University of Pittsburgh, 124 pp.
Emphasizes the tragic narrative and analyzes its elements: tone, ending, distance, approach of the characters to moral values, relation of the characters to fate and destiny, tension, tragic impetus, and the effects of self-knowledge and self-recognition in *Daniel Deronda, The Mill on the Floss*, and *Middlemarch*. Eliot makes tragedy the result of the "interaction of circumstance and character." In contrast, Hardy focuses tragedy on the central character. Eliot tends toward Judaic tragedy whereas Hardy belongs to the tradition of Hellenic tragedy. See *Dissertations Abstracts International* 33, no. 3 (1972):1141A.

1972

28   *George Eliot Fellowship Review.* Edited by Kathleen Adams and Graham Handley. Coventry, Eng.: George Eliot Fellowship.

   Published irregularly since 1971. Includes President's message, book reviews, and essays of historical interest to those interested in Eliot's personal life.

29   GILLIE, CHRISTOPHER. *Longman Companion to English Literature.* London: Longman Group, pp. 171-76, 208-9, 211, 496-97.

   The first essay discusses science and the humanist skeptics, with an emphasis on Charles Hennell's influence on George Eliot. The second essay examines village relationships and country life depicted in *Adam Bede* and *Silas Marner*. Maggie Tulliver's tragedy in *The Mill on the Floss* illustrates the role of womanhood and the constraints on the free development of the original spirit. In *Daniel Deronda*, Eliot makes the marriage of Gwendolen Harleth a test of the "great society's" values and reveals those values as being illusive and static. Includes a brief biography of Eliot and a chronology of her writing and its development.

30   GOLDSBERRY, DENNIS MERRILL. "George Eliot's Use of the Tragic Mode." Ph.D. dissertation, University of North Carolina at Chapel Hill, 134 pp.

   Discusses the tragic mode in *Adam Bede*, *The Mill on the Floss*, *Romola*, and *Middlemarch*. Eliot's universally tragic viewpoint is illustrated by examples from these novels. Emphasizes the "interrelationship of form to theme." Eliot often uses images of light, blindness, and sight to symbolize the progression of the main characters from error to sympathy. See *Dissertations Abstracts International* 34, no. 1 (1973): 273A.

31   GOTTFRIED, LEON. "Structure and Genre in *Daniel Deronda*." In *The English Novel in the Nineteenth Century: Essays on the Literary Mediation of Human Values*. Edited by George Goodin. Urbana: University of Illinois Press, pp. 164-75.

   Studies the structure and genre of *Daniel Deronda* in an attempt to prove that Eliot's purpose in writing was to "poeticize the novel." Eliot meant to present the novel as an art form that contained myth and poetry in order to make the "world of the higher imagination available to modern man." Examines the use of double plotting, heroic myths, the problem of unity, and the elements of romance.

1972

32   GROSSMAN, RICHARD HENRY. "Drama and Background in George Eliot's *Scenes of Clerical Life*." Ph.D. dissertation, University of California, San Diego, 244 pp.

Considers "Amos Barton" as a "tragedy of nature and history, of private life and public life." Reviews Eliot's use of prosaic and poetic language and her organization of narrative modes. "Mr. Gilfil's Love Story" is a tragedy of nature and prophecy of history. The story's poetic drama is compared to *The Winter's Tale*. Ambiguities in the setting of "Janet's Repentence" are discussed. See *Dissertations Abstracts International* 33, no. 10 (1973):5679A.

33   HAGAN, JOHN. "A Re-Interpretation of *The Mill on the Floss*." *PMLA* 87, no. 1 (January):53-63.

Refutes interpretations of *The Mill on the Floss* that the author claims distort the novel's emphasis and oversimplify Eliot's purpose. Eliot sought to present Maggie Tulliver's defeat as stemming from desires for a richer life and her ties to Tom Tulliver, which "makes her renunciation of those desires morally necessary."

34   HAIGHT, GORDON S. "New George Eliot Letters to John Blackwood." *Times Literary Supplement* (London), 10 March, p. 281-82.

Publication of eight letters from Eliot to her publisher, John Blackwood, including some biographical commentary.

35   HALL, MARGARET MILLER. "Modes of Narrative Irony: A Reading of *Middlemarch* and *Madame Bovary*." Ph.D. dissertation. University of Virginia, 158 pp.

Explores how irony functions in *Middlemarch* and Flaubert's *Madame Bovary*. For Eliot, irony has a didactic purpose. For Flaubert, irony is mimetic. See *Dissertations Abstracts International* 32, no. 8 (1972):4564A.

36   HALPERIN, JOHN. "The Language of Meditation: Four Studies in Nineteenth-Century Fiction." Ph.D. dissertation, Johns Hopkins University, 208 pp.

Comparative analysis of the meditation scenes of Jane Austen, George Eliot, George Meredith, and Henry James that assesses these authors' concepts of the operation of the human mind: how preconditioned psychological attitudes contribute to the shaping of ideas. See *Dissertations Abstracts International* 32, no. 12 (1972):6976A. See also 1973.27.

1972

37 HENKLE, DAVID CLARK. "Nietzsche and the Victorians." Ph.D. dissertation, Kent State University, 211 pp.

Presents Nietzsche's views on George Eliot, John Stuart Mill, Jeremy Bentham, Charles Darwin, and Thomas Carlyle. "Eliot, for Nietzsche, was a moralistic female who surrendered God but could not give up her evangelisitic, Christian morality." See *Dissertations Abstracts International* 32, no. 9 (1972):5185A.

38 HIGDON, DAVID LEON. "Eliot's *Daniel Deronda*, Chapter 36." *Explicator* 31, no. 3 (November): Item 15.

Cites similarities in the actions of the characters Lydia, Grandcourt, and Gwendolen with those of the characters in the myth of Medea—Medea, Jason, and Creusa.

39 ____. "The Iconographic Backgrounds of *Adam Bede*, Chapter 15." *Nineteenth-Century Fiction* 27, no. 2 (September):155-70.

A "comparison of the metaphors, objects, and scenic design of *Adam Bede*, chapter 15, a major scene contrasting the egoist and the altruist, with similar scenes in the 'pious literature' establishes a clear influence if indeed not a direct source in Francis Quarles's *Emblem* III, 14."

40 HOLLAND, JOHN GILL. "George Eliot's *Daniel Deronda* with Particular Consideration of the Jewish Element." Ph.D. dissertation, University of North Carolina at Chapel Hill, 346 pp.

Analyzes Judaism as a literary theme in *Daniel Deronda*. Discusses the structure of the two story lines; the significance of coincidence; theater, music, and gambling imagery; and Eliot's didactic realism. Includes a survey of contemporary and critical reviews as well as a synopsis of Eliot's studies in Judaism. See *Dissertations Abstracts International* 33, no. 4 (1972):1727A.

41 HORNBACK, BERT G. "The Moral Imagination of George Eliot." *Papers on Language and Literature* 8, no. 4 (Fall):380-94.

Explores the nature of feeling in *Middlemarch* and the development of sympathy for fellows by the combination of rational knowledge and emotional experience. Dorothea's and Will Ladislaw's marriage is the joining of moral and aesthetic realism. The central theme of the Dorothea sections of the novel is self-transcendence, whereas Ladislaw represents philosophical and aesthetic values.

1972

42   HOROWITZ, LENORE WISNEY. "Present, Past, and Future: The Vision of Society in George Eliot's Novels." Ph.D. dissertation, Cornell University, 268 pp.

Examines "Eliot's experimentation with setting, with types and combinations of characters, with plot, and with such conventions of resolution as marriage and inheritance." Discusses Eliot's views of society. See *Dissertations Abstracts International* 32, no. 8 (1972): 4567A.

43   JACKSON, ARLENE M. "*Daniel Deronda* and the Victorian Search for Identity." *Studies in the Humanities* 3, no. 1 (October):25-30.

In *Daniel Deronda* "George Eliot wished to present her concept of the New Man, product of an age of increasing disorder. Deronda's particular response to modernism is a weakness or vacillation of will, and it is precisely this deficiency, its causes and possible consequences, that George Eliot understood as a most serious danger to the Victorian man. Daniel Deronda is a Victorian in search of a literal, familial identity, but this search also has psychological and social dimensions and is closely related to George Eliot's theory of separateness with communication."

44   KEATING, P.J. *The Working Classes in Victorian Fiction*. London: Routledge & Kegan Paul, pp. 26, 132, 136, 138, 227, 229-31, 246, 247, passim. Orig. pub. London: Routledge & Kegan Paul, 1971.

Examines, particularly in *Felix Holt, the Radical*, how the industrial working class in England during the years 1820 to 1900 is presented in literature. How *Felix Holt, the Radical* was written in response to agitation for working-class enfranchisement in the 1860s. Felix Holt is presented as a working-class intellectual, but the plot places the novel in the working-class romance genre of fiction.

45   KENDA, MARGARET ELIZABETH MASON. "Poetic Justice in the Novels of George Eliot and William Makepeace Thackeray." Ph.D. dissertation, University of Iowa, 238 pp.

Examines Eliot's and Thackeray's belief that poetic justice was a sentimental cliché. Nevertheless, both authors employed it to some degree. "For George Eliot, poetic justice was realistic to the degree of her belief in a moral growth within nature toward a supreme truth that will achieve universal empire and assure the eventual downfall of error. The result in George Eliot's work is that punishment and reward are generally the result of failure or success in the struggle to grow toward sympathy with that general law." See *Dissertations Abstracts International* 32, no. 9 (1972):5232A.

46 McMASTER, JULIET. "*Middlemarch* Centennial Conference. Held at the University of Calgary and The Banff School of Fine Arts, 9-11 Sept. 1971." *Victorian Studies* 15, no. 3 (March):387-89.

Synopsis of papers presented by David Carroll, U.C. Knoepflmacher, and Jerome Beaty at the *Middlemarch* Centennial.

47 MANLEY, SEON, and BELCHER, SUSAN. *O' Those Extraordinary Women! or The Joys of Literary Lib*. Philadelphia: Chilton Book Co., pp. 193-99.

Discussion of Eliot's early life and depiction of her as the first truly modern novelist and as an agnostic. Emphasizes Eliot's need for intellectual expression, and the influence of John Chapman, Herbert Spencer, and George H. Lewes.

48 MANN, KAREN LOUISE B. "Definition Through Form: The Embodiment of George Eliot's Beliefs in the Early Novels." Ph.D. dissertation, University of Pennsylvania, 236 pp.

Examines Eliot's fiction, from *Scenes of Clerical Life* through *Silas Marner*, for her presentation of the elements of pain, relief, love and sorrow. These early novels are examples of Eliot's ability to balance the powers of the imagination with the laws of cause and effect. See *Dissertations Abstracts International* 32, no. 12 (1972):6986A.

49 MARTIN, BRUCE K. "Rescue and Marriage in *Adam Bede*." *Studies in English Literature, 1500-1900*, 12, no. 4 (Autumn):745-63.

Adam Bede concerns itself with Adam's "acquisition of sympathy. The story of Arthur serves as a subplot, to induce behavior in Adam indicative of his moral state, and to create through the crisis involving Hetty, an inescapable condition of suffering, from which his reversal of character can arise. . . ." The rescue of Hetty and marriage to Dinah change Adam.

50 _____. "Similarity within Dissimilarity: The Dual Structure of *Silas Marner*." *Texas Studies in Literature and Language* 14, no. 3 (Fall):479-89.

"An examination of Silas Marner and Godfrey Cass in terms of both similar and dissimilar characteristics to reveal a dimension of structural integrity in the novel. Eliot uses Godfrey as both parallel and

1972

foil to Silas, to universalize certain assumptions about the moral nature and needs of man, while suggesting the varied outcomes of human endeavor."

51   MASON, KENNETH MARCENIUS, Jr. "George Eliot and the Question of Tragic Redemption: A Study of Imaginative Sympathy in *The Mill on the Floss* and *Daniel Deronda*." Ph.D. dissertation, Cornell University, 139 pp.

"*The Mill on the Floss* and *Daniel Deronda* are examined together because Maggie Tulliver and Gwendolen Harleth represent George Eliot's two most comprehensive attempts to focus on the development of a tragic heroine." An analysis of the symbolic pattern of harvest in *The Mill on the Floss* reveals Maggie's imaginative energy and longing. The narrative strategy of *Daniel Deronda* involves Eliot's incorporation of the idea of redemption. See *Dissertations Abstracts International* 33, no. 10 (1973):5735A.

52   MOTTRAM, WILLIAM. *True Story of George Eliot in Relation to Adam Bede, Giving the Real Life History of the More Prominent Characters*. New York: Haskell House, 307 pp. Orig. pub. 1907.

Traces the real-life story of the sources for characters of *Adam Bede*.

53   MUDGE, ISADORE G., and SEARS, M.E., comps. *A George Eliot Dictionary: The Characters and Scenes of the Novels, Stories, and Poems Alphabetically Arranged*. New York: Haskell House, 260 pp. Orig pub. London: George Routledge & Sons; New York: H.W. Wilson, 1924.

Dictionary of characters and place names. Includes a chronological list and synopses of works, as well as a list of books read by Eliot's characters.

54   NICOLL, W. ROBERTSON. Introduction to *The Mill on the Floss*. London: J.M. Dent & Sons; New York: Dutton, pp. v-xi. Orig. pub. 1908.

Discusses contemporary reviews of *The Mill on the Floss* and Eliot's response to criticism. Reviews examine three areas of the novels – auto-biography; an observation on English family life; and the degradation of Maggie in the Stephen Guest episodes.

55   PARRINDER, PATRICK. "The Look of Sympathy: Communication and Moral Purpose in the Realistic Novel." *Novel* 5, no. 2 (Winter):135-47.

Cites Eliot's essay "The Natural History of German Life" and applies her theory of realism and moral philosophy to art. Eliot perceives the active moral function of sympathy and altruism as the artist's or novelist's task.

56   PECK, SUSAN COOLIDGE. "George Eliot's Development as a Psychological Novelist." Ph.D. dissertation, University of Wisconsin, 256 pp.

Considers *Adam Bede*, *The Mill on the Floss*, *Silas Marner*, *Middlemarch*, and *Daniel Deronda* as psychological novels. Assumes there is a "natural evolution from religious to moral to psychological explanations in nineteenth-century thought." Attempts to trace Eliot's development along those lines. See *Dissertations Abstracts International* 32, no. 12 (1972):6997A.

57   REISEN, DIANA MARY COHART. "Pilgrims of Mortality: The Quest for Identity in the Novels of George Eliot." Ph.D. dissertation, Columbia University, 284 pp.

Discussion of Eliot's insights about individuals and their attempt to develop a sense of identity. In the novels *Adam Bede*, *The Mill on the Floss*, *Middlemarch*, and *Daniel Deronda*, Eliot explores English values concerning women, money, and work and how these values molded its citizens. Throughout these works, Eliot uses the ideas of conformity and nonconformity, patterns of personal relationship, and the need for self-generated power in determining identity formation. See *Dissertations Abstracts International* 35, no. 10 (1975):6730A.

58   REISHMAN, JOHN VINCENT, II. "Six Moral Fables: A Study of the Redemptive Vision in George Eliot's Short Fiction." Ph.D. dissertation, University of Virginia, 172 pp.

Classifies six of Eliot's early novels as moral fables and products of an agnostic imagination. In *Silas Marner*, "Brother Jacob," *The Lifted Veil*, "Janet's Repentence," "Mr. Gilfil's Love Story," and "The Sad Fortunes of the Reverend Amos Barton," the most distinctive feature is the allegorical character, who is the extension of the form of the fable. See *Dissertations Abstracts International* 32, no. 8 (1972): 4577A.

1972

59 SANTANGELO, GENNARO A. "Villari's Life and Times of Savonarola: A Source for George Eliot's *Romola*." *Anglia* (Tübingen) 90, no. 1-2:118-31.

Traces sources for *Romola* – Eliot's interest in Italy, the book *La Storia di Girolamo Savonarola* by Pasquale Villari (1859), and Eliot's own moral vision.

60 SCOTT, JAMES E. "George Eliot, Positivism, and the Social Vision of *Middlemarch*." *Victorian Studies* 16, no. 1 (September):59-76.

Examines how Eliot's attitude toward Postivism is central to the structure and character analysis of *Middlemarch* and how it allowed Eliot fictionally to evaluate the Comtean view of social change.

61 SKYE, JUNE. "George Eliot and St. Peter's." *Notes and Queries*, n.s. 19, no. 7 (July):263-64.

Corrects Gordon S. Haight's errors in *George Eliot: A Biography* (1968), in reference to Eliot's description of St. Peter's in *Middlemarch* and the use of liturgical color. In fact, Eliot's description is correct and in accordance with formalities of the Roman Catholic Church.

62 STONE, DONALD DAVID. *Novelists in a Changing World: Meredith, James, and the Transformation of English Fiction in the 1880's*. Cambridge, Mass.: Harvard University Press, pp. 209-13, passim.

Relates historical and philosophical transformations of the 1880s to novels written during that period. Contrasts Henry James and George Eliot as novelists of motive and character analysis rather than of action. Discusses the artistic purpose of James, the ethical purpose of Eliot, and Eliot's influence on James.

63 STRAUSS, DAVID FRIEDRICH. *The Life of Jesus Critically Examined*. Translated by George Eliot. Edited and with an introduction by Peter C. Hodgson. Lives of Jesus Series. Philadelphia: Fortress Press, 812 pp.

George Eliot's 1846 translation includes a critical introduction, bibliographies, annotations, and prefaces to all four German editions. In the introduction, aspects of Eliot's life and her work as a translator are given.

1972

64 SULLIVAN, WILLIAM J. "Piero di Cosimo and the Higher Primitivism in *Romola*." *Nineteenth-Century Fiction* 26, no. 4 (March):390-405.

Piero di Cosimo, the artist in *Romola*, is an actual historical figure whom Eliot uses to embody her aesthetics and to shed light on the moral and philosophical values of Florence, Italy, during the Renaissance. Piero is a primitive within a highly sophisticated culture, whose character suggests a basic naturalness as contrast to the artificiality of his environment.

65 ____. "The Sketch of the Three Masks in *Romola*." *Victorian Newsletter* 41 (Spring):9-13.

Piero di Cosimo's sketch of the Three Masks is analyzed for its contribution to the novel's structure and theme.

66 SWANN, BRIAN. "George Eliot and the Play: Symbol and Metaphor of the Drama in *Daniel Deronda*." *Dalhousie Review* 52, no. 2 (Summer):191-202.

Examines how Eliot uses the theatre as symbolism and metaphor in *Daniel Deronda*, to discriminate ways of regarding the self. The theme of drama is the involvement of people within society; dramatic representation is also an escape. "In *Daniel Deronda*, the further a character gets from the stage the nearer he approaches the true tone of sincere feeling."

67 ____. "*Middlemarch*: Realism and Symbolic Form." *ELH* 39, no. 2 (June):279-308.

Examines historical realism of *Middlemarch* and the scenes of the novel "which might be called symbolic embodiments, since they imbue naturalistic incidents with thematic or symbolic will to stature." Analysis of symbolic acts, gestures, and character as symbol.

68 TEMPLIN, CHARLOTTE HELENE. "The Treatment of Community in the Novels of George Eliot." Ph.D. dissertation, Indiana University, 186 pp.

Eliot's writing is characterized by her "attempt to imagine beneficent community life." Early novels are concerned with "what the individual can do to find self-fulfillment in an already established community with admirable community values." Later novels deal with the "strategies the individual must undertake to promote or create a community which

1972

makes self-fulfillment possible." See *Dissertations Abstracts International* 33, no. 10 (1973):5753A.

69   THOMSON, FRED C. "Politics and Society in *Felix Holt.*" In *The Classic British Novel.* Edited by Howard M. Harper and Charles Edge. Athens: University of Georgia Press, pp. 103-20.
      Discusses the conservative social and political opinions expressed in *Felix Holt, the Radical.* "Placid resistance to change, this gradual transition in mores, just keeping pace with individual enlightenment, is, as George Eliot implies, the wisest course while self-reform and altruistic feeling remain undeveloped in the majority. Political awareness, if not bigoted partisanship, is symptomatic of a spreading sense of community with the rest of the nation, and eventually with the human race."

70   WIESENFARTH, JOSEPH. "*Adam Bede* and Myth." *Papers on Language and Literature* 8, no. 1 (Winter):39-52.
      Ascertains how Hebrew, Greek, and Christian mythology contribute to the realism of *Adam Bede.*

71   WOODCOCK, JOHN A. "The Moral Dimension of Beauty in George Eliot's Heroines." Ph.D. dissertation, State University of New York, Stony Brook, 213 pp.
      Analyzes Eliot's use of two types of feminine beauty—radiant and selfish—as her method of conveying moral judgement of her heroines. Her feelings and attitudes toward feminine beauty reflect on her religious upbringing, theory of aesthetics, her identification with growing feminism and her humanism. See *Dissertations Abstracts International* 32, no. 8 (1972):4639A.

1973

1   ALTICK, RICHARD D. *Victorian People and Ideas.* New York: W.W. Norton & Co., pp. 36-38, 275-80, 304-5, passim.
      Allusions to Victorian literature are explained in an attempt to explore the prevalent topics of the period such as the revolution in class structure and attitudes; the rise of utilitarianism and evangelicalism; the changes in religion, Darwinism, and the Oxford movement; the effects of industrialism; and the place of art and the artist in Victorian society.

2 ANDERSON, ROLAND F. "George Eliot Provoked: John Blackwood and Chapter Seventeen of *Adam Bede.*" *Modern Philology* 71, no. 1 (August):39-47.

Finds chapter 17 of *Adam Bede* to be a statement on the theory of fiction. Anderson believes that provocations by Eliot's publisher, John Blackwood, led Eliot to add the chapter entitled "In Which the Story Pauses a Little." Eliot's aim in inserting the chapter was to have her readers read her theory of fiction without having it disrupt her narrative.

3 BAKER, WILLIAM. "The Kabbalah, Mordecai, and George Eliot's Religion of Humanism." In *Yearbook of English Studies*. Vol. 3. London: Modern Humanities Research, pp. 216-21.

Traces how Kabbalistic doctrine is a significant basis for the relationship between Mordecai and Daniel Deronda. Reviews Eliot's reading and knowledge of *The Kabbalah* and especially the process of the transmigration of the soul.

4 BARTON, ROBERT E. "Saving Religion: A Comparison of Matthew Arnold and George Eliot." Ph.D. dissertation, University of Washington, 241 pp.

"Matthew Arnold and George Eliot were Victorian religious skeptics who sought to transform orthodox Christianity and thereby offer their contemporaries the moral inspiration and guidance of a religious view of life." Both presented a humanistic and secular view of religion that was based on man's moral experience. They differed in that Eliot advocated free inquiry and discussion of all religious questions and Arnold was concerned about the effects on religion of such inquiry. See *Dissertations Abstracts International* 34, no. 7 (1974):4240A.

5 BERNDT, DAVID EDWARD. "'This Hard, Real Life': Self and Society in Five Mid-Victorian *Bildungsromane*." Ph.D. dissertation, Cornell University, 209 pp.

Thematic concerns regarding the relation between self and society and the development of the *bildungsroman* are applied to *The Mill on the Floss*, Dickens's *David Copperfield*, Charlotte Brontë's *Jane Eyre*, and Thackeray's *Henry Esmond*. See *Dissertations Abstracts International* 33, no. 10 (1973):5713A.

1973

6   BEYERS, BRIAN D. "*Adam Bede*: Society in Flux." *Unisa English Studies* 11, no. 3 (September):25-29.
    In *Adam Bede*, Eliot "describes the modes of living of various social classes in a pre-industrial age—modes familiar to her as a child, before religious schism, social change, and industrialization came to disturb the prevailing tranquility of rural England."

7   BÖHM, RUDOLF. "George Eliot: *Adam Bede*." *Der Englische Roman im 19. Jahrhundert: Interpretationen zu Ehren von Horst Oppel*. Edited by Paul Goetsch, Heinz Kosok, and Kurt Otten. Berlin: Erich Schmidt Verlag, pp. 150-64.

8   BOURL'HONNE, P. *George Eliot: Essai de biographie intellectuelle et morale, 1819-1854, influences anglaises et étrangères*. New York: AMS Press, 214 pp. Orig. pub. Paris: Librarie Ancienne Honoré Champion, 1933.
    Traces Feuerbach's influence in the development of Eliot's relationship with Lewes. Finds novels to be negative assertions although Eliot's spirit was positive.

9   BOWLIN, KARLA JANE. "The Brother and Sister Theme in Post-Romantic Fiction." Ph.D. dissertation, Auburn University, 149 pp.
    To demonstrate the post-Romantic theme of sorrow for the loss of childhood and loss of brother or sister, Emily Brontë's *Wuthering Heights*, Eliot's *The Mill on the Floss*, and William Faulkner's *The Sound and the Fury* are examined. The plots of all three novels share the pattern of separation of brother and sister, evoke sympathy, and perceive the separation as unfortunate. See *Dissertations Abstracts International* 34, no. 3 (1973):1232A.

10 CARLISLE, JANICE MARGARET. "The Moral Imagination: Dickens, Thackeray, and George Eliot." Ph.D. dissertation, Cornell University, 266 pp.
    "Mid-Victorian fiction can be defined by the novelist's sense of moral responsibility to his audience." Discusses the moral aesthetic of the fiction of Dickens, Thackeray, and Eliot; the metaphors and analogies used; and how the novelists' concern with the moral need of the reader determines the form of fiction used. See *Dissertations Abstracts International* 34, no. 10 (1974):6630A.

11 CASERIO, ROBERT LAWRENCE, Jr. "Plot, Story and the Novel: Problematic Aspects of English and American Narrative, From

Dickens to Gertrude Stein." Ph.D. dissertation, Yale University, 418 pp.

"Attempts to explain the origin and bearing of a significant antagonism to plot and story in modern writing. . . . George Eliot's sense of life caused her to rebel against Dickens's sense of plot. The ramifications of this are traced . . . by means of a comparison of *Bleak House* and *Felix Holt, the Radical*. These novelists differently evaluate the possibilities of realizing passionate consciousness in some purposeful form of external activity." See *Dissertations Abstracts International* 34, no. 5 (1973):2613A.

12 COLES, ROBERT. "Irony in the Mind's Life; Maturity: George Eliot's *Middlemarch*." *Virginia Quarterly Review* 49, no. 4 (Autumn):526-52.

Stresses Eliot's emphasis in *Middlemarch* of the theme of life's "indefiniteness" and the irony inherent in life's unpredictability. See also 1974.12.

13 CONEY, MARY BRIDGET. "Reflections of English Reform in the Literature of the Eighteen-Seventies." Ph.D. dissertation, Washington University, 222 pp.

Analyzes how the controversy regarding the Reform Bill of 1867 was reflected in the literature of the time. *Daniel Deronda* illustrates the loss of social order and growing moral confusion. See *Dissertations Abstracts International* 34, no. 5 (1973):2552A.

14 CONRAD, PETER. *The Victorian Treasure-House*. London: William Collins Sons, pp. 79-84, 106-8, 119-20, 124-27, 175-77, 209-15.

Studies elements of the novel particular to the Victorian period in *Daniel Deronda* and *Romola*. Discusses realism, methods of pictorial narrative, and the effect of the city on the novel's society.

15 CONWAY, RICHARD HENRY. "The Difficulty of Being a Woman: A Study of George Eliot's Heroines." Ph.D. dissertation, University of Denver, 165 pp.

Focuses on the heroines of George Eliot's novels and finds the author exploring a woman's potential for autonomy in a Victorian culture. Forces antagonistic to the heroines' pursuit of autonomy are either fathers or father-figures. Considers how the heroines become

1973

slowly conscious of the restrictions placed upon them. See *Dissertations Abstracts International* 34, no. 2 (1973):722A.

16   DONOVAN, JOSEPHINE. "Feminist Style Criticism." In *Images of Women in Fiction: Feminist Perspectives*. Edited by Susan Koppelman Cornillon. Bowling Green, Ohio: Bowling Green University Popular Press, pp. 341-54.

Applies Virginia Woolf's argument that nineteenth-century women novelists had no feminist tradition in style from which to write. Cites passages from *The Mill on the Floss* that use a male tone, style, and narrator.

17   DURR, VOLKER O. "The World and Its Protagonists: Goethe's *Wilhelm Meister* and George Eliot's *Middlemarch*." Ph.D. dissertation, Princeton University, 275 pp.

Examines in *Wilhelm Meister* and *Middlemarch* the "interplay of social and spiritual situations and their reflection in fictional alternatives of behavior." Both novels, both *Bildungsromane*, present the reader with normative visions of life. Discussion of their parallel structures and stylistic changes. Differences in the use of language in both novels express the "authors' attitudes towards their respective epochs." See *Dissertations Abstracts International* 34, no. 2 (1973):724A.

18   ELLMANN, RICHARD. "Dorothea's Husbands." *Times Literary Supplement* (London) 16 February, pp. 165-68. Reprinted in *Golden Codgers: Biographical Speculations* (New York and London: Oxford University Press), pp. 17-38.

Biographical critique and investigation of possible prototypes for Dorothea Brooke's two husbands from *Middlemarch*. Casaubon and Ladislaw represent a reversal of roles and functions. Casaubon may have been modeled after either Mark Pattison, Dr. R.H. Brabant, Herbert Spencer, or Robert William Mackay. Prototypes for Will Ladislaw are not as easily discernible. Parallels are drawn to Eliot's two husbands, although her models for the two characters came from a number of acquaintances. Reprinted: 1986.13.

19   ENGEL, MARY TERESA J. "The Literary Reputation of George Eliot in Germany, 1857-1970." Ph.D. dissertation, University of Detroit, 308 pp.

Chronological assessment of critical reponse to George Eliot's fiction by German reviewers. Eliot's contemporaries believed her fiction endorsed mid-nineteenth-century women's rights, English humanitarianism, and Carlylean realism. Twentieth-century reviewers tend to probe into the psychological and thematic aspects of her work. Use of language and methods of characterization are analyzed. English and German criticisms are contrasted. See *Dissertations Abstracts International* 34, no. 12 (1974):7702A.

20 FEENEY, MARY ELIZABETH. "Women in the Major Fiction of George Eliot." Ph.D. dissertation, University of Massachusetts, 253 pp.

    In *Romola*, Eliot presents women in the form of the pure-minded heroine. The women of *Middlemarch* personify Eliot's humanitarianism. The women of *Silas Marner* and *Scenes of Clerical Life* are more interested in marriage than work, but seek the same goal of self-fulfillment as Eliot's other women protagonists. See *Dissertations Abstracts International* 35, no. 1 (1974):446A.

21 FLEISSNER, ROBERT F. "*Middlemarch* and Idealism – Newman, Naumann, Goethe." *Greyfriar* 14:21-26.

    Discusses the saintly idealism of St. Theresa and St. Dorothea in the portrayal of Dorothea Brooke. Finds that the "Key to All Mythology" is in Adolph Naumann, whose name reflects the influence of John Henry Newman. Examines elements of "truth of feeling" and Goethe's "sense of resignation" in *Middlemarch* characters.

22 FRICKE, DOUGLAS C. "Art and Artists in *Daniel Deronda*." *Studies in the Novel* 5, no. 2 (Summer):220-28.

    Summary of Eliot's conception of art and artists in *Daniel Deronda*. The contrast is drawn between the true artist and the artist who presumes his position. Eliot saw that the moral and social nature of art led to one's better understanding of himself and others. Eliot uses art to comment on the artist within Victorian society and to illustrate "the restrictions the insular British world places upon creativity." Discusses conflicts between art and history.

23 FURNISS, JOHN NEILSON. "George Eliot and the Protestant Work Ethic." Ph.D. dissertation, Duke University, 283 pp.

    Eliot's philosophy of work at its most fundamental level is that of the Protestant work ethic. The evidence of Eliot's use of this philosophy of work is traced through *Scenes of Clerical Life, Adam Bede, The Mill on the Floss, Romola, Middlemarch*, and *Daniel*

1973

Deronda. These novels may be viewed as a "continuing dialectic on the issues of work and duty." See *Dissertations Abstracts International* 34, no. 7 (1974):4199A.

24   GARLAND, BARBARA CAROLYN. "Comic Form in 19th-Century English Fiction." Ph.D. dissertation, Indiana University, 331 pp.
Using the literary theories of comedy of Northrop Frye, Susanne Langer, and Nelvin Vos, variations on idealized comic form are studied in nineteenth-century English fiction. *Middlemarch* presents a comic history by juxtaposing plot lines and conferring the complexities of a comic hero upon comic society. See *Dissertations Abstracts International* 33, no. 8 (1973):4412A.

25   GORSKY, SUSAN. "The Gentle Doubters: Images of Women in Englishwomen's Novels, 1840-1920." In *Images of Women in Fiction: Feminist Perspectives*. Edited by Susan Koppelman Cornillon. Bowling Green, Ohio: Bowling Green University Popular Press, pp. 28-54.
Examines prominent female characters who are presented realistically yet who remain individuals. Dorothea Brooke of *Middlemarch*, Mirah of *Daniel Deronda*, Dinah Morris of *Adam Bede*, Milly Barton of *Scenes of Clerical Life*, and Maggie Tulliver of *The Mill on the Floss* are described in relation to stereotypic female characterizations.

26   GOTTLIEB, AVIVAH. "George Eliot's 'Casaubon Tints.'" In *Further Studies in English Language and Literature*. Vol. 25. Edited by A.A. Mendilow. Jerusalem: Magnes Press, Hebrew University, pp. 189-213.
Examines sources for and readings about the characterization and origin of Casaubon.

27   HALPERIN, JOHN. "George Eliot (1819-1880)." In *The Language of Meditation: Four Studies in Nineteenth-Century Fiction*. Elms Court, Eng.: Arthur H. Stockwell, pp. 51-93.
Examines meditation scenes in *Middlemarch* and *Daniel Deronda* to discover Eliot's heroines' "education in the art of moral vision." The heroines' self-awareness is usually reached as the result of a parting with the male character. See also 1972.36.

28 HARDY, BARBARA. "Rituals and Feelings in the Novels of George Eliot." W.D. Thomas Memorial Lecture Delivered at the University College of Swansea on 6 February 1973. Swansea, Wales: University College of Swansea, 15 pp.

Identifies Eliot's use of ritual – weddings, funerals, and holidays – to place life within the seasons; to stress the value of religion; to stress the unity of the family; and to show psychological response to change and to bonding. Reprinted: 1982.34.

29 HEILBRUN, CAROLYN G. *Toward a Recognition of Androgyny*. New York: Alfred A. Knopf; Harper Colophon Books, pp. 73-74, 82-86.

Discusses androgynous elements of *Middlemarch* and Eliot's abandonment of the androgyny theme in *Daniel Deronda*. Eliot's own embodiment of "masculine strength of mind and feminine impulses" is discussed in the chapter dealing with the woman as hero.

30 HIGDON, DAVID LEON. "Failure of Design in *The Mill on the Floss*." *Journal of Narrative Technique* 3, no. 3 (September):183-92.

Finds the open ending of *The Mill on the Floss* to be unsatisfactory in relation to the symmetrical design of the novel's unity of action, idea, and structure.

31 ———. "*Sortes Biblicae* in *Adam Bede*." *Papers on Language and Literature* 9, no. 4 (Fall):396-405.

Examines Dinah Morris's three uses of "opening the Bible" as a form of sortilege known as bibliomancy. The practice of *sortes biblicae* individualizes Dinah's character, develops historical structure, and develops thematic structure.

32 HILL, D.M. "Why Did Mr. Keck Edit 'The Trumpet'?" *Neuphilologische Mitteilungen* 74:714-15.

"Mr. Keck and 'The Trumpet', editor and newspaper respectively in *Middlemarch*, are associated by name through the plant 'angelica sylvestris,' sometimes called the 'trumpet-keck.'... By using this association of names George Eliot was augmenting the picture of Mr. Keck as a boy playing games...."

33 JACKSON, ARLENE M. "Dor[o]thea Brooke of *Middle March* [sic]: Idealism and Victorian Reality." *Cithara* 12, no. 2:91-102.

"The idealism of *Middlemarch*'s Dorothea Brooke and the pain and joy of the idealistic struggle with the Victorian condition make [her] a revealing study of George Eliot's own struggle with life. . . . Eliot criticizes the idealist and warns against the dangers of self-interest, emotional excess, and intellectual error. . . . The renunciation of heroic desire is a part of this realistic approach to life."

34 JAMES, GLENN JOSEPH. "Walter Scott and George Eliot: A Common Tradition." Ph.D. dissertation, Emory University, 256 pp.

Discusses the influence of Walter Scott on Eliot's fiction. Analyzes Scott's *The Heart of Midlothian* and Eliot's *Adam Bede* – their similar plots and use of the pastoral tradition. The similar uses of compassion and human estrangement are studied further in *Silas Marner* and Scott's *The Black Dwarf*. See *Dissertations Abstracts International* 34, no. 7 (1974):4207A.

35 KATZ, JUDITH NINA. "Rooms of Their Own: Forms and Images of Liberation in Five Novels." Ph.D. dissertation, Pennsylvania State University, 180 pp.

Five novels – *Middlemarch*, Woolf's *The Waves*, Austen's *Pride and Prejudice*, Charlotte Brontë's *Jane Eyre*, and Burney's *Evelina* – are studied in terms of female liberation. Symbols of enclosed containers are described as images that both entrap and liberate their inhabitants. See *Dissertations Abstracts International* 34, no. 3 (1973):1283A.

36 KRAFT, STEPHANIE BARLETT. "Women and Society in the Novels of George Eliot and Edith Wharton." Ph.D dissertation, University of Rochester, 168 pp.

Studies the relation in George Eliot's and Edith Wharton's fiction and their treatment of the problems of women in restrictive social environments. The novels of both authors contain examples of women who adjust positively to their society, yet who are limited in what they can accomplish by their lack of experience and naïveté. Disillusionment as a maturational stage is examined in relation to *Romola*. See *Dissertations Abstracts International* 34, no. 5 (1973):2632A.

37 LASKI, MARGHANITA. *George Eliot and Her World*. New York: Charles Scribner's Sons, 128 pp.

Illustrated biography makes substantial use of pictorial material to tie Eliot's works to the Victorian era. Makes references to sexual and social codes of mid-Victorian society in discussions of her liaison with George H. Lewes, late marriage to John Cross, and relationship with John Chapman.

38 LEAVIS, F.R. *The Great Tradition: George Eliot, Henry James, Joseph Conrad.* New York: New York University Press, pp. 28-125. Orig. pub. London: Chatto & Windus; New York: Doubleday, 1954.
    Examination and critical analysis of Eliot's early works, *Romola, Middlemarch,* and *Daniel Deronda,* in relation to *The Portrait of a Lady.* Cites Henry James's opinions of Eliot's writings. Eliot's serious attitude toward life gives her novels a Tolstoyian quality.

39 LEE, ROBIN. "Irony and Attitudes in George Eliot and D.H. Lawrence." *English Studies in Africa* 16, no. 1:15-21.
    Compares the relationship between irony and attitude in the works of Eliot and D.H. Lawrence. "George Eliot's irony implies her relative certainty of her view of things and of her control over her material."

40 LINEHAN, KATHERINE BAILEY. "George Eliot's Use of Comedy and Satire." Ph.D. dissertation, Stanford University, 354 pp.
    Analyzes the function of comedy and satire in Eliot's fiction. Chronologically traces the development of humor in her attempt to promote tolerance and sympathy. Eliot uses humor to relieve the reader from the tension of the main plot. See *Dissertations Abstracts International* 34, no. 9 (1974):5919A.

41 LODGE, DAVID. Introduction to *Scenes of Clerical Life.* Harmondsworth, Eng.: Penguin Books, pp. 7-32
    Discusses development of *Scenes of Clerical Life* and Eliot's indebtedness to Sir Walter Scott and Jane Austen. In her debut novels, Eliot presented orthodox religion as a "metaphorical vehicle for humanistic values. . . ." Examines various leitmotifs used in the stories – animal and bird imagery, weather imagery, and references to the heart.

42 MILLS, NICOLAUS. "Nathaniel Hawthorne and George Eliot." In *American and English Fiction in the Nineteenth Century: An Anti-Genre Critique and Companion.* Bloomington and London: Indiana University Press, pp. 52-73.

Analyzes the theme of redemptive knowledge in Hawthorne's *The Scarlet Letter* and Eliot's *Adam Bede*. To understand the nature of religious transformation as a consequence of the dilemma of the fall, the author provides examples of the novels' descriptions of society and characters.

43   NELSON, CAROLYN CHRISTENSEN. "Patterns in the *Bildungsroman* as Illustrated by Six English Novelists from 1814 to 1860." Ph.D. dissertation, University of Wisconsin, 175 pp.

Study of six novels in the *Bildungsroman* tradition to explain how personal education changed in relation to the individual's development, his family, society, and its institutions. Eliot's *The Mill on the Floss* is a tragedy in that the individual seeks to liberate himself from society but is ultimately destroyed by stronger, outside forces. See *Dissertations Abstracts International* 33, no. 7 (1973):3597A.

44   NEWTON, K.M. "Byronic Egoism and George Eliot's 'The Spanish Gypsy.'" *Neophilologus* 57, no. 4 (October):388-400.

Study of Byronic characters in Eliot's poetry, particularly in the character Armgart of "Armgart" and the character Don Silva of "The Spanish Gypsy."

45   _____. "The Role of the Narrator in George Eliot's Novels." *Journal of Narrative Technique* 3, no. 2 (May):97-107.

Argues that the narrator is not Eliot, but is in fact a distinct character within the novels' structure. Eliot meant for the narrator to be a part of the artistic structure. Believes Eliot saw the narrator as male in *Scenes of Clerical Life* and *Adam Bede*, but as having no relation to gender in the later novels. The narrator is characterized as an historical novelist.

46   OLSEN, TILLIE. "Silences: When Writers Don't Write." In *Images of Women in Fiction: Feminist Perspectives*. Edited by Susan Koppelman Cornillon. Bowling Green, Ohio: Bowling Green University Popular Press, pp. 97-112. Orig. pub. in *Harper's* 231, no. 1385 (October 1965).

Olsen discusses the creative process and the writer's trauma when unnatural silence occurs. Notes Eliot's long period of not writing before pursuing her first work.

1973

47   PALKO, ALBERT J. "Latter-Day Saints: George Eliot's New Saint Theresa in Image and Symbol." Ph.D. dissertation, University of Notre Dame, 216 pp.

Eliot dramatizes the conflict between pagan and Christian myth in her heroines, whose task is to reconcile the opposing myths. Through symbols and images associating Romola, Esther Lyon, Dorothea Brooke, and Gwendolen Harleth, Eliot re-creates important elements of prior myths and creates a new myth of Saint Theresa. See *Dissertations Abstracts International* 34, no. 7 (1974):4277A.

48   PATERSON, JOHN. *The Novel as Faith: The Gospel According to James, Hardy, Conrad, Joyce, Lawrence, and Virginia Woolf*. Boston: Gambit, pp. 8-19, 75, 150-75, 185-282 passim.

Authors Henry James, Joseph Conrad, D.H. Lawrence and Virginia Woolf expound on Eliot's novels as an expression of faith in the quality of natural and human existence. A theory of fiction and its conscious and unconscious processes as it applies to the English novel is presented.

49   PEARCE, T.S. *George Eliot*. Edited by Kenneth Grose. Literature in Perspective. Totowa, N. J.: Rowan & Littlefield, 152 pp.

An account of Eliot's life is given so that her personality and point of view is made evident to readers of her novels. A review of the novel up to the time of Eliot's first fictional writing is provided to demonstrate what she brought to that form.

50   PRATT, LINDA RAY. "The Abuse of Eve by the New World Adam." In *Images of Women in Fiction: Feminist Perspectives*. Edited by Susan Koppelman Cornillon. Bowling Green, Ohio: Bowling Green University Popular Press, pp. 155-74.

Examines the Edenic myth and compares the character development of women in English novels, such as *Middlemarch*, with those of American novels, such as those by Henry James.

51   QUENNELL, PETER. *A History of English Literature*. Springfield, Mass.: G & C Merriam Co., pp. 291, 292, 357-61, 363.

Biographical sketch of Eliot and short discussion of *Adam Bede, Felix Holt, the Radical*, "Amos Barton," *Daniel Deronda*, "Janet's Repentance," *Middlemarch, The Mill on the Floss*, "Mr. Gilfil's Love Story," and *Romola*. Emphasizes Eliot's commitment to literary realism, the influence of Herbert Spencer and Auguste Comte, and her sympathy with the poor. Her stories are of seduction and repentence, with the characters embodying the values of the whole community.

52 ROAZEN, DEBORAH HELLER. "George Eliot and Wordsworth: 'The Natural History of German Life' and Peasant Psychology." *Research Studies of Washington State University* 41, no. 3 (September):166-78.

Wordsworth's and Eliot's views of peasantry are analyzed. For Wordsworth, "human feelings exist in their purest, most untampered state in the primitive peasant; as man becomes progressively more civilized, his feelings become less authentic, less spontaneous." For Eliot, "the peasant mentality is so dominated by custom and tradition as to leave no room for authentic individual feeling; civilization, far from eroding such feeling, is instead responsible for developing it."

53 SABISTON, ELIZABETH. "The Prison of Womanhood." *Comparative Literature* 25:336-51.

Examines the developing consciousness in the heroines of Jane Austen (Emma Woodhouse), Gustave Flaubert (Emma Bovary), Eliot (Dorothea Brooke), and Henry James (Isabel Archer). The isolative predicament the four heroines find themselves in is either spatial, social, sexual, or educational. The dilemma of female isolation and creativity is analyzed with regard to "tensions between opposites in her own character."

54 SAVOIA, DIANELLA. "Le immagini dell'acqua nel linguaggio di George Eliot." *Aevum* (Milan) 47, no. 3-4 (May-August):343-61.

55 SHAW, PATRICIA. "Humour in the Novels of George Eliot." *Filologia moderna* (Madrid) 13, no. 48 (June):305-35.

Study of humour in Eliot's novels of closed societies – *Scenes of Clerical Life, Adam Bede, The Mill on the Floss, Silas Marner,* and *Middlemarch.* Humorous possibilities regarding dialects, expressions, comic character-presentation, death, self-righteousness, and exaggeration are cited by extensive quotes.

56 SQUIRES, MICHAEL. "*Adam Bede* and the Locus Amoenus." *Studies in English Literature* 13, no. 4 (Autumn):670-76.

Describes Eliot's use of the *locus amoenus* ("lovely place") in *Adam Bede.* In chapters 12 and 13, this device "strengthens the novel's relationship to traditional pastoral and valuably illuminates her artistic method by showing how, in syncretic fashion, she fuses pastoral conventions and Christian morality."

57 STEPHEN, Sir LESLIE. *George Eliot*. English Men of Letters. Edited by John Morley. New York: AMS Press, 206 pp. Orig. pub. New York: Macmillan, 1902.
    A biography, and an examination of each novel.

58 STEWART, KAY LANETTE. "The Rhetoric of the Confession: Essays on Theory and Analysis." Ph.D. dissertation, University of Oregon, 246 pp.
    Uses *Middlemarch* and other examples of the "detached process-directed narrative novel" to construct a theory of literature. See *Dissertations Abstracts International* 34, no. 9 (1973):5997A.

59 STUMP, REVA. *Movement and Vision in George Eliot's Novels*. New York: Russell & Russell, 232 pp. Orig. pub. Seattle: University of Washington Press, 1959.
    How the rhythm of Eliot's novels is established and perpetuated by a pattern of vision imagery. In-depth study of two antithetical movements, one toward and one away from vision, and the structure they create in *Adam Bede*, *The Mill on the Floss*, and *Middlemarch*. Analysis of how imagery, theme, and dramatic action work together to produce these movements.

60 SWANN, BRIAN. "*Middlemarch* and Myth." *Nineteenth Century Fiction* 28, no. 2 (September):210-14.
    Discussion of how myth informs the structure of *Middlemarch* by referring to the classical myths of the rape of Persephone and the tale of Ariadne. Elements of myth are instrumental in connecting the people of a small town of the 1830s to Greece–which add to the elements of human fellowship and the archetypal patterns of human response to crisis situations.

61 ____. "*The Mill on the Floss* and the Form of Tragedy." *English Miscellany*. Vol. 24. Edited by Mario Praz. Rome: Edizioni di Storia e Letteratura, pp. 199-232.
    "George Eliot's theory of tragedy can be divided into two aspects: that tragedy is due to the clash between the individual and the general, and that it is the result of hereditarily irreconcilable qualities." Analysis of *The Mill on the Floss* finds Maggie to be a "rebel without

understanding why or how, and every passionate choice, up to her moment of enlightenment and beyond, turns out to be a wrong one."

62 SWINDEN, PATRICK. "Deaths and Entrances." In *Unofficial Selves: Character in the Novel from Dickens to the Present Day*. New York: Harper & Row, pp. 26-61.

Eliot's elements of realism in *Daniel Deronda, Felix Holt, the Radical, Middlemarch*, and *The Mill on the Floss* are analyzed and compared to those of Dickens. Characters by both novelists are examined – their appearances and the effects of their deaths upon other characters and upon the plot. Differing methods used by Eliot and Dickens allow the reader to respond to the characters' various responses to the world.

63 SWINNERTON, EMILY. *George Eliot: Her Early Home*. Folcroft, Pa.: Folcroft Library Editions, 48 pp. Orig. pub. London: R. Tuck, n.d.

Compilation of illustrations of scenes from Eliot's youth, with Eliot's descriptions of each site or references to them in her works. Illustrations by Lilian Russell, G.G. Kilburne, and Patty Townsend.

64 SZANTO, ALISON ANDREW. "Between Liberalism and Democracy: George Eliot's Novels and the Structure of Mid-Victorian Social Reality." Ph.D. dissertation, University of California, San Diego, 324 pp.

"This analysis of the narrative structures of George Eliot's novels attempts to demonstrate a relationship between these structures and the underlying social structure of the period in which the novels were written." Political, economic, and social changes during the 1870s greatly altered society. Eliot's changes in the structure of *Middlemarch* and *Daniel Deronda* express these changes and are contrasted with her earlier novels in which she had established a definite narrative pattern. See *Dissertations Abstracts International* 34, no. 7 (1974):4220A.

65 THUENTE, DAVID R. "Channels of Feeling: George Eliot's Search for the Natural Bases of Religion." Ph.D. dissertation, University of Kentucky, 247 pp.

Surveys Eliot's early novels to "relate settings, characters, incidents, and themes to the primary philosophic impulse behind their composition." *Adam Bede, The Mill on the Floss*, and *Silas Marner* portray man's religious consciousness as it exists in a "natural" context, independent of supernatural agencies. Eliot's novels grew out of her own religious changes and her perceptions of those changes in relation to society. See *Dissertations Abstracts International* 34, no. 8 (1974):5207A.

66 TUMAN, MYRON CHESTER. "*Frederick the Great, Romola, The Ring and the Book* and the Mid-Victorian Crisis in Historicism." Ph.D. dissertation, Tulane University, 313 pp.

Considers Carlyle's *Frederick the Great*, Eliot's *Romola*, and Browning's *The Ring and the Book* in terms of differing attitudes about the nature of history. Defines and analyzes the mid-Victorian crisis in historicism and traces the historical structure of each work. See *Dissertations Abstracts International* 34, no. 11 (1974):7251A.

67 WARD, STANLEY SIDNEY. "Pattern and Personality: A Study of Split Structure in the Novels of George Eliot." Ph.D. dissertation, Harvard University.

Cited but not abstracted in *Dissertation Abstracts International* (1973).

68 WHITLOCK, ROGER DENNIS. "Charles Dickens and George Eliot: Moral Art in the 'Age of Equipose.'" Ph.D. dissertation, University of Washington, 158 pp.

Examines the similarities in Dickens's and Eliot's work as influenced by the changes in the literary tastes of England in the 1850s and 1860s. *Hard Times* and *Silas Marner* are both moral fables that attack utilitarianism. *The Mill on the Floss* and *Great Expectations* are about childhood and growing up and how the natural self must be sacrificed to the social self. *Daniel Deronda* and *Our Mutual Friend* are novels about the tensions and dilemmas of contemporary life. See *Dissertations Abstracts International* 35, no. 1 (1974):484A.

69 WIESENFARTH, JOSEPH. "The Medea in *Daniel Deronda*." *Die neuren Sprachen* (Frankfurt) 22 (February):103-8.

Cites parallels between characters of Euripides' *Medea* – Jason, Medea, and Creusa – and *Daniel Deronda*'s Grandcourt, Lydia, and Gwendolen.

70 WILLIAMS, RAYMOND. "Knowable Communities." In *The Country and the City*. Oxford and New York: Oxford University Press, pp. 165-181.

1973

Examines the knowable community within country life in Eliot's *Adam Bede* and *The Mill on the Floss*. Studies plot constructions, language, setting, and country action. Reflects on the traditions of the English country worker and his social and economic relationships. Reprinted: 1977.51; 1986.59.

71   WOLFE, THOMAS PINGREY, II. "The Inward Vocation: An Essay on George Eliot's *Daniel Deronda*." Ph.D. dissertation, Rutgers University, 116 pp.

"The double plot of *Daniel Deronda* reflects a division of George Eliot's sensibility between impulses of rebellion against, and submission to, the demands of traditional moral authority. The careers of the two central characters, Gwendolen Harleth and Daniel Deronda, enact diametrically opposed relations to a primary figure of moral authority, the father. The artistic failure of the Deronda part of the novel comes from George Eliot's strained idealization of and identification with Deronda, who embodies her impulses to submission." See *Dissertations Abstracts International* 34, no. 10 (1974):6610A. Reprinted: 1976.63.

1974

1   BASCH, FRANÇOISE. "Seduction in Elizabeth Gaskell and George Eliot." In *Relative Creatures: Victorian Women in Society and the Novel*. New York: Schocken Books, pp. 243-68.

Eliot's female heroines are studied because they form a psychological and intellectual transition between Victorian stereotypes of the spinster, wife/mother, and impure woman, and the characters of outright feminists. Victorian fictional characters are studied from three points of view—the wife/mother, the impure woman, and the single woman. Eliot's Hetty Sorrel, in *Adam Bede*, is studied in two stages—before and after her seduction and the revelation of her pregnancy.

2   BEATY, JEROME. "George Eliot." In *The English Novel: Select Bibliographical Guides*. Edited by A.E. Dyson. London: Oxford University Press, pp. 246-63.

Select bibliography of Eliot's texts, critical studies and commentary, biographies and letters, bibliographies, and background readings.

1974

3   BEER, PATRICIA. *Reader, I Married Him: A Study of the Women Characters of Jane Austen, Charlotte Brontë, Elizabeth Gaskell and George Eliot*. New York: Barnes & Noble; Harper & Row Publishers, 213 pp.

Examines the work of four women novelists to show how they depict women and their situation in society. The lives of the authors and influence of society on their writings is described. Criticism of novels and presentations of heroines and minor female characters. Studies the "Woman Question" and what the authors thought in real life and the ideas they implied in their works.

4   BELL, BRENDA JOYCE HARRISON. "The Figure of the Child in the Novels of George Eliot." Ph.D. dissertation, University of South Carolina, 201 pp.

Eliot's depiction of children and parent/child relationships are examined. In *The Mill on the Floss*, Eliot convincingly recreates childhood based upon her own memories. In *Silas Marner*, Eliot creates, in the child, a symbol of ties that bind a person to the outside world. See *Dissertations Abstracts International* 35, no. 10 (1975):6701A.

5   BIČANIČ, SONIA. "Selfishness and Self-Affirmation in Rosamond Vincy and Gwendolen Harleth." *Studia romanica et anglica zagrabiensia*, no. 38 (December):115-26.

Traces the similarities and differences in characters Rosamond Vincy and Gwendolen Harleth. Use of flower imagery and elements of selfishness describe Rosamond. Gwendolen quests for the discovery of self.

6   BUCKLEY, JEROME HAMILTON. "George Eliot: A Double Life." In *Season of Youth: The Bildungsroman from Dickens to Golding*. Cambridge, Mass.: Harvard University Press, pp. 92-115.

Examination of the genre of "growing up and finding one's place in the world." *The Mill on the Floss* is about a double life, "a sort of contrapuntal *Bildungsroman*, comparing and contrasting hero and heroine as each moves into young adulthood."

7   BUSH, GERTRUDE EVA BLOSER. "*Middlemarch* and the Tradition of the English Provincial Novel." Ph.D. dissertation, University of Wisconsin at Madison, 239 pp.

Examines traditions of the provincial novel in *Middlemarch*. *Middlemarch* is compared to Gaskell's *Wives and Daughters*, Margaret

1974

Oliphant's *Miss Marjoribanks*, Harriet Martineau's *Deerbrook*, and Trollope's *Doctor Thorne*. See *Dissertations Abstracts International* 35, no. 6 (1974):3672A.

8   CARTER, DUNCAN ALBERT. "The Drama of Self: Role-Playing in the Novels of George Eliot." Ph.D. dissertation, University of Illinois at Urbana-Champaign, 210 pp.
     Examines dramatic imagery and role-playing in Eliot's fiction. *Middlemarch* and *Daniel Deronda* use modern role-theory to portray social and psychological determinism, the projection of self into non-self roles, and the relation of self to the everyday life. Discusses the dangers of acting by the egoist. See *Dissertations Abstracts International* 35, no. 7 (1975):4420A.

9   CLINE, C.L. "Qualifications of the Medical Practitioners of *Middlemarch*." In *Nineteenth Century Literary Perspectives: Essays in Honor of Lionel Stevenson*. Edited by Clyde de L. Ryals. Durham, N.C.: Duke University Press, pp. 271-81.
     "Considers the physicians and surgeons who practiced in *Middlemarch*, the kind of training which they must have undergone, and their general status and that of their profession at the time."

10   COHAN, STEVEN MICHAEL. "Fiction and the Creation of Character." Ph.D. dissertation, University of California at Los Angeles, 256 pp.
     Survey of the self and the socialization of the self in the English novel. A comparative analysis of *The Mill on the Floss* and *Mrs. Dalloway* examines the effect of narrative form on the reader's image of a character. See *Disserations Abstracts International* 35, no. 3 (1974):1616A.

11   COLBY, VINETA. *Yesterday's Woman: Domestic Realism in the English Novel*. Princeton, N.J.: Princeton University Press, pp. 202-9, 250-52.
     Demonstrates how the domestic novel, particularly *Scenes of Clerical Life*, transcends sect and dogma to explain the human condition. Eliot uses evangelicalism as symbolism to study guilt, self-examination, conscience and moral character development. Evangelicalism is the medium by which feelings of sympathy, love, and kindness are demonstrated but repressed by life's conditions.

1974

12   COLES, ROBERT. "Maturity: George Eliot's *Middlemarch*." In *Irony in the Mind's Life: Essays on Novels by James Agee, Elizabeth Bowen and George Eliot*. Charlottesville: University of Virginia Press, pp. 154-210.

Based on the Page-Barbour Lectures (University of Virginia, 1973). Examines the authors from childhood to maturity, to better understand irony in faith, social, psychological, and political ideals. *Middlemarch* centers on the theme of life's indefiniteness and the search to find coherence in unrelated phenomena. Maturity is perceived by Eliot to be the analysis and psychological reflection on "indefiniteness," as achieved by Dorothea Brooke. See also 1973.12.

13   CRAIG, DAVID [M.]. "Fiction and the 'Rising Industrial Classes.'" In *The Real Foundations: Literature and Social Change*. New York: Oxford University Press, pp. 132-42.

Studies of literature within the context of understanding the age in which it was written. Eliot's expression of repressed love and desire in *Scenes of Clerical Life* is discussed. Includes Eliot's comments on Brontë's *Jane Eyre*. Eliot writes in "Essays" about the unreality of social novels that "profess to represent the people as they are" within the industrial culture and conditions of England. In dealing with the industrial epoch, *Felix Holt, the Radical* presents, in the speeches of the trade-unionist and of Felix, two types of radicalism – individual political utterance (social propaganda) and Eliot's own type of idealized humanism.

14   DECAVALCANTE, FRANK. "Sexual Politics in Four Victorian Novels." Ph.D. dissertation, Kent State University, 210 pp.

Studies sexual politics and the roles of women characters in *The Mill on the Floss*, Trollope's *The Eustace Diamonds*, George Meredith's *Diana of the Crossways*, and George Gissing's *The Odd Women*. These novels illustrate a change in the depiction of the female characters who strive for independence and the emerging tolerance in Victorian society of this independence. See *Dissertations Abstracts International* 35, no. 3 (1974):1618A.

15   DIGNON, HUGH ALEXANDER. "Love and Courtship in the Novels of George Eliot, Thomas Hardy, and D.H. Lawrence: A Comparative Study." Ph.D. dissertation, New York University, 485 pp.

1974

Traces the changing attitudes toward love and courtship in works by Eliot, Hardy, and Lawrence. In *Adam Bede*, *The Mill on the Floss*, *Middlemarch*, and *Daniel Deronda*, Eliot's characters exploit their sexual attraction for egoistic purposes. Marriages fail because they were not based on love. Eliot believed men and women were equal in their moral responsibilities and choices. See *Dissertations Abstracts International* 35, no. 7 (1975):4425A.

16   DYLLA, SANDRA MARIE. "Jane Austen and George Eliot: The Influence of Their Social Worlds on Their Women Characters." Ph.D. dissertation, University of Wisconsin-Milwaukee, 330 pp.

Studies the development of Austen's and Eliot's women characters and the effects of their own social worlds on their characters. An examination of class structure and consciousness, education and economic structures, and the effect of courtship and marriage on a woman's status in society. Both authors pay close attention to their heroines' growing self-knowledge. See *Dissertations Abstracts International* 36, no. 2 (1975):899A.

17   EISNER, GRETA. "George Eliot: The Problem Novels." Ph.D. dissertation, University of California, Irvine, 160 pp.

Detailed reading and analysis of *Romola, Felix Holt, the Radical*, and *Daniel Deronda* to determine the "problematics of fictional structure and design." Refutes the commonly held notion that these three works are "aesthetically unrealized novels." See *Dissertations Abstracts International* 35, no. 11 (1975):7253A.

18   EMERY, LAURA COMER. "Creative Conflict in George Eliot's Middle Novels." Ph.D. dissertation, University of California at Berkeley.

Cited but not abstracted in *Dissertation Abstracts International* (1974). See 1976.21

19   ERMARTH, ELIZABETH [DEEDS]. "Incarnations: George Eliot's Conception of 'Undeviating Law.'" *Nineteenth-Century Fiction* 29, no. 3 (December):273-86.

Attempts to make clear the paradox of the 'undeviating law' of moral consequences and the idea of freedom. "Eliot distingushes two senses of the word 'law' and two realms of law which are analogous, but distinct – the cultural (or moral) and the natural (or material); that within the realm of culture the only law is the embodied presence of the world itself."

20 _____. "Maggie Tulliver's Long Suicide." *Studies in English Literature* 14, no. 4 (Fall):587-601.

Perceives Maggie Tulliver to be a victim and unwilling participant in her "suicide." The combination of sexist norms and reliance on approval causes Maggie to grow up weak and afraid of conflict. Her self-denial is seen as her "long suicide." Examines how being female is central to Maggie's tragedy.

21 FAVILLE, JOHN NYE. "The Rhetoric of Characterization in the Novels of Charles Dickens, George Eliot, and Joseph Conrad." Ph.D. dissertation, University of California at Berkeley.

Cited but not abstracted in *Dissertations Abstracts International* (1974).

22 FELTES, N.N. "Community and the Limits of Liability in Two Mid-Victorian Novels." *Victorian Studies* 17, no. 4 (June):355-69.

Presents from an historical point of view the influence upon novels of the altering forms of community. Studies *The Mill on the Floss* for social and economic relations in St. Ogg in 1829-30 and how these relations changed in the 1840s and 1850s. Contrasted and compared with Dickens's *Little Dorrit*. How social analysis can explain how "later novels reflect their changed historical context."

23 FUERMANN, WARREN BRYAN. "The Novels of George Eliot: A Critical Commentary." Ph.D. dissertation, University of Illinois at Urbana-Champaign, 484 pp.

Critical commentary of all of Eliot's novels based on Eliot's social and ethical thought, her treatment of landscape, the use of the omniscient author, and her concept of traditions and history. Attempts to give the reader a general account of Eliot's major preoccupations and their development. See *Dissertations Abstracts International* 35, no. 11 (1975):7254A.

24 FULMER, C[ONSTANCE] M[ARIE]. "Contrasting Pairs of Heroines in George Eliot's Fiction." *Studies in the Novel* 6, no. 3 (Fall):288-94.

Analyzes contrasting pairs of heroines in Eliot's fiction. Heroine-pairs are described with regard to moral maturity, levels of egotism, and mannerisms. The women are consistent representations of Eliot's symbolical scenes and character types. "With her contrasting pairs of heroines, she preaches the negative effects of selfishness and the broadening, positive effects of sympathetic understanding."

25   GODWIN, GAIL. "Would We Have Heard of Marian Evans?" *Ms*. 3 (September):72-5.
     Biographical portrait of George Eliot traces her relationships, development, and use of a pseudonym. Focus is on male/female and strength/weakness of Eliot and her characters. Contrasts between the novelist and the characters Maggie Tulliver and Dorothea Brooke are highlighted.

26   GRANT, JUDITH ANN SKELTON. "The Nature of Duty and the Problem of Passion in the Works of George Eliot." Ph.D. dissertation, University of Toronto (Canada).
     Explores Eliot's religious period, her sense of liberation following her reading of Wordsworth, and the revolution of her ideas about social, moral, and intellectual development. Applies these elements of Eliot's background to the development of the relationship between duty and passion in *Adam Bede*, *The Mill on the Floss*, *Romola*, *Daniel Deronda*, and *Middlemarch*. See *Dissertations Abstracts International* 38, no. 6 (1977):3481A.

27   HAIGHT, GORDON S. "Original Mss. Bound-In." *Times Literary Supplement* (London), 15 March, p. 264.
     Documents Haight's search for bound-in manuscripts and leaves of the *Spanish Journal* for the supplementary eighth volume of *The George Eliot Letters* (Yale University Press).

28   _____. "Poor Mr. Casaubon." In *Nineteenth Century Literary Perspectives: Essays in Honor of Lionel Stevenson*. Edited by Clyde de L. Ryals. Durham, N.C.: Duke University Press, pp. 255-70.
     Analysis of *Middlemarch* character Edward Casaubon and his marriage, at age 48, to 19-year-old Dorothea Brooke.

29   HALDANE, ELIZABETH SANDERSON. *George Eliot and Her Times, A Victorian Study*. Folcroft, Pa.: Folcroft Library Editions, 326 pp. Orig. pub. London: Hodder & Stoughton, 1927.
     Biography of Eliot relates her work to the times she lived in.

30 HALPERIN, JOHN. "George Eliot." In *Egoism and Self-Discovery in the Victorian Novel: Studies in the Ordeal of Knowledge in the Nineteenth Century*. New York: Burt Franklin, pp. 125-92.

Makes clear the theme of "moral and psychological expansion of protagonists who begin in self-absorption and move, through the course of a tortuous ordeal of education, to more complete self-knowledge." Eliot's constant theme is that one must live without illusion and truly know oneself or else one is trapped within the parameters of egoism. Theme is traced through *Adam Bede*, *Middlemarch*, and *Daniel Deronda*.

31 HARDWICK, ELIZABETH. "Seduction and Betrayal." In *Seduction and Betrayal: Women and Literature*. New York: Random House, pp. 177-208.

Examines the fate of Hetty Sorrel of *Adam Bede*, who is involved in promiscuous love. Hetty's story is an example of the plot of existence wherein her susceptibility makes her life a consequence of seduction. Her lack of spiritual depth causes the reader to find her exasperating and without much sympathy.

32 HATTON, JOHN CHARLES. "Sympathy and Form in George Eliot's Early Novels." Ph.D. dissertation, University of California at Berkeley.

Cited but not abstracted in *Dissertations Abstracts International* (1974).

33 HIGDON, DAVID LEON. "Sortilège in George Eliot's *Silas Marner*." *Papers on Language and Literature* 10, no. 1 (Winter):51-57.

Examines the practice of drawing lots in *Silas Marner*. "It bridges folk superstition and religious practice . . . and focuses on the elements of chance and providence."

34 HOFFMANN, LEONORE NOLL. "A Delicate Balance: The Resolutions to Conflict of Women in the Fiction of Four Women Writers in the Victorian Period." Ph.D. dissertation, Indiana University, 266 pp.

Contrasts the heroines' resolution of conflict as handled by Charlotte Brontë, George Eliot, Olive Schreiner, and George Egerton. Models of fictional responses to sacrifice are compared. Finds *The Mill on the Floss* uses self-sacrifice as a means of assertion, which is

1974

perceived to be an unsatisfactory and conventional resolution. See *Dissertations Abstracts International* 35, no. 7 (1975):4432A.

35   HOLLAHAN, EUGENE. "The Concept of 'Crisis' in *Middlemarch*." *Nineteenth-Century Fiction* 28, no. 4 (March):450-57.
    Examples of the concept and use of the word 'crisis' on fifteen occasions in *Middlemarch*. Illustration of crucial junctures between subplots, individual and collective crises, and local crisis situation, and how these citations of crisis demonstrate the inevitable conflicts of life. Analysis of the significance of crisis in the novel's plot, elements of suspense, and psychological and moral complexities.

36   JOHN, JOSEPH. "Pan-Humanism in the Novels of George Eliot." Ph.D. dissertation, Marquette University, 272 pp.
    Eliot's pan-humanism – her concern with and for the entire human race – is compared with the theories of Tennyson, Butler, Meredith, and Hardy. Based on secular theophany, Eliot's pan-humanism is centered on her belief in sympathy and the evolutionist thought of a holistic, nonsupernatural metaempiricism. For Eliot, "moral growth is a process of evolution from the 'moral stupidity' of the inborn egoism of human nature toward a proper correlation of the self with the life of mankind represented by one's immediate human fellows." See *Dissertations Abstracts International* 36, no. 1 (1975):316A.

37   LEDLIE, OLIVE. "George Eliot's Narrative Technique in the Dramatic Delineation of Her Mentors." Ph.D. dissertation, Rice University, 268 pp.
    Examines Eliot's narrative modes and stylistic devices. Discusses Eliot's theory of fiction, her concept of realism, and her moral view of art. Focus is on specific exemplars throughout her fiction who represent the author's values. See *Dissertations Abstracts International* 35, no. 4 (1974):2229A.

38   MacMULLEN, CORNELIA ELIZA. "The Psychological Basis of George Eliot's Ethics." Ph.D. dissertation, New York University, 122 pp.
    Cited but not abstracted in *Dissertation Abstracts International* (1974).

39 MAROTTA, KENNY RALPH. "The Literary Relationship of George Eliot and Harriet Beecher Stowe." Ph.D. dissertation, Johns Hopkins University, 291 pp.

Comparison of the similarities in the novels of Eliot and Stowe. Emphasizes the authors' use of typology–the use of Biblical characters to interpret day-to-day life. Both women employ religious motifs as part of their fictional method. See *Dissertations Abstracts International* 35, no. 6 (1974):3751A.

40 MARTIN, ROBERT BERNARD. "George Eliot, Leslie Stephen, and George Meredith." In *The Triumph of Wit: A Study of Victorian Comic Theory*. London: Oxford University Press, pp. 82-100.

Examines the change in comic theory in Victorian fiction from sentimental humor to a more intellectual humor. Eliot's essay "German Wit: Heinrich Heine" is analyzed. "Without specifically alluding to the almost complete dominance of sentimental humour, George Eliot sets out to destroy the idea that there is anything in humour that necessarily demands sympathy; indeed, as she points out, it may be cruel and savage." Eliot believes that wit and humour "overlap and blend. . . ."

41 MEIN, MARGARET. "George Eliot." In *A Foretaste of Proust: A Study of Proust and His Precursors*. London: Saxon House, pp. 121-42.

Examines Eliot's influence on Marcel Proust's development of a theory of memory and the transposition of a sense of duration. How Eliot's values influence Proust's sense of free will and the role of chance.

42 MILDER, GAIL EASON. "'Sublime Resignation': George Eliot and the Role of Women." Ph.D. dissertation, Harvard University.

Cited but not abstracted in *Dissertations Abstracts International* (1974).

43 MILLER, J. HILLIS. "Narrative and History." *ELH* 41, no. 3 (Fall):455-73.

Argues that, in *Middlemarch*, Eliot sees history as "an act of repetition in which the present takes position of the past and liberates it for a present purpose, thereby exploding the continuum of history."

44 MILNER, IAN. "Dickens's Style: A Textual Parallel in *Dombey and Son* and *Daniel Deronda*." *Philologica pragensia* 17, no. 4:209-10.

1974

Cites metaphorical and literal similarities, surface details, and similarities in the narrative modes of *Dombey and Son* and *Daniel Deronda*.

45 MOFFAT, MARY JANE, and PAINTER, CHARLOTTE, eds. "George Eliot (1819-1880)." In *Revelations: Diaries of Women*. New York: Random House, pp. 218-24.

Sample of Eliot's journal includes "How I Came to Write Fiction" in entries written between December 1857 and March 1858.

46 MORGAN, KATHLEEN E. "The Ethos of Work in Nineteenth Century Literature." *English* 23, no. 116 (Summer):47-54.

Discusses the work ethic in individual craftsmen such as Adam Bede, Felix Holt, and Caleb Garth of *Middlemarch*, where the individual's satisfaction comes from his work.

47 MURDOCH, JOHN. "English Realism: George Eliot and the Pre-Raphaelites." *Journal of the Warburg and Courtland Institutes* 37:313-29.

Traces qualities of English realism in painterly forms of the Pre-Raphaelites and literary forms of Eliot in their presentations of the everyday, working world.

48 NEUMANN, HENRY. "Villains in the English Novel from Aphra Behn to Eliot: A Classification and a Study in the Development of Certain Types." Ph.D. dissertation, New York University.

Cited but not abstracted in *Dissertation Abstracts International* (1974).

49 NEWTON, K.M. "George Eliot, George Henry Lewes, and Darwinism." *Durham University Journal* 66, no. 3 [n.s. 35, no. 3] (June):278-93.

Examines Eliot's and Lewes's response to Darwinism. Although Eliot accepted Darwin's theory of evolution, she was opposed to what she felt were its dangerous consequences (i.e., the implications of natural selection). "The main effect of Darwinism on George Eliot's novels was to reinforce her preoccupation with egoism." This is traced in *Felix Holt, the Radical, Daniel Deronda*, and *Middlemarch*.

50 PARIS, BERNARD J. "Inner Conflicts of Maggie Tulliver." In *A Psychological Approach to Fiction: Studies in Thackeray, Stendhal,*

George Eliot, Dostoevsky, and Conrad. Bloomington and London: Indiana University Press, pp. 165-89.

In an attempt to understand the neurotic processes of *The Mill on the Floss*, psychological theories of Karen Horney and Abraham Maslow are used to analyze characters and the consciousness of the implied author. Maggie Tulliver represents a "disparity between representation and interpretation, between the implied author as a creator of mimetic portraits and the implied author as analyst and judge. Movements from one neurotic solution to another are interpreted as processes of growth and education."

51   QUICK, JONATHAN R. "*Silas Marner* as Romance: The Example of Hawthorne." *Nineteenth-Century Fiction* 29, no. 3 (December):287-98.

Cites parallels between *Silas Marner* and Nathaniel Hawthorne's *The Scarlet Letter*. In both novels, the authors' aim is to record individual psychological struggles with expiation and guilt. Romance mystery qualities of apparently causeless circumstances occur in both novels. Similarities in structure, style, and characterization are described. How Hawthorne's use of shadows, to bring the commonplace and the mysterious together before Hester Prynne, was an influence on Eliot's formulation of *Silas Marner*.

52   ROGAL, SAMUEL J. "Hymns in George Eliot's Fiction." *Nineteenth-Century Fiction* 29, no. 2 (September):173-84.

Discussion of examples of hymns, metrical versions of the Psalms, and commentary on attitudes toward hymnody and psalmody in Eliot's "Amos Barton," *Adam Bede*, and "Janet's Repentence."

53   ROQUEMORE, JOSEPH H. "Historicism in George Eliot's Fiction." Ph.D. dissertation, University of New York at Buffalo.

Cited but not abstracted in *Dissertation Abstracts International* (1974).

54   SHUMAKER, RONALD CLAIR. "The Rhetoric of George Eliot's Fiction." Ph.D. dissertation, University of Pittsburgh, 172 pp.

Examines the recurrent triangular pattern in *Scenes of Clerical Life*, *Adam Bede*, *Middlemarch*, *Felix Holt, the Radical*, and *Daniel Deronda*. The pattern involves two characters – one representing egoism, the other representing renunciation – between whom a third character must choose. The realistic, romantic, and mixed modes of

1974

treatment and Eliot's rhetorical stance reflect the dialectical pattern. See *Dissertations Abstracts International* 35, no. 4 (1974):2299A.

55   SIEFERT, SUSAN ELIZABETH. "The Dilemma of the Talented Woman: A Study in Nineteenth-Century Fiction." Ph.D. dissertation, Marquette University, 197 pp.

Considers the atypical heroines, Dorothea Brooke of *Middlemarch* and Maggie Tulliver of *The Mill on the Floss*. Studies how these women reconcile their personal aspirations with those of a society that is adverse to such aspirations. Examines each heroine's success or failure in terms of self-image and the integration of self and society. See *Dissertations Abstracts International* 36, no. 1 (1975):285A.

56   SMALLEY, BARBARA. *George Eliot and Flaubert: Pioneers of the Modern Novel*. Athens: Ohio University Press, 240 pp.

How Flaubert's *Madame Bovary* and Eliot's *Middlemarch* were pioneers in the development of the modern psychological narrative. Both use the process of putting the significant action of the novel within the thoughts of the characters. Human illusion depicted against stark reality, a twofold consciousness, is described as "binocular vision." Discusses patterns of romantic egoism in *Middlemarch*, their impact on the modern novel, and its use of internalized drama.

57   SMITH, CORLESS ANN. "George Eliot and the Romantic Enterprise." Ph.D. dissertation, University of Missouri, Columbia, 147 pp.

Demonstrates Eliot's Romantic presentation of the theory of knowledge and the world. Eliot espoused a theory of the relationship between mind and matter, used the metaphor of the mystical marriage, and wrote about the evolution of consciousness. Eliot's basic subject deals with the form of cognition. Along with the Romantic poets, she sought to fuse the ideal and the real, as demonstrated by the relationship of humanity to nature. See *Dissertations Abstracts International* 36, no. 1 (1975):286A.

58   SQUIRES, MICHAEL. "*Adam Bede*: 'A Great Temple and a Sacred Song.'" In *The Pastoral Novel: Studies in George Eliot, Thomas Hardy, and D.H. Lawrence*. Charlottesville: University Press of Virginia, pp. 53-85.

Shows specific connections between *Adam Bede* and the traditional pastoral and how the pastoral is modified to meet the demands of the novel. Uses structural and textual methods to study the novel's language. *Adam Bede*'s pastoralism is evident in the city/country contrast, characterization, in the use of the *locus amoenus* and the concentric circles of pastoral romance, in the use of the imagery of nature, in the use of temporal and spatial distance, and in the use of detail.

59 _____. "*Silas Marner*: 'A Snug Well-Wooded Hollow.'" In *The Pastoral Novel: Studies in George Eliot, Thomas Hardy, and D.H. Lawrence*. Charlottesville: University Press of Virginia, pp. 86-105.

Studies pastoral qualities of *Silas Marner* – its structural pattern, regional contextualization, and characterization. Refers to Wordsworth's influence in Eliot's use of realism in her presentation of rural life. The double plot is the device used to tell the narratives.

60 STANG, MAURICE. "The German Original of a George Eliot Poem." *Notes & Queries*, n.s. 21, no. 1 (January):15.

Eliot's verse translation "Question and Answer" was originally published in Klauer-Klattowski's *German Poetical Anthology*, which served as Eliot's introduction to German lyrical poetry.

61 STEELE, KAREN BETH. "Social Change in George Eliot's Fiction." Ph.D. dissertation, Brown University, 208 pp.

Explains Eliot's ideas of social organization and change and how her ideas were formulated in her fiction. The sociological formulations of Ralf Dahrendorf and Anthony F.C. Wallace are used to illustrate Eliot's belief that the parts of the whole social organization are combined units of opposing interests. *Adam Bede, Middlemarch*, and *The Mill on the Floss* portray conflicts in authority relationships. *Daniel Deronda, Romola*, and *Felix Holt, the Radical* deal with social coercion and restructuring. See *Dissertations Abstracts International* 35, no. 11 (1975):7329A.

62 SUKENICK, LYNN. "Sense and Sensibility in Women's Fiction: Studies in the Novels of George Eliot, Virginia Woolf, Anaïs Nin, and Doris Lessing." Ph.D. dissertation, City University of New York, 346 pp.

Discusses the self-conscious approach to feelings and sensibility taken by Eliot, Woolf, Nin, and Lessing. Their understanding of women's sensibility, emotion, intuition, and sympathy intensifies the

1974

moral concerns of their novels. See *Dissertations Abstracts International* 35, no. 7 (1975):4563A.

63   SULLIVAN, WILLIAM J. "Allusion to Jenny Lind in *Daniel Deronda*." *Nineteenth-Century Fiction* 29, no. 2 (September):211-14.
   Eliot's reference to soprano Jenny Lind, in *Daniel Deronda*, is misleading and incongruous. It is a comment on Gwendolen Harleth's "selfishness and narrow horizons," in that Eliot's earlier reviews of Jenny Lind found her to be more concerned with her own ambition than the advancement of her art.

64   _____. "Music and Musical Allusion in *The Mill on Mill on the Floss*." *Criticism* 16, no. 3 (Summer): 232-46.
   Considers Eliot's use of music, either as commentary or as metaphor, to define the emotional life of Maggie Tulliver and as a literal event in the narrative sequence. How Eliot uses musical references in the abstract and to reveal structure and theme. Most important are the allusions to romantic operas of Handel, Keble, Haydn, Bellini, and Kempis.

65   SUSMAN, MAXINE SYLVIA. "Interpretations of Jewish Character in Renaissance and Recent Literature." Ph.D. dissertation, Cornell University, 288 pp.
   Studies the recurrent motifs of humor, isolation, and the law in the Jewish characters of *Daniel Deronda*. See *Dissertations Abstracts International* 35, no. 2 (1974):1063A.

66   SWANN, BRIAN. "George Eliot's Ecumenical Jew, or, The Novel as Outdoor Temple." *Novel: A Forum on Fiction* 8, no. 1 (Fall):39-50.
   Perceives *Daniel Deronda* to be Eliot's consummation of all her ideals and hopes for the human race. "In *Daniel Deronda*, she tried to pull together the parts of a world that had been shattered when she lost her faith in transcendentalism, a loss that forced the burden of meaning on the individual mundane consciousness."

67   TOMLINSON, T[HOMAS] B[RIAN]. "Love and Politics in the Early-Victorian Novel." *Critical Review* (Melbourne) 17:127-39.
   Compares the inherent failures of Gaskell's *Mary Barton* (1848) and *North and South* (1854-55), Disraeli's *Sybil* (1845), and Eliot's *Felix Holt, the Radical*.

1974

68   UNGER, WILLIAM EUGENE, Jr. "Implied Authors and Created Readers in Thackeray, Trollope, Charlotte Brontë, and George Eliot." Ph.D. dissertation, Ohio State University, 448 pp.

Compares methods used by Thackeray, Trollope, Eliot, and Brontë in their attempt to "create readers who would fully share the values advocated by the novels themselves." Examines *Scenes of Clerical Life, Adam Bede, The Mill on the Floss, Silas Marner, Romola,* and *Felix Holt, the Radical,* in which an implied author is progressively developed. Includes a survey of Victorian criticism and theories regarding the intrusive author. See *Dissertations Abstracts International* 35, no. 5 (1974):2956A.

69   WARNER, FRANCES CLAIRE. "Toward *Middlemarch*: The Heroine's Search for Guidance as Motif in the Earlier Novels of George Eliot." Ph.D. dissertation, University of Illinois at Urbana-Champaign, 190 pp.

Discusses the search for guidance as an important theme in Eliot's early narrative structures. Uses Eliot's early novels to discuss her presentation of this theme and how *Middlemarch* was the perfecting of Eliot's weaving of the search for affection and the search for moral and intellectual guidance. Similarities between *Romola* and *Middlemarch* are developed. See *Dissertations Abstracts International* 35, no. 7 (1975):4462A.

70   WILLIAMS, IOAN. "The Development of Realist Fiction: From Dickens to George Meredith." In *The Realist Novel in England: A Study in Development.* London: Macmillan Press.

Defines realist fiction and George Henry Lewes's theory of realism. This theory states that "Life and Art must be seen as complete and meaningful in themselves, but this can only be done when the individual learns to achieve unity and harmony within himself." Reprinted: 1975.84.

71   _____. "George Eliot: The Philosophy of Realism." In *The Realist Novel in England: A Study in Development.* London: Macmillan Press.

Analyzes Eliot's applications of Lewes's theory of realism in the novels *Adam Bede* and *The Mill on the Floss*. Her writings balance the real and the ideal, poetry and science, religion and reason, and the subjective and objective forces of experience. Reprinted: 1975.85.

1974

72 WING, GEORGE. "The Motto to Chapter XXI of *Daniel Deronda*: A Key to All George Eliot's Mythologies?" *Dalhousie Review* 54, no. 1 (Spring):16-32.

Suggests that the motto to Chapter XXI of *Daniel Deronda* expresses Eliot's main anxiety. The chapter is concerned with social problems of the rural privileged, in particular the power of their ignorance.

73 WITEMEYER, HUGH. "George Eliot, Naumann, and the Nazarenes." *Victorian Studies* 18, no. 3 (December):145-58.

Identifies Adolf Naumann, the German painter of the Rome chapters of *Middlemarch*, and his historical prototypes. Eliot drew upon her religious experience and evaluation of Nazarene painters Johann Friedrich Overbeck and Josef von Führich to formulate the character Naumann. How Naumann's career adheres to the historical patterns of aspiration and failure set by the main characters of the novel.

74 ZAK, MICHELE WENDER. "Feminism and the New Novel." Ph.D. dissertation, Ohio State University, 350 pp.

Perceives both Eliot and Henry James as the forerunners in experimenting with dialectical relationships between feminine and masculine principles. See *Dissertations Abstracts International* 34, no. 8 (1974):5215A.

75 ZIMMERMAN, BONNIE SUE. "Appetite for Submission: The Female Role in the Novels of George Eliot." Ph.D. dissertation, State University of New York, Buffalo, 257 pp.

Evaluates Eliot in the context of the nineteenth-century feminist movement. Feminist criticism of character development, plot and structure, and themes of *Adam Bede, The Mill on the Floss, Middlemarch*, and *Daniel Deronda*. "Asserts that the role of women is essential to George Eliot's vision of all social and artistic questions. A concentration on the inner lives of the heroines in the context of the novels' social world and internal structure suggests a total perspective on George Eliot as a major social novelist." The manner in which Eliot's melancholy compromises her novels is studied as well as why she could not take a stronger stand on women's issues. See *Dissertations Abstracts International* 35, no. 3 (1974):1639A.

1975

1 ADAM, IAN. "The Structure of Realisms in *Adam Bede.*" *Nineteenth-Century Fiction* 30, no. 2 (September):127-49.
Procedural and subject realism are distinguished in *Adam Bede*. Background details, local anecdotes, and inclusiveness in time define realities of the novel. Use of pictorial and analytic realism gives the work structural significance and cohesion.

2 ____, ed. *This Particular Web: Essays on Middlemarch*. Toronto: University of Toronto Press, 121 pp.
Five essays on *Middlemarch* consider Eliot's authorial irony and character. Articles cited separately.

3 AUERBACH, NINA. "Incarnations of the Orphan." *ELH* 42, no. 3 (Fall):395-419.
Briefly describes Eliot's treatment of the orphan-myth evident in Eppie of *Silas Marner* and Dorothea of *Middlemarch*. Finds that Eliot treats orphanhood in "too idiosyncratic a fashion."

4 ____. "The Power of Hunger: Demonism and Maggie Tulliver." *Nineteenth-Century Fiction* 30, no. 2 (September):150-71.
Analysis of *The Mill on the Floss* as Gothic romance. "Maggie Tulliver's recurrent pattern of action is to enter worlds and explode them. Her destructive aura takes shape in the associations of demonism, witchery and vampirism. . . . Maggie spiritually feasts upon the world she lives in." The language of hunger and thirst is used to define her. Reprinted: 1985.1.

5 AUSTER, HENRY. "George Eliot and the Modern Temper." In *The Worlds of Victorian Fiction*. Edited by Jerome H. Buckley. Cambridge, Mass., and London: Harvard University Press, pp. 75-101.
Analyzes Eliot's growth and modern elements in her later works – *Romola, Felix Holt, the Radical, Daniel Deronda*, and *Middlemarch*. The emergence of Eliot's modern view in her literature is evident in her "concern with the plight of the individual in a world of changing and decaying values, her acute sense of the erosion in society of long-established traditions and her realism." Another modern element is her flexible and subtle use of the narrative, which provides

1975

Eliot an avenue for expressing her bent towards philosophy and psychology.

6   BAKER, WILLIAM. *George Eliot and Judaism*. Edited by Dr. James Hogg. Salzburg, Austria: Institut für Englische Sprache und Literatur, Universität Salzburg, 273 pp.
     Traces Eliot's sources for her knowledge regarding Judaism and Zionism as presented in *Daniel Deronda* and her essay "The Modern Hep! Hep! Hep!" Cites influence of Strauss, Spinoza, Heine, and Feuerbach.

7   _____. "George Eliot's Projected Napoleonic War Novel: An Unnoted Reading List." *Nineteenth-Century Fiction* 29, no. 4 (March):453-60.
     Examination of Eliot's holograph notebook, now in the Carl H. Pforzheimer Library (New York). Notebook contains two reading lists that allude to Eliot's unfinished novel dealing with the Napoleonic War, military law, corporal punishment, desertion, and religious freedom in Ireland.

8   _____. "John Walter Cross to Herbert Spencer, Dec. 23, 1880: An Unpublished Letter Concerning George Eliot's Death." *English Language Notes* 13, no. 1 (September):39-40.
     A previously unpublished letter from John Walter Cross to Herbert Spencer details the manner of Eliot's death on 22 December 1880.

9   _____. "'Problematic Thinker' to a 'Sagacious Philosopher'; Some Unpublished George Henry Lewes-Herbert Spencer Correspondence." *English Studies* 56, no. 3 (June):217-21.
     Publication of four letters between Lewes and Spencer sheds light on their relationship and Eliot's relationship to them.

10 BAMBER, LINDA. "Self-defeating Politics in George Eliot's *Felix Holt*." *Victorian Studies* 18, no. 4 (June):419-35.
     Felix Holt, the Radical deals with claims of public and private morality. Yet Felix never pays the price for his actions that Eliot felt was the cost of social reform. The problem of a corrupt man representing a good cause is peripheral to Felix Holt because he supports neither the bad man nor the good cause. The plot of the novel ensures that politics are secondary to personal relationships. But Eliot's

1975

creation of unified images leads to artisitic and political conflict because Eliot's own tragic vision was unreconciled.

11   BAUMGARTEN, MURRAY. "From Realism to Expressionism: Toward a History of the Novel." *New Literary History* 6, no. 2 (Winter):415-27.

Discusses the narrator and his role as a character/mediator and the narrator's influence on the realism of *Middlemarch*.

12   BEDICK, DAVID R. "The Changing Role of Anxiety in the Novel." Ph.D. dissertation, New York University, 244 pp.

Surveys the thematic structure of anxiety in *Daniel Deronda*. The bad marriage is the tense and anxious situation that is built from the opening chapters. See *Dissertations Abstracts International* 36, no. 6 (1975):3682A.

13   BEER, GILLIAN. "Myth and the Single Consciousness: *Middlemarch* and *The Lifted Veil*." In *This Particular Web: Essays on Middlemarch*. Edited by Ian Adam. Toronto: University of Toronto Press, pp. 91-115.

"Argues that *The Lifted Veil* is a fictional manifestation of one of those collapses of confidence to which Eliot was subject throughout her life. She traces her escape from depressive vision through her recognition in *Middlemarch* of human reality as extraordinarily complex and ultimately irreducible." Examines *Middlemarch*'s sense of finding value in sympathetic human relationships in order to achieve unity.

14   BEETON, RIDLEY. "Joseph Conrad and George Eliot: An Indication of the Possibilities." *Polish Review* 20, no. 2-3:78-86.

Cites affinities in the works and careers of Conrad and Eliot. Compares passages from *Nostromo* and *Romola* for similarities in style; from *Middlemarch* and *Nostromo* and *Lord Jim* for statements on morality; and from *Daniel Deronda* and *Under Western Eyes* for similarities in structure.

15   BENSON, JAMES D. "Sympathetic Criticism: George Eliot's Response to Contemporary Reviewing." *Nineteenth-Century Fiction* 29, no. 4 (March):428-40.

Re-examines Eliot's response to her critics and finds Eliot resentful of her contemporaries who "fragment the unity of her fiction."

1975

Eliot believed that sympathy should be an element of responsible criticism so that the critic could avoid a fragmentary approach.

16 BOLSTAD, ROBERT MONTELLE. "The Passionate Self in George Eliot's *Adam Bede, The Mill on the Floss*, and *Daniel Deronda*." Ph.D. dissertation, University of Washington, 149 pp.
Critical analysis of *Adam Bede, The Mill on the Floss, Daniel Deronda*, and Eliot's letters shows conflicts between the community and individuals who resist the community's demand for self-renunciation in an attempt to live as free individuals. "Eliot's ideal of self-renunciation makes unrealistic demands upon egocentric human instincts." See *Dissertations Abstracts International* 37, no. 2 (1976):980A.

17 BONAPARTE, FELICIA. *Will and Destiny: Morality and Tragedy in George Eliot's Novels*. New York: New York University Press, 221 pp.
Eliot's protagonists, concerned with the tragedy in common life, personify man's limitations and projections of self. Actions and their consequences determine human will, moral judgement, and destiny in her novels, which can be perceived as individual Greek tragedies. "The collision of will and destiny which revealed man's tragic condition also taught him what restraints he must put on his will if he hoped to make the best compromise he could with an indifferent but powerful enemy." Argues that Eliot is a moral determinist whose tragic novels are not compatible with her beliefs. Explores Eliot's theory of the universality of human tragedy and demonstrates how it is portrayed in Eliot's fiction.

18 BRADLEY, ANTHONY G[ERARD]. "Family as Pastoral: The Garths in *Middlemarch*." *Ariel* 6, no. 4 (October):41-51.
Contemplates the Garth family and its "attempt to make pastoral a function of character. . . . The Garths' function is to provide from the outset an unambiguous moral yardstick for the other members of a society nonetheless modern for being provincial. . . ."

19 BULLEN, J.B. "George Eliot's *Romola* as a Positivist Allegory." *Review of English Studies* 26, no. 104 (November):425-35.
Considers the relationship between the structure of *Romola* and current mid-nineteenth-century interpretation of history – particularly the influence of Auguste Comte's *Philosophie Positive*. *Romola*'s allegorical account of the development of man's moral consciousness is

traced to Comte's account of moral evolution. Eliot attempted to fictionalize abstract Positivist theory. "Coming first under the polytheistic influences of her father and husband, then under the monotheistic influences of her brother and Savonrola, Romola emerges finally from her experience as the embodiment of a new way of life . . . and remarkable for her Positivist characteristics."

20   BURSTEIN, JANET HANDLER. "Journey Beyond Myth: The Progress of the Intellect in Victorian Mythography and Three Nineteenth-Century Novels." Ph.D. dissertation, Drew University, 199 pp.

Studies the evolutionary theme of the "progress of the intellect" in *Daniel Deronda*, Hardy's *Jude the Obscure*, and Conrad's *Lord Jim*. *Daniel Deronda* "reveals the ambivalence provoked by both the inadequacy of mythic modes of thought and language in a modern world and the decided limitations of abstract theoretical speculation." See *Dissertations Abstracts International* 36, no. 5 (1975):2838A.

21   CARROLL, DAVID. "*Middlemarch* and the Externality of Fact." In *This Particular Web: Essays on Middlemarch*. Edited by Ian Adam. Toronto: University of Toronto Press, pp. 73-90.

Examines the idea of the disengaged mind – one that has overcome egoism and is challenging reality. Studies how characters interpret their worlds. "Underlines the characters' perceptions as above all generative of consequences and shows the novelist at crucial points associating them with the demonology and angelology of the Gothic novel."

22   CRAIG, DAVID M. "A Study of Endings of Selected Nineteenth-Century Novels." Ph.D. dissertation, University of Notre Dame, 200 pp.

Identifies the mechanisms and meanings of endings in *Daniel Deronda*, Dickens's *Bleak House*, Stevenson's *The Master of Ballantrae*, and James's *The Golden Bowl*. Eliot tries to write an ending that goes along with the novel's sense of experience. Eliot uses the two devices of the *in medias res* opening and the "chipped off" ending. See *Dissertations Abstract International* 36, no. 6 (1975):3675A.

23   CUNNINGHAM, VALENTINE. "George Eliot." In *Everywhere Spoken Against: Dissent in the Victorian Novel*. London: Oxford University Press, pp. 143-89.

1975

Examines fictional accounts, in *Adam Bede* and *Felix Holt, the Radical*, of religious nonconformity within real historical contexts. Eliot's scientific and sociological interest in the working classes stems from her early Evangelical background, but her experience with dissent and dissenters was extensive and influential.

24 DORIA, PATRICIA JAMISON. "Narrative Persona in George Eliot and Henry James." Ph.D. dissertation, University of Texas at Austin, 221 pp.
"A detailed technical analysis of comparable passages from *Middlemarch* and James's *The Portrait of a Lady* reveals both the complex fluidity of voice in Eliot's omniscient narration and the similar tension of narrative attitudes which compose James's more effaced voice." See *Dissertations Abstracts International* 36, no. 10 (1976):6671A.

25 EDWARDS, MICHAEL. "George Eliot and Negative Form." *Critical Quarterly* 17, no. 2 (Summer):171-79.
Concentrates on the negative forms in *Felix Holt, the Radical*, which are governed by a tragic sequence. The book fails to affirm personal integrity by reenacting a process of failure.

26 ELIASBERG, ANN PRINGLE. "The Victorian Anti-Heroine: Her Roles in Selected Novels of the 1860's and 1870's." Ph.D dissertation, City University of New York, 333 pp.
Describes feminist concerns and altering patterns of sexual and domestic life in *The Mill on the Floss*, *Daniel Deronda*, and *Middlemarch*. "In each novel a central female figure, the anti-heroine, exposes through her experience of life and love the contradictory demands and limits placed on women by Victorian law and the middle-class social code." See *Dissertations Abstracts International* 36, no. 3 (1975): 1495A.

27 ERMARTH, ELIZABETH [DEEDS]. "Method and Moral in George Eliot's Narrative." *Victorian Newsletter* 47 (Spring):4-8.
Distinguishes between author, narrator, and narrative while considering the moral implications of Eliot's narrative treatment.

28 FAIREY, WENDY WESTBROOK. "The Relationship of Heroine, Confessor and Community in the Novels of George Eliot." Ph.D. dissertation, Columbia University, 238 pp.

Examines Eliot's recurrent theme of the heroine trying to reunite herself with her community with the help of a sympathetic father figure. Discussion of Eliot's own pessimism and difficulty in establishing and maintaining the heroine-confessor relationship throughout her fiction. See *Dissertations Abstracts International* 36, no. 3 (1975):1523A.

29 FRANCONE, CAROL BURR. "Women in Rebellion: A Study of the Conflict Between Self-Fulfillment and Self-Sacrifice in *Emma, Jane Eyre*, and *The Mill on the Floss*." Ph.D. dissertation, Case Western Reserve University, 188 pp.

Studies "the causes behind the literary and human rebellion" in Eliot's Maggie Tulliver. Eliot created, in Maggie, a believable character who cannot resolve society's need for self-sacrifice while trying to acquire self-fulfillment. See *Dissertations Abstracts International* 36, no. 7 (1975):4507A.

30 FREEMAN, JANET HELFRICH. "Story, Teller, and Listener: A Study of Six Victorian Novels." Ph.D. dissertation, University of Iowa, 224 pp.

Demonstrates the relations between the story, the teller, and the listener in *The Mill on the Floss* and *Silas Marner*. This approach to analyzing the narrative device differs from the usual analyses that perceive the narrator to be omniscient. See *Dissertations Abstracts International* 36, no. 8 (1976): 5315A.

31 GREENBERG, ROBERT A. "Plexuses and Ganglia: Scientific Allusion in *Middlemarch*." *Nineteenth-Century Fiction* 30, no. 1 (June):33-52.

Description of the effects of Eliot's scientific allusions and references on the political issues of *Middlemarch*. All of the allusions (i.e., to agriculture, chemistry, medicine, and physiology) refer to their direct or indirect influence upon reform.

32 GRIFFITH, GEORGE V. "The Idea of Progress and the Fiction of George Eliot." Ph.D. dissertation, Southern Illinois University, 304 pp.

Discusses Eliot's attitude toward progress and how she establishes conflict and plot to put forth her ideas on progress. Traces her idea of moral progress and how linguistic structures dramatize her

1975

concept of fiction. See *Dissertations Abstracts International* 36, no. 12 (1976):8073A.

33   HAIGHT, GORDON S. "George Eliot's 'Eminent Failure,' Will Ladislaw." In *This Particular Web: Essays on Middlemarch*. Edited by Ian Adam. Toronto: University of Toronto Press, pp. 22-42.
      Examines evaluative problems in Eliot's heroic characterization of Will Ladislaw. Defends him against the novel's critics.

34   HARDY, BARBARA. "*Middlemarch* and the Passions." In *This Particular Web: Essays on Middlemarch*. Edited by Ian Adam. Toronto: University of Toronto Press, pp. 3-21.
      Discusses the love relationship between Will Ladislaw and Dorothea Brooke. "Her heroine's idealism and sexuality seem to fuse, bringing critical objections of authorial identification." Eliot uses passionate statements to reveal the characters' outer expressions and inner lives. Study of the relations of feelings between author and characters. Reprinted 1982.28.

35   ____. *Tellers and Listeners: The Narrative Imagination*. London: Athlone Press, pp. 22-28, 74-78, 120-24, 133-38, 177-80.
      Assesses Eliot's interest in the moral implications of memory in *The Mill on the Floss*. Considers how Eliot used benign public conversation in *Silas Marner*, wherein she is "anatomizing exile and community."

36   HELLENBERG, NELLIEMAY MILES. "The Role of Nature in George Eliot's Fiction." Ph.D. dissertation, University of Oregon, 365 pp.
      Discusses the importance of external nature in Eliot's novels. Her concept of nature encompassed her philosophy that only through identification with nature can man realize his role in the evolutionary process. Emphasis is on the influence external nature has on human nature. The role of nature is discussed progressively throughout Eliot's development. See *Dissertations Abstracts International* 36, no. 9 (1976):6113A.

37   HERBERT, CHRISTOPHER. "Preachers and the Schemes of Nature in *Adam Bede*." *Nineteenth-Century Fiction* 29, no. 4 (March):412-27.

Analysis of the pairing of *Adam Bede*'s two preachers, Dinah Morris and Mr. Irwine, as exemplars of religious philosophies that are judged and discussed throughout the novel. The preachers comment on moral and metaphysical questions of the plot. Dinah's theory rests on the belief that Nature is corrupt; Irwine's Wordsworthian theory of Nature is sympathetic and beneficial to man.

38   HOFFELD, LAURA D. "The Servant Heroine in 18th and 19th Century British Fiction: The Social Reality and Its Image in the Novel." Ph.D. dissertation, New York University, 259 pp.
      Examines the nature of the servant heroine, public awareness of her, and ways in which the author treats her. Hetty Sorrel, of *Adam Bede*, is perceived as the erring servant. See *Dissertations Abstracts International* 36, no. 6 (1975):3730A.

39   HOROWITZ, LENORE WISNEY. "George Eliot's Vision of Society in *Felix Holt, the Radical.*" *Texas Studies in Literature and Language* 17, no. 1 (Spring):175-91.
      Analysis of the use of industrial England of the 1830s as setting for *Felix Holt, the Radical*. Set in the first year of elections following the Reform Bill of 1832, the novel presents a wide range of social problems and political philosophies. "The novel creates a broad myth of social transition, suggesting the selective incorporation of past values into a new social order." Eliot merges the political plot, the novel's myth of social transition and the historical changes upon a hierarchical society.

40   JACKSON, R.L.P. "George Eliot, J.S. Mill and Women's Liberation." *Quadrant* 94 [19, no. 2] (March-April):11-33.
      Dicusses women's liberation with reference to *Daniel Deronda* and John Stuart Mill's essay "The Subjection of Women."

41   JONES, JESSE C. "The Use of the Bible in George Eliot's Fiction." Ph.D. dissertation, North Texas State University, 294 pp.
      Identifies and analyzes Eliot's use of Scripture in her novels. Traces Eliot's acquisition of biblical knowledge; her use of the Bible for symbolism and characterization; her use of biblical phrases and allusions; her use of biblical themes of "duty, sowing and reaping, sympathy, renunciation, conversion, and suffering." See *Dissertations Abstracts International* 36, no. 5 (1975):2846A.

1975

42   JONES, PETER. "George Eliot and Philosophy." In *Philosophy and the Novel: Philosophical Aspects of "Middlemarch," "Anna Karenina," "The Brothers Karamazov," "à la recherche du temps perdu," and of the Methods of Criticism.* Oxford: Clarendon Press, pp. 50-69.
     Considers philosophical remarks by Eliot in her essays and letters, and the sources of these remarks.

43   _____. "Imagination and Egoism in *Middlemarch.*" In *Philosophy and the Novel: Philosophical Aspects of "Middlemarch," "Anna Karenina," "The Brothers Karamozov," "à la recherche du temps perdu," and the Methods of Criticism.* Oxford: Clarendon Press, pp. 7-50.
     By examining "the imagination-vocabulary in *Middlemarch*, the numerous references to images and imaging, to conjectures, inclination, preconceiving, foreseeing, fashioning, and fancying, it is discovered that other prominent notions are subsumable under the concept of imagination – notions such as possibilities and plans, conscience and unconsciousness, even power and providence."

44   JUMEAU, ALAIN. "Les romans de George Eliot: Genèse d'une tradition critique." *Études anglaises* (Paris) 28, no. 2 (April/June):190-202.

45   KIELY, ROBERT. "The Limits of Dialogue in *Middlemarch.*" In *The Worlds of Victorian Fiction.* Edited by Jerome H. Buckley. Cambridge, Mass., and London: Harvard University Press, pp. 103-23.
     Surveys Eliot's use of language, dialogue, and metaphor in *Middlemarch*. Feuerbach's theories on language are applied to Eliot's objective in using words to communicate – not as rhetoric. "Despite its double plot and careful pairing of characters, *Middlemarch* ... is a masterpiece of interrupted dialectics. ..."

46   KNOEPFLMACHER, U.C. "The Counterworld of Victorian Fiction and *The Woman in White.*" In *The Worlds of Victorian Fiction.* Edited by Jerome H. Buckley. Cambridge, Mass., and London: Harvard University Press, pp. 351-69.
     Analyzes Wilkie Collins's *The Woman in White* for its anarchic and asocial counterworld and how Eliot and other nineteenth-century writers use alternatives to civilized conventions. Eliot's portrayal of unrestrained egotism is revealed in her criticism of provincial societies.

47 _____. "Fusing Fact and Myth: The New Reality of *Middlemarch*." In *This Particular Web: Essays on Middlemarch*. Edited by Ian Adam. Toronto: University of Toronto Press, pp. 43-72.

Perceives *Middlemarch* as a combination of fact and myth and that it attempts to be a poem in prose. Examines influence of Eliot's readings, editorship, and translating on the evolution of *Middlemarch*.

48 _____. "*Middlemarch*: An Avuncular View." *Nineteenth-Century Fiction* 30, no. 1 (June):53-81.

Mr. Casaubon, Arthur Brooke, Peter Featherstone, Bulstrode, and Sir Godwin Lydgate "pervert the traditional role of father substitute . . . assigned to the uncle or avunculus in an ordered universe." The inadequate father substitute is the method by which Eliot dramatizes the orphaned condition of nineteenth-century intellectuals who lack a sense of identity with ancestors. *Middlemarch*, as a study of kinship, accounts for Eliot's personal interest in the variables of social and familial relationships. See also 1976.61.

49 LEDLIE, OLIVE. "Caleb Garth and George Eliot's Meliorism." *Research Studies of Washington State University* 43, no. 2 (June):126-29.

Considers the characterization of Caleb Garth, of *Middlemarch*, and his importance to the novel. The pessimistic theme of vocation is countered by Garth, who represents the positive elements of reform and an adherence to the concept of duty.

50 LERNER, LAURENCE. "Literature and Money." In *Essays and Studies*. London: John Murray, pp. 106-22.

Discusses details of domestic economy and Eliot's functional and moral views of money in *Middlemarch*. "In order to be above money, you need to have it . . . the true meaning of money is something a professional man has to earn bit by bit, and family man has to spend with care." Reprinted: 1982.45.

51 LEVENSON, SHIRLEY FRANK. "The Artist and the Woman in George Eliot's Novels." Ph.D. dissertation, Brandeis University, 462 pp.

Discusses the relationship between male artist and distressed woman protagonist in *The Mill on the Floss*, *Middlemarch*, and *Daniel Deronda*. In each case, the artist is the confessor-figure to whom the heroine turns. The artists have aesthetic sensibilities that symbolize

1975

their sympathetic natures. The three protagonists all lack the ability to apply their intellectual and emotional capabilities to some useful work. See *Dissertations Abstracts International* 36, no. 5 (1975):2849A.

52   LONGERBEAM, LARRY SIMPSON. "Seduction as Symbolic Action: A Study of the Seduction Motif in Six Victorian Writers." Ph.D. dissertation, George Peabody College, 196 pp.
      Examines patterns and functions of the seduction motif in *Adam Bede*. The conflicts between the upper- and middle-classes over seduction demonstrate the superiority of middle-class morality, power, economics, and social position. See *Dissertations Abstracts International* 36, no. 4 (1975):2222A.

53   MacANDREW, ELIZABETH, and GORSKY, SUSAN. "Why Do They Faint and Die? The Birth of the Delicate Heroine." *Journal of Popular Culture* 8, no. 4 (Spring):735-45.
      Contrasts the characterizations of Maggie Tulliver and her cousin Lucy in *The Mill on the Floss*. Applies theories of Gothic techniques and symbolism to the novel and attributes psychological significance to the realistic growth of the heroines of sentimentalism.

54   McDANIEL, JUDITH ADAIR. "Fettered Wings Half Loose: Female Development in the Victorian Novel." Ph.D. dissertation, Tufts University, 205 pp.
      Discusses the three situational categories fictional Victorian women were placed in by George Eliot and other Victorian writers. Heroines of *Felix Holt, the Radical* and *Adam Bede* find themselves in situations in which marriage is the desirable destiny. *Middlemarch* explores the traditional role definitions for its heroine, although she too marries. The third category examines women alone in the novels *The Mill on the Floss* and *Daniel Deronda*. See *Dissertations Abstracts International* 36, no. 3 (1975):1530A.

55   McELLIGOTT, MARY BRADLEY. "English Novels of the Eighteen-Seventies." Ph.D. dissertation, New York University, 430 pp.
      Analyzes the inspiration for *Daniel Deronda*, its method of publication, critical reaction to it, and social applications of the theories of the 1870s to themes and problems within the novel. The duality of *Daniel Deronda* illustrates certain dualities in the decade. See *Dissertations Abstracts International* 36, no. 6 (1975):3735A.

56 MAHAR, MARGARET ANNE. "The Shape of a History: Eliot, Hardy, and Lawrence." Ph.D. dissertation, Yale University, 201 pp.

Uses historical metaphors to analyze the "inner and outer forms" of *Adam Bede*, *Daniel Deronda*, *The Mayor of Casterbridge*, *Jude the Obscure*, *Sons and Lovers*, and *Women in Love*. Eliot uses a dialectical vision of history to present her belief that history is a continuing process with no beginning or end. Her characters are shaped by, and in turn shape, history. See *Dissertations Abstracts International* 36, no. 6 (1975):3734A.

57 MAKURATH, PAUL A., Jr. "Symbolism of the Flood in Eliot's *The Mill on the Floss*." *Studies in the Novel* 7, no. 2 (Summer):298-300.

A variety of symbolic meanings is attached to the climactic flood in *The Mill on the Floss*.

58 MARCUS, STEVEN. "Human Nature, Social Orders, and 19th Century Systems of Explanation: Starting with George Eliot." *Salmagundi* 28 (Winter):20-42.

"Examines certain of the modes, methods, and devices through which George Eliot establishes her account of the human world. These fictional, linguistic and conceptual arrangements and conventions can be demonstrated as bearing upon the meaning of her novels, upon the novel in the 19th century as a whole, and even perhaps upon the idea of the novel itself."

59 _____. "Literature and Social Theory: Starting in With George Eliot." In *Representations: Essays on Literature and Society*. New York: Random House, pp. 183-213.

Identifies modes and devices Eliot used to illustrate her view of human society. Study of "fictional, linguistic and conceptual arrangements and conventions" to demonstrate the meaning of Eliot's novels, the nineteenth-century novel, and the idea of the novel itself. Applies Eliot's theoretical views of society to *Scenes of Clerical Life*.

60 MARGULIES, JAY WARREN. "The Marriage Market: A Study of Variations of the Marriage Plot Convention in Novels by Austen, Thackeray, Eliot, James, and Hardy." Ph.D. dissertation, University of California at Berkeley.

Cited but not abstracted in *Dissertation Abstracts International* (1975).

1975

61   MAYNARD, JOHN. "Broad Canvas, Narrow Perspective: The Problem of the English Historical Novel in the Nineteenth Century." In *The Worlds of Victorian Fiction*. Edited by Jerome H. Buckley. Cambridge, Mass., and London: Harvard University Press, pp. 237-65.

Discusses the genre of the English historical novel and its failure to "confront the realities of history." In *Romola* and *Middlemarch*, Eliot approaches the genre by dealing "with the uses of history to the individual and, in turn, the uses of the individual to history."

62   MILLER, J. HILLIS. "Optic and Semiotic in *Middlemarch*." In *The Worlds of Victorian Fiction*. Edited by Jerome H. Buckley. Cambridge, Mass., and London: Harvard University Press, pp. 125-45.

Explores the structural metaphor of the web in *Middlemarch* – particularly the application of this theme to the range of social relationships in the novel. Discusses Eliot's metaphorical use of the stream and the microscope. Studies large-scale and small-scale structures as being intertwined within the Middlemarch society – infinitely subdividable. The totality of this society is watched over by the omniscient narrator, a separate being empowered to see the whole. Reprinted: 1986.48; 1987.28.

63   MILLS, RUSSELL. "Settings in Fiction: A Study of Five English Novels." Ph.D. dissertation, Indiana University, 259 pp.

Applies a theory of fictional settings – rhetorical and representational function – to *Middlemarch*. Eliot has a broad perspective of her society and demonstrates historical, philosophical, and scientific changes on man in society. See *Dissertations Abstracts International* 36, no. 11 (1976):7442A.

64   MINTZ, ALAN L. "George Eliot and the Novel of Vocation in England." Ph.D. dissertation, Columbia University, 287 pp.

Eliot uses vocation as a major theme in her late fiction. Discusses the issue that Eliot's concept of work is in contradiction with individualism. This theme is most evident in the major characters of *Middlemarch*, with its ideas for reform and philanthropy. "Among the 'workers' of the novel, by no means the least important is the novelist herself, who continually compares the success of her vocational endeavor (the novel) with the failures and imperfections of those of the characters." See *Dissertations Abstracts International* 36, no. 12 (1976):8077A. See also 1978.37.

65 MOERS, ELLEN. "Denaro, lavoro, e piccole donne: Il realismo femminile." *Communità* (Milan) 30:179-205.

66 ____. "Performing Heroinism: The Myth of *Corinne*." In *The Worlds of Victorian Fiction*. Edited by Jerome H. Buckley. Cambridge, Mass., and London: Harvard University Press, pp. 319-50.
     Eliot's perceptions and commentary on the novel *Corinne*, written by Mme. de Staël in 1807. The myth of Corinne is "the fantasy of the performing heroine" and is the basis for understanding Eliot's conception of heroism in *The Mill on the Floss, Adam Bede, Daniel Deronda*, and *Middlemarch*. Reprinted in part: 1976.45.

67 NEWTON, K.M. "Historical Prototypes in *Middlemarch*." *English Studies* 56, no. 5 (October):403-8.
     Discusses historical figures, Dorothea and Friedrich Schlegel, who influenced characterizations of Dorothea Brooke and Will Ladislaw of *Middlemarch*.

68 PERAZZINI, RANDOLPH JAMES. "Prophecy in Fiction." Ph.D. dissertation, Cornell University, 301 pp.
     Analyzes the concept of prophecy in *Middlemarch*. See *Dissertations Abstracts International* 36, no. 10 (1976):6676A.

69 POSTLETHWAITE, DIANA LYNN. "The Novelist as a Woman of Science: George Eliot and Contemporary Psychology." Ph.D. dissertation, Yale University, 275 pp.
     Analyzes the influence of the birth of scientific psychology on the novels of Eliot. In *Adam Bede* and "The Lifted Veil," Eliot questions the objectivity of the science of psychology. *Middlemarch* intertwines the complex nature of characters. Eliot attempts, in *Daniel Deronda*, to hypothesize on the inseparable qualities of subject and object and the ideal and the real. See *Dissertations Abstracts International* 37, no. 1 (1976):337A.

70 PRICE, THEODORE. "The Ugly Duckling: Recurrent Themes in George Eliot." Ph.D. dissertation, Rutgers University, 165 pp.
     The recurrent pattern of the hero as Jesus, the villain as Satan, and the heroine as Mary Magdalene is traced through *Romola, Felix*

Holt, the Radical and *Daniel Deronda.* "In this pattern, the heroine's soul is contended for by hero and villain; she is tempted by the powers of darkness; she is saved by having the right life revealed to her by the Jesus hero. Savonarola, Felix Holt and Daniel Deronda are the Jesuses; Romola, Esther Lyon, and Gwendolen Harleth are the Mary Magdalenes; Tito Melema, Harold Transome and Grandcourt are the Devils." See *Dissertations Abstracts International* 36, no. 5 (1975):2854A.

71 PUTZELL [-KORAB], SARA M[OORE]. "An Antagonism of Valid Claims: The Dynamics of *The Mill on the Floss*." *Studies in the Novel* 7, no. 2 (Summer): 227-44.

Maggie and Tom Tulliver's problems stem from the conflict of the conservative/progressive forces in history and thus result in "contributions to the evolutionary or historical process." In the ending of the novel, "Eliot emphasizes the continuity between the history of the brother and sister and the 'onward tendency of human things' as represented by the community of St. Ogg. . . . The many antitheses of *The Mill on the Floss* might be read dualistically as unresolved if Eliot had not repeatedly stressed union as the ultimate product of conflict."

72 RAINWATER, MARY JANICE. "Emily Dickinson and Six Contemporary Writers: Her Poetry in Relation to Her Readings." Ph.D. dissertation, Northwestern University, 281 pp.

Studies Emily Dickinson's readings and comments on the poetry and novels of George Eliot. See *Dissertations Abstracts International* 36, no. 7 (1976): 4479A.

73 RANCE, NICHOLAS. "Popular Politics in George Eliot's Historical Novels of the 1860s." In *The Historical Novel and Popular Politics in Nineteenth-Century England*. Barnes & Noble Critical Studies, edited by Michael Egan. New York: Barnes & Noble, pp. 102-36.

Historical novels *Romola* and *Felix Holt, the Radical* argue that the evolution of man's moral nature is divorced from politics. Man's moral nature is the only true progress. "In *Romola*, all value is located in the individual divorced from a society which there is no serious attempt to portray, and what might seem a characteristic disjunction of the historical romance is carefully contrived. . . . *Felix Holt* is much concerned with education of one kind or another."

74 REDINGER, RUBY V. *George Eliot: The Emergent Self.* New York: Alfred A. Knopf, 540 pp.

Emphasis is on Eliot's "emergence" as a great novelist and great person. Description of her emotional and creative growth and the development of her literary techniques, with most attention given to the early works. Biographical account of her early family relationships, particularly with her brother Isaac, life with George Lewes, and her writing career. How Eliot's use of a pseudonym is seen as the "symbolic birth" of the author. Studies the influence of Evangelicalism on her attitudes, ideas, and sentence structure. Recreates her confrontation with her need to write and the consciousness that made her overly critical of her own work.

75 ROBERT, NEIL. *George Eliot: Her Beliefs and Her Art*. Pittsburgh: University of Pittsburgh Press, 240 pp.

Considers the influence of Comte, Feuerbach, Evangelical Christianity, and evolutionary theory upon Eliot's novels. Gives a sympathetic and detailed review of each novel and considers how the above-mentioned influences, enhance, or detract from her artistic work.

76 SERLEN, ELLEN. "The Rage of Caliban: Realism and Romance in the Nineteenth-Century Novel." Ph.D. dissertation, State University of New York at Stony Brook, 275 pp.

"George Eliot's *Middlemarch* deals with human illusions, the subjective ways in which we view our world, and 'vision,' the most positive of illusions and the way to an ideal existence in the real world." See *Dissertations Abstracts International* 36, no. 2 (1975): 911A.

77 SHAFFER, ELINOR S. "*Daniel Deronda* and the Conventions of Fiction." In *"Kubla Khan" and "The Fall of Jerusalem": The Mythological School in Biblical Criticism and Secular Literature, 1770-1880*. Cambridge: Cambridge University Press, pp. 225-91.

Finds that Coleridge's 'Kubla Khan' and *Daniel Deronda* were "shaped by the higher critical movement." Examines Neoplatonism, Coleridge's syncretic style, Orientalism, and the basis of the form of *Daniel Deronda*.

78 SPACKS, PATRICIA MEYER. *The Female Imagination*. New York: Alfred A. Knopf, pp. 36-57, 72-77, 229-39, 319-21, passim.

Recount of the twofold interworkings of psychic power and social passivity that overcome Maggie Tulliver of *The Mill on the Floss*. Uses literary and psychological analysis to explore patterns in literature by women and the way imagination and traditional female

1975

preoccupations and roles make a difference in women's writings. Eliot's perceptions on adolescence, career vs. marriage, passivity, and power relations as embodied in *Daniel Deronda, Middlemarch,* and *Silas Marner.*

79 SPEER, RODERICK S. "*Middlemarch*: Dorothea's Nickname." *American Notes and Queries* 14, no. 3 (November):40-41.
    Ugly duckling and bird imagery associated with Dorothea Brooke is source for her nickname, Dodo, used by her sister Celia. Significant is the fact that the dodo bird is an extinct species.

80 SUTHERLAND, J.A. "Lytton, John Blackwood, and the Serialization of *Middlemarch*." *Bibliotheck* (Edinburgh) 7, no. 4:98-104.
    Discusses George Henry Lewes, Bulwer-Lytton and John Blackwood's sequential publication of *Middlemarch* in eight bimonthly books.

81 TESLER, RITA WEINBERG. "George Eliot and the Inner-Self." Ph.D. dissertation, New York University, 234 pp.
    Eliot's concept of the "inner-self" – the subconscious – was influenced by George Henry Lewes's *The Physical Basis of the Mind.* Her novels are "experiments with different personalities in different situations," in which she tries to formulate a method of combining one's inner self with moral purpose. In *Daniel Deronda,* Eliot strongly puts forth the idea that one's subconscious determines one's will to do good. See *Dissertations Abstracts International* 36, no. 4 (1975):2229A.

82 TORGOVNICK, MARIANNA. "Novelistic Conclusions: Epilogues in Nineteenth-Century Novels." Ph.D. dissertation, Columbia University, 249 pp.
    Examines the thematic and aesthetic uses of the epilogue in *Middlemarch.* The epilogue transforms endings by making them more thoughtful and adding new perspectives on the human experience. See *Dissertations Abstracts International* 36, no. 12 (1976):8041A.

83 TOTH, EMILY. "The Independent Woman and 'Free' Love." *Massachusetts Review* 16, no. 4 (Autumn): 647-64.
    Demonstrates how Eliot's heroines either conform or die and are not allowed independence or love. In neither *The Mill on the Floss* nor *Middlemarch* is sexuality a part of the potentially independent

woman's life. This is attributed to the dichotomy of women's roles and a lack of contraception during the nineteenth-century.

84 WILLIAMS, IOAN. "The Development of Realist Fiction: From Dickens to George Meredith." In *The Realist Novel in England: A Study in Development*. Pittsburgh: University of Pittsburgh Press, pp. 115-38.
Reprint of 1974.70.

85 ____. "George Eliot: The Philosophy of Realism." In *The Realist Novel in England: A Study in Development*. Pittsburgh: University of Pittsburgh Press, pp. 169-83.
Reprint of 1974. 71.

86 WILLIAMS, KRISTI FAYLE. "The Idealized Heroine in Victorian Fiction." Ph.D. dissertation, Brown University, 210 pp.
Studies the theories of fiction of Eliot, Dickens and Thackeray and how they dealt with the conflict between realism and idealization. Considers why Eliot, though committed to realism, resorted to idealization in critical parts of her fiction and how this affected her work. See *Dissertations Abstracts International* 37, no. 1 (1976):346A.

1976

1 ADAMS, KATHLEEN; BLACK, CYRIL; and CECIL, DAVID. "A George Eliot Memorial." *Times Literary Supplement* (London), 11 June, p. 707.
Documents, in a letter, a move by the George Eliot Fellowship to memorialize Eliot with a stone in the Poet's Corner of Westminster Abbey.

2 ARGYLE, GISELA. "German Key to Life in *Middlemarch*." *Ariel* 7, no. 4 (October):51-68.
"The criticism of life and art in *Middlemarch* functions in a German context. Eliot's treatment of such ideas as culture and self-culture, of scope and versatility, dilettantism and disinterestedness, is part of the Victorian tradition of showing by way of German examples what one may do in life and art."

1976

3   AUSTEN, ZELDA. "Why Feminist Critics Are Angry with George Eliot." *College English* 37, no. 6 (February):549-61.
Feminist critics disagree with Eliot's handling of Dorothea Brooke in *Middlemarch* because she did not allow Dorothea to do what she, Eliot, did in real life. Critics feel Eliot should have had Dorothea reflect herself rather than the real values of the Victorian culture. Feminist critics believe Eliot should portray active and ambitious women who take advantage of alternatives to their lifestyle – as Eliot did in her own life.

4   BAKER, WILLIAM. "George Eliot and Hebrew – Some Source Materials." *Studies in Bibliography and Booklore* 11, no. 1-2 (Winter):75-84.
Examines three types of materials available to Eliot in her study of Jews and Hebrew – biographical Hebraic sources; Hebrew available in her Judaica reading; and her personal collection of Hebrew-language books.

5   _____. *Some George Eliot Notebooks: An Edition of the Carl H. Pforzheimer Library's George Eliot Holograph Notebooks, Mss. 707, 708, 709, 710, 711*. Vol. 1. Edited by Dr. James Hogg. Salzburg, Austria: Institut für Englische Sprache und Literatur, 337 pp.
Edition of MS. 707 of the George Eliot holograph notebooks owned by the Carl H. Pforzheimer Library, New York. Describes the notebooks and textual notes. Appendixes include two unnoted George Eliot reading lists and a guide to her readings between 1875 and 1879.

6   BEATY, JEROME. "On First Looking into George Eliot's *Middlemarch*." In *The Victorian Experience: The Novelists*. Edited by Richard A. Levine. N.p.: Ohio University Press, pp. 151-76.
The first part of this essay concerns Beaty's own reading process for *Middlemarch* and his personal experience in reading Eliot. The second part of the essay examines Eliot's presentation of the relationship between sociopolitical questions and the life of an individual, and the historical experience of *Middlemarch*.

7   BEETON, D.R. "George Eliot's Published Translations." *Unisa English Studies* 14, no. 2-3 (September):22-28.
Evaluates Eliot's translations of Strauss's *Das Leben Jesu* and Feuerbach's *Das Wesen des Christendums* and the effect of the two philosophers on Eliot's thought.

1976

8   ____. "Some Notes on George Eliot's Manuscripts. *"Unisa English Studies* 14, no. 1 (April):1-17.
    Surveys British Museum's holdings of Eliot's manuscripts of fiction, poetry, and essays for indication of her artistic development. Compares published and manuscript texts.

9   BLAKE, KATHLEEN. *"Middlemarch* and the Woman Question." *Nineteenth-Century Fiction* 31, no. 3 (December): 285-312.
    Analysis of criticism against *Middlemarch* as a feminist novel. Qualifies the novel as feminist and deals with the "Woman Question" in four counterarguments in which she assesses sexual stereotypes and the issue of sex, feminist views of the period, marriage and education for women, and women's narrowing of prospects. Reprinted: 1987.3.

10   BUMP, JEROME. "Hopkins, Pater, and Medievalism." *Victorian Newsletter* 50 (Fall):10-15.
    Uses *Romola* to provide an analogy for Gerard Manley Hopkins's "attempted synthesis of the medieval and the classical . . . for Eliot wished to make Hellenism rather than Hebraism the subordinate element of the marriage."

11   BUTLER, PATRICIA ANNE. "Despondency Corrected: George Eliot, Romantic." Ph.D. dissertation, University of Texas at Austin, 222 pp.
    Clarifies Eliot's affinity with the spirit of Romanticism. Demonstrates her anxiety over spiritual attenuation and "that her creative response to the distress of this form of disenchantment parallels Wordsworth's in its vigorous striving for a transcending ethic of compensation." See *Dissertations Abstracts International* 37, no. 5 (1976):2890A.

12   CALDER, JENNI. "Women of the Period." In *Women and Marriage in Victorian Fiction*. London: Thames & Hudson; New York: Oxford University Press, pp. 120-31.
    Profiles George Eliot within the social context of the Victorian era. Discusses Eliot's writings about marriage and her relationships with Lewes and Cross. Examines Eliot's interest in the response of the community to its heroes and heroines in *Middlemarch* and *Daniel Deronda*.

1976

13   CHRIST, CAROL. "Aggression and Providential Death in George Eliot's Fiction." *Novel* 9, no. 2 (Winter):130-40.
      Examines the patterns and concept of providential death in "Mr. Gilfil's Love Story," *Romola*, and *The Mill on the Floss*. In each story, death satisfies the survivor's aggression while removing that person from a hostile situation. By using providential death to avoid aggression, Eliot puts limitations on the heroic and tragic capabilities of her heroines.

14   COLLINS, KENNY KAYLE. "Experimental Method and the Epistemology of *Middlemarch*." Ph.D. dissertation, Vanderbilt University, 544 pp.
      Studies the experimental method of the narrator and the empirical epistemology of *Middlemarch*. Perceives the experience of the novel to be the "instructive closeness to the workings of the scientific mind on its course of knowing . . . George Eliot meant *Middlemarch* to be, for its narrator and reader as well, an act of knowledge at once artisitc and experimental." See *Dissertations Abstracts International* 37, no. 9 (1977):5843A.

15   DEAKIN, MARY HANNAH. *Early Life of George Eliot*. Folcroft, Pa.: Folcroft Library Editions, 188 pp. Orig. pub. 1913.
      Biography of Eliot's life before beginning her writing career. Material is drawn from her early and later letters.

16   DeLAURA, DAVID J. "Froude's Translation of Goethe: An Addition and a Possible George Eliot Attribution." *Bibliographical Society of America: Papers* 70 (October):518-19.
      Cites Eliot's notation, from Haight's *The George Eliot Letters* (New Haven, Conn.: Yale University Press, 1954), which dates Froude's translation of Goethe's *Elective Affinities* before 1850.

17   DODGE, KIRSTEN ATKINSON. "Transformation: Deliverance or Death, Structure and Theme in George Eliot's *Daniel Deronda*." Ph.D. dissertation, University of Texas at Austin, 289 pp.
      Examines the combined identity of Daniel and Gwendolen. How Eliot uses mystery and magic to reveal the chasm between individual desire and forms of art, religion, and culture "through which this desire can be discovered and expressed. Both Daniel and Gwendolen have been disinherited, witness the failure of forms of identification, and

incorporate elements of good and evil." See *Dissertations Abstracts International* 37, no. 8 (1977):5139A.

18   DOHENY, JOHN. "George Eliot and Gwendolen Harleth." *Recovering Literature* 5, no. 2 (Fall):19-37.

Traces biographical and fictional parallels in Eliot's dislike of the typical Victorian beauty who sought no moral purpose and used beauty as a tool.

19   DOI, KOCHI. "*Middlemarch* Ni Tsuite." *Eigo Seinen: The Rising Generation* 121:114-18.

In Japanese.

20   DUNHAM. ROBERT H. "Silas Marner and the Wordsworthian Child." *Studies in English Literature* 16, no. 4 (Autumn):645-59.

Analysis of Wordsworth's presence and influence in *Silas Marner*. A romantic statement, *Silas Marner* uses a motto from Wordsworth's "Michael" to place the character Eppie in a Wordsworthian context. Eppie's natural piety allows Silas to acquire a child's wondering vision in his rebirth.

21   EMERY, LAURA COMER. *George Eliot's Creative Conflict: The Other Side of Silence*. Berkeley: University of California Press, 235 pp.

Applies Freudian concepts – father/daughter relationships, regressive needs, confrontation – to Eliot's inner conflicts and developing self-awareness as expressed in *The Mill on the Floss*, *Silas Marner, Felix Holt, the Radical, Romola*, and *Middlemarch*. See also 1979.38.

22   FAULKNER, PETER. "George Eliot, George Meredith and Samuel Butler." In *Humanism in the English Novel*. New York: Barnes & Noble, pp. 42-70.

"George Eliot's ethical idealism led her to write novels conceived in humanistic terms." Her treatment of the religion of humanity is paralleled with the treatments of humanism by George Meredith and Samuel Butler.

23   GAEDDERT, LOUANN B. *All-in-All: A Biography of George Eliot*. New York: E.P. Dutton, 138 pp.

1976

Biography of Eliot relies heavily on her correspondence and Gordon Haight's *The George Eliot Letters* (New Haven, Conn.: Yale University Press, 1954).

24 GANDESBERY, JEAN JOHNSON. "Versions of the Mother in the Novels of Jane Austen and George Eliot." Ph.D. dissertation, University of California, Davis, 210 pp.

Illustrations of the types of maternal power and influence evident in *Middlemarch* and Austen's *Mansfield Park*. A four-part typology defines the maternal types and concludes that "motherhood is but a delusive measure of authority and self-identity." See *Dissertations Abstracts International* 37, no. 6 (1976):3640A.

25 GRAVER, SUZANNE L. "George Eliot and the Idea of Community." Ph.D. dissertation, University of Massachusetts, 381 pp.

Explores the contradictions and problems in Eliot's ideas regarding community. Her writings reveal a "disparity between observed reality and an imagined ideal of community." See *Dissertations Abstracts International* 37, no. 9 (1977):5849A.

26 HAIGHT, GORDON S. "The Carlyles and the Leweses." In *Carlyle and His Contemporaries: Essays in Honor of Charles Richard Sanders*. Edited by John Clubbe. Durham, N.C.: Duke University Press, pp. 181-204.

Describes the relationship between George Eliot, George Henry Lewes, and Thomas Carlyle. Presents correspondence between the Leweses and Carlyles.

27 HALPERIN, JOHN, and KUNERT, JANET. *Plots and Characters in the Fiction of Jane Austen, the Brontës, and George Eliot*. Hamden, Conn.: Archon Books, Shoe String Press; Folkestone, Eng.: Wm. Dawson & Sons, 282 pp.

Chronological information, summaries of the fiction, and a catalogue of characters of Eliot's novels and major shorter fiction. Reference guide for information regarding dates, plots, and characters.

28 HARDY, BARBARA. "*Middlemarch*: Public and Private Worlds." *English* 25, no. 121 (Spring):5-26.

Discusses the "plurality of personal worlds" as presented in *Middlemarch*. "George Eliot's way of connecting outer and inner, public and private, historic and unhistoric, is to locate and understand the link within the individual consciousness." Reprinted: 1982.29; 1987.14.

29 HEINDEL, LINDA HEEFNER. "*Daniel Deronda*: Eliot's Debt to Feuerbach." Ph.D. dissertation, Lehigh University, 226 pp.

    Daniel Deronda illustrates Eliot's belief in the philosophy of Ludwig Feuerbach and the empirical approach to life. Through her handling of time sequence, plot structure, characterization and themes that convey human reason, will, and love, Eliot involved her readers in a sympathetic comprehension of the human condition. See *Dissertations Abstracts International* 37, no. 11 (1977):7142A.

30 HEMMINGER, MARILYN LEWIS. "George Eliot's *Daniel Deronda*: A Study of Vision and Form." Ph.D. dissertation, University of Pittsburgh, 261 pp.

    Eliot uses satire to define the moral fabric of the real and ideal societies of *Daniel Deronda*. The polarization of the values of Gwendolen's English society against Mordecai's historical vision of Judaism juxtaposes the relationship between vision and form. Eliot changes the standard conventions of the nineteenth-century realistic novel and adds romantic elements to come up with a mixed mode that is a measure of "what [her] thought and emotion may be capable of." See *Dissertations Abstracts International* 38, no. 1 (1977):281A.

31 JURGRAU, THELMA L. "'Pastoral' and 'Rustic' in the Country Novels of George Sand and George Eliot." Ph.D. dissertation, City University of New York, 474 pp.

    Compares the differences in the pastoral novels of Sand and Eliot. Clarifies the definition of pastoral and rustic and contrasts the works of Sand and Eliot accordingly. See *Dissertations Abstracts International* 37, no. 1 (1976):284A.

32 KENDRICK, WALTER M. "Balzac and British Realism: Mid-Victorian Theories of the Novel." *Victorian Studies* 20, no. 1 (Autumn):5-24.

    Comments on Eliot's knowledge and disapproval of the work of Balzac. Eliot, because of her affinity for realism, saw Balzac as presenting a destructive resolution of the conflict between the aesthetic and moral values of art.

1976

33 KER, I.T. "George Eliot's Rhetoric of Enthusiasm." *Essays in Criticism* 26, no. 2 (April):134-55.

Eliot's major failures as a novelist were the consequences of her early religious convictions and how these convictions determined her perceptions of life. Study of conversions in "Janet's Repentence" and *Adam Bede*, wherein Eliot uses an "Evangelical-type conversion as the mode of self-liberation." Eliot's writings are examined from the point of view of an agnostic writing within a Christian framework. Particular attention is given to the "higher religion of enthusiasm" in *Romola*.

34 KISCHNER, MICHAEL SERGE. "Spinozism in Three Novels of George Eliot: *Adam Bede, The Mill on the Floss*, and *Silas Marner.*" Ph.D. dissertation, University of Washington, 220 pp.

Discusses the philosophy of Spinoza and biblical criticism within the philosophical and psychological contexts of *Adam Bede, The Mill on the Floss*, and *Silas Marner. Adam Bede* illustrates Spinoza's theory of rationalism. Characters in *The Mill on the Floss* are connected by superstitions and Spinoza's associations between virtue/vice and power/impotence are applied. *Silas Marner* contains Spinozan elements from the two previous novels. These culminate in man's salvation resulting because of self-understanding. See *Dissertations Abstracts International* 38, no. 3 (1977):1412A.

35 KROPF, CARL R. "Time and Typology in George Eliot's Early Fiction." *Studies in the Novel* 8, no. 4 (Winter):430-40.

Elements of time – permanence/impermanence, timeliness, sequence, change, impending disaster, and tense – are studied in *Adam Bede* and *Scenes of Clerical Life*. Eliot uses biblical typology to depict the triumph of human experience over sequential time.

36 KRUTZ-AHLRING, INGRID. *Literatur als Kommunikation: Zur Frage der historischen und psychosozialen Vermittlung positivistischer Denkweisen in Literatur and Literaturkritik.* Giessen, W. Germany: Focus Verlag, 388 pp.

37 KUDO, YOSHIMI. "Mizu No Image Wo Megutte: *The Mill on the Floss* to *The Ambassadors.*" *Eigo Seinen: The Rising Generation* (Tokyo) 121:439-42.

In Japanese.

1976

38 LANGBAUM, ROBERT. "The Art of Victorian Literature." In *The Mind and Art of Victorian England*. Edited by Josef L. Altholz. Minneapolis: University of Minnesota Press, pp. 16-34.

Examines Victorian realism and the use of dramatic monologue in *Adam Bede*.

39 LASKI, MARGHANITA. "The Music of *Daniel Deronda*." *Listener* (London) 96 (23 September):373-74.

Discusses musical elements and sources of *Daniel Deronda*, as presented in an English radio broadcast (Radio 3, 22 September 1976).

40 LOTHAMER, EILEEN. "Science and Pseudo-science in George Eliot's 'The Lifted Veil.'" *Extrapolation* 17, no. 2 (May):125-32.

How Eliot negatively used pseudoscience and science to posit her theme of the religion of humanity.

41 McCOBB, E.A. "Aaron Bernstein's *Mendel Gibbor*: A Minor Source for *Daniel Deronda*?" *English Language Notes* 14, no. 1 (September):42-43.

Cites similarities, differences, and the influence of Aaron David Bernstein's character Jankele Klesmer (Musikant) from his *Mendel Gibbor* (Berlin, 1865) upon the musician Julius Klesmer of *Daniel Deronda*.

42 McFARLANE, FRANCES M. "La réforme et les réformes dans *Adam Bede*." *Études anglaises* (Paris) 29, no. 2 (April-June):152-66.

43 MAROTTA, KENNY [RALPH]. "*Adam Bede* as Pastoral." *Genre* 9, no. 1 (Spring):59-72.

Discusses literal and allegorical definitions of the pastoral elements of *Adam Bede*.

44 MILLER, J. HILLIS. "Narrative and History." In *ELH Essays for Earl R. Wasserman*. Edited by Ronald Paulson and Arnold Stein. Baltimore: Johns Hopkins University Press, pp. 165-83.

Assesses *Middlemarch* for elements of deconstruction of the assumptions of realism in fiction, history, and the writing of history. "History takes its place in *Middlemarch* as one theme parallel to a chain of other themes . . . religion, love, science, art, and superstition."

1976

45   MOERS, ELLEN. *Literary Women*. Garden City, N.Y.: Doubleday & Co., pp. 35-39, 42-53, 152-56, 173-77, 180-85, 192-200, 250-55, 287-90, passim.

Surveys literary traditions that came about because of female awarenesses and assertions. Reviews changes women writers have brought to the development of heroines who embody the realties and fantasies of women's lives. Explains why Eliot was moved to write about Jews in *Daniel Deronda*. Discusses Eliot's perceptions on the novel *Corinne* (de Staël, 1807). Reprinted from: 1975.66.

46   PAGE, NORMAN. "The Great Tradition Revisited." In *Jane Austen's Achievement: Papers Delivered at the University of Alberta*. Edited by Juliet McMaster. New York: Barnes & Noble, pp. 44-63.

Discusses Jane Austen's influence on Eliot and Austen's place in English literature.

47   PERRY, DONNA MARIE. "From Innocence through Experience: A Study of the Romantic Child in Five Nineteenth-Century Novels." Ph.D. dissertation, Marquette University, 241 pp.

Studies the figure of the Romantic child in C. Brontë's *Jane Eyre*, Dickens's *David Copperfield*, Eliot's *The Mill on the Floss*, Dickens's *Great Expectations*, and James's *What Maisie Knew*. "All five novels suggest the ambiguities of innocence. . . ." Examines how each author explores the child's consciousness. Eliot provides a mature narrative to put the child's view into perspective. See *Dissertations Abstracts International* 37, no. 6 (1976):3599A.

48   ROOKE, CONSTANCE. "Beauty in Distress: *Daniel Deronda* and *The House of Mirth*." *Women and Literature* 4, no. 2 (Fall):28-39.

Considers Eliot's influence on Edith Wharton's *The House of Mirth*. Compares parallels in vocabulary and characters from *Daniel Deronda*.

49   SABIN, MARGERY. "*Middlemarch*: Beyond the Voyage to Cythera." In *English Romanticism and the French Tradition*. Cambridge, Mass., and London: Harvard University Press, pp. 237-57.

Comparative criticism of the characters Dorothea Brooke of *Middlemarch* and Emma Bovary of *Madame Bovary*.

50 SCHOENWALD, RICHARD L. "G. Eliot's Love Letters; Unpublished Letters from George Eliot to Herbert Spencer." *New York Public Library Bulletin* 79, no. 3 (Spring):362-71.

Reprint of Eliot's letters to Spencer, in order of their composition, sheds light on their evolving relationship.

51 STERN, MICHAEL DAVID. "The Sociological Imagination and the Forms of Fiction: Social Structure in the Novels of Dickens, Trollope, and Eliot." Ph.D. dissertation, Yale University, 351 pp.

Analyzes the "historically-determined relationship between classical sociological thought and the classical European novel." A comparison of classical sociology and Victorian fiction as a response to industrialization and democratization in Europe between 1830 and 1920. Assesses Eliot's fiction, which integrated objective scientific analysis and subjective human behavior. See *Dissertations Abstracts International* 38, no. 1 (1977):250A.

52 SUTHERLAND, J.A. "Marketing *Middlemarch*." In *Victorian Novelists and Publishers*. Chicago: University of Chicago Press, pp. 188-205.

Describes production process of *Middlemarch* and the publisher/author relationship between Eliot and John Blackwood.

53 SWANN, BRIAN. "*Silas Marner* and the New Mythus." *Criticism* 18, no. 2 (Spring):101-21.

Analysis of *Silas Marner* as an anticipation of *Middlemarch* and *Daniel Deronda* because of its concern with the form of experience over its content. The subjects are mythic in that they show inner revelations. "Silas is a hero awaiting an awakening." Examines mythic structure, the limits of tragedy, and miraculous images – such as solar imagery. Eliot puts forth a religion which constitutes "the heart of mankind."

54 TOMLINSON, T[HOMAS] B[RIAN]. "'Fits of Spiritual Dread': George Eliot and Later Novelists." In *The English Middle-Class Novel*. London: Macmillan Press; New York: Barnes & Noble, pp. 114-30.

Analysis of George Eliot's perception of the influence of the circumstances of country society on women's sensitivities and fears. In *Daniel Deronda*, Gwendolen Harleth is bored by the idea of a domestic life and is often uncontrollably and physically repulsed by forms of love and tenderness. Discusses how Eliot was aware of the "possibilities in

1976

human nature for inconsistent, even vicious behavior of a kind that is not unconnected with impulses that dominate some of the best of the Gwendolen/Grandcourt scenes." Examines unstable elements in Eliot's writing and the society in which she lived. Examines Eliot, Hardy, Conrad, and James and their development of tendencies of middle-class confidence and solidity.

55   . "Love and Politics in the English Novel,1840s-1860s." In *The English Middle-Class Novel*. London: Macmillan Press; New York: Barnes & Noble, pp. 69-82.
        Explains why the themes of love and politics failed in the novels *Felix Holt, the Radical*, Disraeli's *Sybil*, and Gaskell's *North and South* and *Mary Barton*.

56   . "*Middlemarch* and Modern Society." In *The English Middle-Class Novel*. London: Macmillan Press; New York: Barnes & Noble, pp. 102-13.
        Contrasts *Middlemarch* with Dickens's *Great Expectations*. *Middlemarch* depicts a struggle between individualism (i.e., Dorothea and Lydgate) and the conservative, corporate unity of Middlemarch citizens. The novel demonstrates an acceptance of modern society. Discusses the failure of idealists in the novel.

57 TRICKETT, RACHEL. "Vitality of Language in Nineteenth-Century Fiction." In *The Modern English Novel: The Reader, the Writer, and the Work*. Edited by Gabriel Josipovici. New York: Barnes & Noble, pp. 37-53.
        Defines the language of the narrative in Dickens's *Bleak House* and Eliot's *Middlemarch*. Finds that "Eliot's imagination is continually checked and sometimes confused by her conscious or didactic intention. The shift from narrative to commentary is always deliberate but not always stylistically successful. . . . Exploring experience is a meditative, analytic process in her books."

58 TRUDGILL, ERIC. *Madonnas and Magdalens: The Origins and Development of Victorian Sexual Attitudes*. New York: Holmes & Meier Publishers, pp. 226-27, 229, 258-59, 262-64.
        A study of the discrepancies between actual Victorian social attitudes and literary attitudes. Patterns of literary prudery and the imagery of the Madonna are traced in *The Mill on the Floss, Felix Holt, the Radical*, and *Scenes of Clerical Life*.

1976

59 WATSON, CHARLES N., Jr. "The 'Accidental' Drownings in *Daniel Deronda* and *An American Tragedy*." *English Language Notes* 13, no. 4 (June):288-91.

Comments on coincidences in plot and timely accidents common to Dreiser's *An American Tragedy* and Eliot's *Daniel Deronda*. Eliot's influence on Dreiser is evident in their mutual concern for the psychology of the moral life.

60 WIESENFARTH, JOSEPH. "Legend in *The Mill on the Floss*." *Texas Studies in Literature and Language* 18, no. 1 (Spring):20-41.

How *The Mill on the Floss* retells the legend of St. Ogg and the legend of the flood as a tragedy that reaffirms life. Through this legendary approach to the novel, the reader can better accept the drowning conclusion of Maggie and Tom Tulliver.

61 _____. "*Middlemarch* (Commentary)." *Nineteenth-Century Fiction* 30, no. 4 (March):572-73.

Adds to, by use of historical reference, Knoepflmacher's interpretation of avuncular relationships in *Middlemarch*. Refers to 1975.48.

62 WITEMEYER, HUGH. "English and Italian Portraiture in *Daniel Deronda*." *Nineteenth-Century Fiction* 30, no. 4 (March):477-94.

In *Daniel Deronda*, Eliot "describes her English characters in terms of the English portrait tradition and her Jewish characters in terms of Italian, especially Venetian, painting. The pictorial descriptions contribute to both the characterization and themes of the novel." Eliot attempts to convince her English readers that the Jews deserve the respect given to other Mediterranean non-Protestants. Her English characters are portrayed as being affected, worldly, and unflattering.

63 WOLFE, THOMAS P[INGREY], III. "The Inward Vocation: An Essay on George Eliot's *Daniel Deronda*." In *Literary Monographs*. Vol. 8, *Mid-Nineteenth Century Writers: Eliot, DeQuincey, Emerson*. Edited by Eric Rothstein and Joseph Anthony Wittreich, Jr. Madison: University of Wisconsin Press, pp. 1-46, 195-98.

Reprint of 1973.71.

64 YUEN, MARIA. "Two Crises of Decision in *Jane Eyre*." *English Studies* 57, no. 3 (June):215-26.

1976

Compares the decisions made by Jane Eyre and Maggie Tulliver. The decisions involve their whole personalities, experiences and backgrounds, and reflect the heroines' discoveries of self-identity. Draws a parallel between Jane Eyre's decision whether to live with Rochester as his unmarried wife and Eliot's own personal decision regarding similar circumstances surrounding her relationship with George Henry Lewes.

1977

1   ANDRONNE, MARY JANE PETERSEN. "Legacies of Clerical Life: A Study of Clerical, Artistic, and Domestic Figures in the Novels of George Eliot." Ph.D. dissertation, University of Pennsylvania, 316 pp.

Analyzes the transformation of the early works' clerical ideals and standards into the domestic and artistic values of Eliot's later works. The growth of imagination and individual moral development are primary themes used by Eliot in all fiction following *Adam Bede*. See *Dissertations Abstracts International* 38, no. 3 (1977):1402A.

2   ARGYLE, GISELA. "German Elements in the Fiction of George Eliot, Gissing and Meredith." Ph.D. dissertation, York University (Canada).

An account of Eliot's, Gissing's, and Meredith's knowledge and opinions of Germany. References to Germany in the fiction of these authors are evident in German characters, books, music, art and setting. The symbolic use of Germany represents their affinity with German philosophies regarding life, art, realism and idealism. See *Dissertations Abstracts International* 38, no. 11 (1978):6710A.

3   ATKINS, DOROTHY J. "George Eliot and Spinoza." Ph.D. dissertation, University of Nebraska-Lincoln, 211 pp.

Explores the influence of Spinoza's philosophy and system of ethics in Eliot's novels. Liberating knowledge reveals a progress that can be likened to Spinoza's three types of knowledge – "imagination or opinion, reason, and intuition." Eliot portrays characters who strive for freedom in a deterministic world. See *Dissertations Abstracts International* 38, no. 8 (1978):4837A. See also 1978.3.

4   BEETON, D.R. "George Eliot: Select Bibliography." *Unisa English Studies* 15, no. 1 (April):39-44.
    Works of Eliot arranged chronologically under topics. Works dealing with Eliot arranged alphabetically under topics. Reviews Redinger's *George Eliot: The Emergent Self*. See also 1975.74.

5   BENET, MARY KATHLEEN. "George Eliot and George Henry Lewes." In *Writers in Love*. New York: Macmillan Publishing, pp. 113-83.
    Portrait of Eliot and Lewes as a couple whose achievements are directly related to their relationship. Controversial view of the sexual nature of Eliot's writings and how her immersion into life and a loving relationship generated her writing.

6   BERGER, MORROE. *Real and Imagined Worlds: The Novel and Social Science*. Cambridge, Mass., and London: Harvard University Press, pp. 17-18, 32-33, 146-49, 151-52, 156-58, 216-19, passim.
    Examines how the novel tells about social life. Passages on Eliot describe her interest in women's status in marriage and in novels; social class structure; the family and society; law, religion, kinetics and science; social causation; psychoanalysis; truth in fiction and the use of metaphor; and herself as a critic of society.

7   BLYTHE, DAVID EVERETT. "Household Gods: Domesticity in the Novels of George Eliot." Ph.D. dissertation, University of North Carolina at Chapel Hill, 343 pp.
    Considers the importance of home in the themes, metaphors, and characterizations of *The Mill on the Floss*, *Adam Bede*, and *Daniel Deronda*. "Every character whose virtues Eliot extolls reaches fulfillment either by achieving a happy homelife amid modest circumstances, and/or by seeking to make lives better for others." See *Dissertations Abstracts International* 38, no. 6 (1977):3509A.

8   BURNETT, T.A.J. "Brother and Sister: New George Eliot Letters." *British Library Journal* 3, no. 1 (Spring):24-28.
    Overview of letters describing Eliot's relationship with her brother, Isaac Evans.

9   DALY, MARY GAY. "Foundresses of Nothing: Narrators, Heroines and Renunciation in George Eliot's Novels." Ph.D. dissertation, Yale University, 285 pp.

1977

Describes the renunciation of each of Eliot's heroines and analyzes the narrator's responses to the characters' efforts to understand the narrator's changes. Examines patterns of renunciation in *Adam Bede, The Mill on the Floss, Felix Holt, the Radical, Daniel Deronda*, and *Middlemarch*. Studies sacrifices and their rewards, renunciation as a means to fend off fear, and the narrator's control. See *Dissertations Abstracts International* 39, no. 3 (1978):1583A.

10   DeBRUYN, JOHN R. "George Eliot and Alice Helps: Two Unpublished Letters." *Notes and Queries* 24 (October):409-11.
Publication of two letters from Eliot to her "spiritual mother," Alice Helps. The letters shed new detail on their developing friendship.

11   DRAPER, R.P., ed. *George Eliot: "The Mill on the Floss" and "Silas Marner."* Casebook series. London: Macmillan Press, pp. 234-51.
Consists of modern critical readings (1948-1970), comments on the novels by Eliot, and reviews and opinions by Eliot's contemporaries.

12   FAST, ROBIN RILEY. "Getting to the Ends of *Daniel Deronda*." *Journal of Narrative Technique* 7:200-17.
Identifies the differing methods and motives of the two plots of *Daniel Deronda*. How, stylistically and thematically, the two plots are distinct.

13   FERNANDO, LLOYD. "George Eliot: 'Emotional Intellect' in a Widening Ethic." In *"New Women" in the Late Victorian Novel.* College Park, Pa., and London: Pennsylvania State University Press, pp. 26-63.
Examines Eliot's letters for her views on women's nature and role in society. "*The Mill on the Floss* and *Daniel Deronda* deal centrally with the moral issues of women's freedom in a static society. They rest on aspects of a profound theory of the human sensibility which gives an equal place to the contribution women can make to the quality of life."

14   FLEETWOOD, JANET RYE. "The Spiderweb and the Beehive: A Study of Multiplicity in George Eliot's *Middlemarch* and Tolstoy's *Anna Karenina*." Ph.D. dissertation, Indiana University, 191 pp.
Defines the multiplicity of *Middlemarch* and *Anna Karenina* and how the expansiveness of both works is carefully organized to explore human destiny. *Anna Karenina* is arranged in a definite hierarchy and *Middlemarch* is a balance – the former is likened to a beehive, the latter

to a spiderweb. Analyzes four forms of multiplicity: triple-plot structure; multiple points of view; multiple character revelations; and multiple self-identities. See *Disserations Abstracts International* 38, no. 8 (1978):4841A.

15 FREEMAN, JANET H[ELFRICH]. "Authority in *The Mill on the Floss*." *Philological Quarterly* 56, no. 3 (Summer):374-88.
   Analyzes the role of the narrator in *The Mill on the Floss* as an important participant in the novel. Discusses how the element and passage of time affects the narrator as well as the main characters. Draws contrasts between Maggie Tulliver's and the narrator's accumulated memories and concerns for their futures.

16 FULMER, CONSTANCE MARIE. *George Eliot: A Reference Guide*. Reference Guides in Literature. Boston: G. K. Hall, 255 pp.
   Annotated bibliography of published critical writings written between 1858 and 1971. Includes indexes to Eliot's works, titles, authors, and subjects.

17 GINSBURG, MICHAEL PELED. "Free Indirect Discourse: Theme and Narrative Voice in Flaubert, George Eliot, and Verga." Ph.D. dissertation, Yale University, 270 pp.
   Uses Flaubert's *Madame Bovary*, Eliot's *Middlemarch*, and Verga's *Imalavoglia* to demonstrate that free indirect discourse "repeats on the linguistic level central thematic preoccupations of the text, and that it is always concomitant with other rhetorical or narrative structures similar in function to it." In *Middlemarch*, free indirect discourse asserts the shift in point of view and "repeats on the level of a single utterance the problem of the relation between author and text." See *Disserations Abstracts International* 39, no. 4 (1978):2236A.

18 HARTNOLL, PHYLLIS. *Who's Who in George Eliot*. Who's Who in Literature Series. New York: Taplinger Publishing, 183 pp.
   Alphabetically arranged list of characters from Eliot's novels. Each entry discusses character traits and characters' contribution to the story.

19 HIGDON, DAVID LEON. "Process Time." In *Time and English Fiction*. Totowa, N.J.: Rowman & Littlefield, pp. 15-44.

1977

Eliot's handling of time as process and chronological time, in *Adam Bede* and *Daniel Deronda*, is a symbol of character development and causality.

20   HOCHMAN, BARUCH. "From *Middlemarch* to *The Portrait of a Lady*: Some Reflections on Henry James and the Traditions of the Novel." *Hebrew University Studies in Literature* 5, no. 1 (Spring):102-26.

Comparison of the parallels in *The Portrait of a Lady* and *Middlemarch* and the differences in the authors' handling of similar themes and techniques.

21   HOLLOWAY, JOHN. Introduction to *Silas Marner*. London: J.M. Dent & Sons; New York: Dutton, pp. v-xix.

Comments on the novel's realism and representation of an English village in the nineteenth century. Discusses how English Congregationalism affected the complex microcosm of the English provincial culture. Points out patterning and symmetries of Silas Marner and Nancy Lammeter.

22   HUNT, LINDA SUSSMAN. "Ideology, Culture, and the Female Novel Tradition; Studies in Jane Austen, Charlotte Brontë, and George Eliot as Nineteenth-Century Women Writers." Ph.D. dissertation, University of California at Berkeley, 254 pp.

Explores the novelistic tradition of English women writers who wrote in response to changing ideas of the Victorian woman. The womanly ideal both nourished and warped women's lives but provided literary themes and inspirations for its women writers. Studies Eliot's relationship with the female subculture and the tradition of female fiction, and the positive and negative implications of that relationship. See *Dissertations Abstracts International* 39, no. 2 (1978):897A.

23   JOHNSON, E.D.H. "The Truer Message: Setting in *Emma*, *Middlemarch*, and *Howard's End*." In *Romantic and Modern: Revaluations of Literary Tradition*. Edited by George Bornstein. Pittsburgh: University of Pittsburgh Press, pp. 197-205.

Illustrates the impact of natural settings on the changing social structure as demonstrated in scenes of change in *Middlemarch*, Austen's *Emma*, and Forster's *Howard's End*.

1977

24 JONES, ROBERT ALAN. "The Rural Mirror: George Eliot, Jeremias Gotthelf and George Sand as Novelists of Country Life." Ph.D. dissertation, University of Illinois at Urbana-Champaign, 348 pp.

Mid-nineteenth-century rural novels of Eliot, Jeremias Gotthelf, and George Sand seriously and realistically portray country laborers in their working environments. Compares social and literary origins, moral instruction, social vision, thematic and narrative structure, psychological realism, and character idealization in Gotthelf's *Uli der Knecht*, Sand's *La Petite Fadette*, and Eliot's *Adam Bede*. See *Dissertations Abstracts International* 38, no. 1 (1977):245A.

25 KNOEPFLMACHER, U.C. "Mutations of the Wordsworthian Child of Nature." In *Nature and the Victorian Imagination*. Edited by U.C. Knoepflmacher and G.B. Tennyson. Berkeley: University of California Press, pp. 391-425.

Examines the influence of the Wordsworthian triangle of Nature, child, and adult in *Silas Marner* and *The Mill on the Floss*. Both novels were influenced by the poem "Michael."

26 LARKIN, MAURICE. "Eliot's Moral Dialectic." In *Man and Society in Nineteenth-Century Realism: Determinism and Literature*. Totowa, N.J.: Rowman & Littlefield, pp. 179-81.

Reviews Eliot's perception of the three stages of moral development and her application of this theme in *Middlemarch*.

27 ____. "The Industrial Revolution." In *Man and Society in Nineteenth-Century Realism: Determinism and Literature*. Totowa, N.J.: Rowman & Littlefield, pp. 74-88.

Discusses the effects of the Industrial Revolution in England and on Eliot's realism in *Felix Holt, the Radical* and *Middlemarch*.

28 ____. "A *Modus Vivendi*? George Eliot." In *Man and Society in Nineteenth-Century Realism: Determinism and Literature*. Totowa, N.J.: Rowman & Littlefield, pp. 89-97.

Analyzes Eliot's attempts to find a "foundation for morality in a determinist world." Her development was based on a synthesis of religion and science.

29 LEVINE, GEORGE [L.]. "High and Low: Ruskin and the Novelists." In *Nature and the Victorian Imagination*. Edited by U.C.

1977

Knoepflmacher and G.B. Tennyson. Berkeley: University of California Press, pp. 137-70.

Describes Eliot's imaginative landscapes and how they compare and differ from those of John Ruskin. Their treatments of the roadside cross are detailed.

30 LIDDELL, ROBERT. *The Novels of George Eliot*. New York: St. Martin's Press, 193 pp.

Recounts each novel and its narrative. Argues that Eliot's "greatest achievement lies in those characters whose dilemmas stem from their high ethical aspirations, and that Eliot analyzed their conflicts of conscience by the method of casuistry, resolving them by accomodating principles to specific cases and recognizing a higher and lower ethical norm."

31 LINKOVICH, STANLEY ANTONE. "The Romantic Image in the Novels of George Eliot." Ph.D. dissertation, University of Toronto (Canada).

Eliot's handling of artistic imagery provides a way to "relate her artistic views and practices to romanticism." Imagery of mountains, the Wandering Jew, music, the drifting boat, freedom, and the dream are discussed as indications of Eliot's ambivalence toward her own themes. See *Dissertations Abstracts International* 39, no. 4 (1978):2293A.

32 MESHER, DAVID R. "Rabbinical References in *Daniel Deronda*." *Notes and Queries* 24 (October):407-9.

Citations of rabbinical references in *Daniel Deronda* shed insight into Eliot's depth of knowledge in Talmudic studies and Jewish culture. Allusions to the *Talmud* and *Midrash* are divided into three categories: those traced to a secondary source; those that imply an unknown secondary source; and those for which the original work was Eliot's probable source.

33 MILLER, DAVID ALBERT. "Narrative and Its Discontents: Jane Austen, George Eliot, and Stendhal." Ph.D. dissertation, Yale University, 335 pp.

"The 'narratable' ... is possible only within a logic of insufficiency, disequilibrium and deferral, and traditional novelists typically desire worlds of greater stability and wholeness than such a logic intrinsically provides. Moreover, the suspense that constitutes the narratable comes to imply a suspensiveness of signification, so that what is finally threatened is no less than the possibility of a full or definitive meaning. Thus, novelists such as Jane Austen and George Eliot need to postulate a controlling perspective of narrative closure. . . ." See *Dissertations Abstracts International* 39, no. 3 (1978):1534A.

34 MOLDSTAD, DAVID. "George Eliot's *Adam Bede* and Smiles's *Life of George Stephenson*." *English Language Notes* 14, no. 3 (March):189-92.

Cites details from Samuel Smiles's *Life of George Stephenson* (London, 1857) which influenced Eliot's characterization of *Adam Bede*.

35 NJOKU, MATTHIAS CHIMEZIE. "George Eliot: The Technique of Unfolding Character from Within." Ph.D. dissertation, University of Alberta (Canada).

Cited but not abstracted in *Dissertation Abstracts International* (1977).

36 PASCAL, ROY. "Victorians: The Thackeray-type Narrator: George Eliot – Author and Narrator." In *The Dual Voice: Free Indirect Speech and Its Functioning in the Nineteenth-Century European Novel*. Totowa, N.J.: Rowman & Littlefield, pp. 78-89.

Examines Eliot's use of free indirect speech as a method of evoking the thought of characters and the double role of the narrator.

37 PUTZELL [-KORAB], SARA MOORE. "Victorian Views of Man in the Novels of Charlotte Brontë and George Eliot." Ph.D. dissertation, Emory University, 533 pp.

Analyzes Eliot's Hegelian view of human nature and the latitudinarian view held by Charlotte Brontë. Although both novelists present characters who "suffer as they act to realize their ideas of themselves and to do their duty, these individualists have quite different ideas about who they are, why they suffer, and what they should do with their lives." See *Dissertations Abstracts International* 38, no. 8 (1978):4851A.

38 ROAZEN, DEBORAH HELLER. "*Middlemarch* and the Wordsworthian Imagination." *English Studies* 58, no. 5 (October):411-25.

In her presentation of the basic aesthetics and moral issues, Eliot continues, in *Middlemarch*, to demonstrate Wordsworthian

1977

elements. "Her resolute affirmation of the value to be found in ordinary experience remains constant. ... The fundamentally Wordsworthian concern with unity of vision and integrity of personality remains central in *Middlemarch*."

39 RONALD, ANN. "George Eliot's Florentine Museum." *Papers on Language and Literature* 13, no. 3 (Summer):260-69.
    Finds *Romola* to be a failure because Eliot relied too much on pictorial details. Eliot loses the narrative because of an overextension of the visual arts.

40 SHOWALTER, ELAINE. "Feminine Heroines: Charlotte Brontë and George Eliot." In *A Literature of Their Own: British Women Novelists from Brontë to Lessing.* Princeton, N.J.: Princeton University Press, pp. 100-32.
    Describes women novelists and their characters against the backdrop of women of their time. Reviews the female literary tradition and how the development of that tradition is similar to other literary subcultures. Includes Eliot's perceptions on the feminine literature of her day ("Silly Novels by Lady Novelists"). Compares Eliot and Brontë – Eliot being in the Austen tradition of a studied, intellectual, and cultivated author.

41 SKILTON, DAVID. "Victorian Views of the Individual: The Brontës, Thackeray, Trollope, and George Eliot." In *The English Novel: DeFoe to the Victorians.* Newton Abbot, Eng.: David & Charles; Totowa, N.J.: Barnes & Noble, pp. 136-62.
    Finds Eliot's novels to be the "profoundest examination of the nineteenth-century individual in relation to his or her environment and, in their constant working out of her religious humanism in action, the greatest fictional embodiment of any philosophical position in the language."

42 SMITH, JANE S. "The Reader as Part of the Fiction: *Middlemarch*." *Texas Studies in Literature and Language* 19, no. 2 (Summer):188-203.
    Discusses Eliot's technique of placing the reader in the twofold position of being an outside observer and of being within the confines of the narrative. How this placement of the reader is vital to the narrative technique is analyzed in relation to *Middlemarch* and Brontë's

Jane Eyre. Examines the role of the reader as fictive reader, and the psychological adjustments and identification that entails.

43 STWERTKA, EVE MARIE. "The Web of Utterance: *Middlemarch*." *Texas Studies in Literature and Language* 19, no. 2 (Summer):179-87.

Studies the roles of the narrator and reader and the elements of utterance and speech in *Middlemarch*. Analysis of how speech expresses the metaphors of open/closed space and of the web being spun. Dorothea's elucidation and generalizations provide insight into her inner thoughts, which are punctuated by the silent, meditative passages.

44 SUKENICK, LYNN. "On Women and Fiction." In *The Authority of Experience: Essays in Feminist Criticism*. Edited by Arlyn Diamond and Lee R. Edwards. Amherst: University of Massachusetts Press, pp. 28-44.

Eliot asserted that it is "an immense mistake to maintain that there is no sex in literature" and that "a woman has something specific to contribute" to literature, despite the fact that she retained a masculine pseudonym. Eliot pleaded for women to rebuke generalizations that prejudice men against them – "women have not to prove that they can be emotional and rhapsodic, and spiritualistic; everyone believes that already. They have to prove that they are capable of accurate thought, severe study, and continuous self-demand." Discusses sexual and gender misconceptions in literature, as well as Eliot's treatment of neuter gender, women's intellect, and feminism.

45 SWANN, CHARLES S.B. "Evolution and Revolution: Politics and Form in *Felix Holt* and *The Revolution in Tanner's Lane*." In *Literature, Society, and the Sociology of Literature*. Edited by Francis Barker. Proceedings of the conference held at the University of Essex, July 1976. Colchester: University of Essex, pp. 75-92.

Detailed comparison of Mark Rutherford's *The Revolution in Tanner's Lane* (1887) and *Felix Holt* and the theme of political revaluation. Analyzes different presentations of form and political attitude. "Eliot pins her faith on evolution and tries to underpin it by claiming a semi-scientific sanction for this view, while Rutherford can allow for the possibility or at least the desirability of radical change whether in an individual-conversion or in a society-revolution."

1977

46 THOMSON, PATRICIA. "The Two Georges." *George Sand and the Victorians: Her Influence and Reputation in Nineteenth-Century England.* New York: Columbia University Press, pp. 152-84.
    Evaluates the influence of George Sand on Eliot and compares their careers and writing styles.

47 TJOA, HOCK GUAN. *George Henry Lewes: A Victorian Mind.* Cambridge, Mass.: Harvard University Press, 172 pp.
    Analysis of Lewes's moral and philosophical theories.

48 WALLACE, ROBERT K. "Probable Source for Dorothea and Casaubon: Hester and Chillingworth." *English Studies* 58, no. 1 (February):23-25.
    Cites parallels between and influences of Hawthorne's characters Hester Prynne and Chillingworth of *The Scarlet Letter* (1850) and the *Middlemarch* characters of Dorothea Brooke and Casaubon.

49 WIESENFARTH, JOSEPH. *George Eliot's Mythmaking.* Heidelberg: Carl Winter Universitäts-verlag, 280 pp.
    Mythic analysis of each of Eliot's novels and poems and the archetypal patterns of the pagan, Christian, and Hebrew myths. "The canon of George Eliot's fiction presents a mythology of fellow-feeling which exhibits phases of creation, destruction, redemption, and longing for Paradise, and that these phases subsume specific biblical and classical myths into their structure."

50 ____. "George Eliot's Notes for *Adam Bede*." *Nineteenth-Century Fiction* 32, no. 2 (Spring):127-65.
    Notes deemed pertinent to *Adam Bede* are printed. Commentary on the notes discusses facts about Eliot's reading habits, research, and character influences.

51 WILLIAMS, RAYMOND. "The Knowable Community in George Eliot's Novels." In *Towards a Poetics of Fiction.* Edited by Mark Spilka. Bloomington and London: Indiana University Press, pp. 225-38.
    Examines the knowable community within country life in *Adam Bede* and *The Mill on the Floss.* Studies plot construction, language, setting, and country action. Reprint of 1973.70.

52 WOLFF, ROBERT LEE. "Eric and Janet: Two Studies in Repentence." In *Gains and Losses: Novels of Faith and Doubt in Victorian England*. New York: Garland, pp. 220-37.

Discusses religious issues in Eliot's fiction and how her writing reflects her own religious experience. Examines *Scenes of Clerical Life*. Traces sources for characters, Eliot's opposition to Evangelicals, and Evangelical heroes.

53 YEE, CAROLE ZONIS. "Feminism and the Later Heroines of George Eliot." Ph.D. dissertation, University of New Mexico, 281 pp.

Finds feminist attributes in heroines of *Romola, Felix Holt, the Radical, Middlemarch*, and *Daniel Deronda*, when studied within their aesthetic contexts. When Romola, Esther Lyon, Dorothea Brooke, and Gwendolen Harleth become aware of the fact that their personal lives are bound to the historical forces surrounding them, they learn to act in their own interests, asserting their individuality and experiencing kinship with others. Uses critical methodology of Murray Krieger to discuss heroines' resolution of conflicts. See *Dissertations Abstracts International* 38, no. 6 (1977):3526A.

54 YOUNGREN, VIRGINIA ROTAN. "Moral Life in Solitude: A Study of Selected Novels of Jane Austen, Charlotte Brontë, Elizabeth Gaskell, and George Eliot." Ph.D. dissertation, Rutgers University, 172 pp.

Even though the novelists discussed here move out of the home, they maintain a point of view that puts value on introspection and private, moral perspective. They saw their work as being defined by their experience as women and that, as novelists, they had moral influences and obligations. See *Dissertations Abstracts International* 38, no. 2 (1977):814A.

55 ZEMAN, ANTHEA. *Presumptuous Girls: Women and Their World in the Serious Woman's Novel*. London: Weidenfeld & Nicolson, pp. 32-33, 56-60, 93-94, 100-101, 159-63, passim.

Considers Eliot's heroines and her comments on marriage and religion in this study of women writers who wrote as witnesses to their particular times.

56 ZICHY, FRANCIS ANTHONY. "The Novelist's Purpose: Sympathy and Judgment in the Novels of George Eliot." Ph.D. dissertation, Harvard University.

1977

Cited but not abstracted in *Dissertations Abstracts International* (1977).

57 ZIMMERMAN, BONNIE S[UE]. "'Radiant as a Diamond': George Eliot, Jewelry, and the Female Role." *Criticism* 19 (Summer):212-22.
Analysis of Eliot's use of jewelry as a metaphor and symbol of the female role in *Middlemarch, Adam Bede*, and *Daniel Deronda*. Through control of imagery, jewelry and ornamentation come to symbolize "woman's struggle to transform her hard lot into the duty, sympathy, and devotion that exalt human life."

1978

1 ALLEY, HENRY. "Allusion as a Technique of Characterization in *Middlemarch* and *Daniel Deronda*." *Greyfriars* 19:29-39.
Points out that Eliot's allusions to the heroic past do not necessarily denigrate the present. "Eliot uses the world of allusion to draw herself away from her characters and to elevate the more modern world of her fictional account by suggesting that its hardships and relations are more intricate than those of the past."

2 ALTICK, RICHARD. "Anachronisms in *Middlemarch*: A Note." *Nineteenth-Century Fiction* 33, no. 3 (December):366-72.
Illustrates anachronisms found in *Middlemarch*, despite Eliot's research and attention to authentic topical detail.

3 ATKINS, DOROTHY [J.]. *George Eliot and Spinoza*. Salzburg Studies in English Literature. Edited by Dr. James Hogg. Salzburg, Austria: Institut für Englische Sprache und Literatur, Universität Salzburg, 188 pp.
Discusses the influence of Spinoza's ethical doctrine on Eliot's novels, in particular *Adam Bede*. Assesses the ideas of freedom and bondage as Eliot applied them in *Felix Holt, the Radical* and *Daniel Deronda*, after having translated Spinoza's *Ethics*. See also 1977.3

4 AUERBACH, NINA. "Artists and Mothers: A False Alliance." *Women and Literature* 6, no. 1 (Spring):3-15.

1978

Considers artisitic (writing) and biological (mothering) creativity as separate entities. For Eliot and Jane Austen, the role of author was not a metaphoric submission to childlessness. Both authors found writing to be "more spacious, more adult, more inclusive."

5 ____. *Communities of Women: An Idea in Fiction*. Cambridge, Mass., and London: Harvard University Press, pp. 22-23, 28, 42, 43, 155, 195-96, passim.

Characterizes the community of women as a literary image that rebukes the traditional hypothesis that women live for and through men to attain position within the community. Communities of women in literature illustrate the hopes and fears of realistic self-sufficiency. Discusses Eliot's relationship with Edith Simcox and George Henry Lewes.

6 BENSON, JAMES D. "*Romola* and the Individuation Process." *Colby Library Quarterly* 14, no. 2 (June):54-71.

Argues, by means of Jungian analysis, for the positive development of the character Romola. Identifies Romola's mechanisms for projection and repression and her stages of individuation.

7 CHAPMAN, RAYMOND, and GOTTLIEB, ELEANORA. "A Russian View of George Eliot." *Nineteenth-Century Fiction* 33, no. 3 (December):348-65.

Translation of Sophía Kovalevskaia's journal in which she gives an account of her visits with George Eliot and her impressions of the author. Journal provides comment on Victorian English literary society and Eliot's novels.

8 CHASE, CYNTHIA. "The Decomposition of the Elephants: Double-Reading *Daniel Deronda*." *PMLA* 93, no. 2 (March):215-27.

"A letter to the hero in *Daniel Deronda* offers an interpretation of George Eliot's novel, an account of its rhetorical principles: the Deronda plot discloses not the effects of causes but the present causes of past effects. This metaleptic plot structure contradicts the linking of origin, cause and identity affirmed in the story of Deronda's Jewish birth. The story must shift between constative and performative conceptions of language and must finally invoke the notion of an actual, nonlinguistic fact or act. The relevant referent is Deronda's circumcision. . . ." Reprinted: 1986.10. See also 1978.50.

1978

9 COHAN, STEVEN. "Narrative Form and Death: *The Mill on the Floss* and *Mrs. Dalloway*." *Genre* 11, no. 1 (Spring):109-29.

Maintains that the narrative needs an ending for form and that endings are "little deaths." Justifies Eliot's ending by suggesting that not only does the narrative make death inevitable, but the reader hopes for Maggie's death as the option that life cannot give her. Victorian linear form copes with death because of the Victorian belief in progress.

10 COHEN, SUSAN REGINA. "'The Family Procession': Generational Structures in the Novels of George Eliot." Ph.D. dissertation, Yale University, 211 pp.

Illumination of Eliot's imaginative involvement of the family in her novels. In the early novels, she focuses on the immediate nuclear family and, in later works, she writes about the genealogical lines. Throughout all of her works she negates the family model and interrupts the genealogical flow by including bastards, adopted, orphaned, and abandoned children—all violating the simple family scheme. See *Dissertations Abstracts International* 40, no. 1 (1979):265A.

11 COLLINS, K[ENNY] K[AYLE]. "G.H. Lewes Revised: George Eliot and the Moral Sense." *Victorian Studies* 21, no. 4 (Summer):463-92.

How Eliot writes about ethical questions based upon her revisions of Lewes's manuscript for *Problems of Life and Mind*. Similarities between Eliot's moral perceptions in her fiction and Lewes's manuscript are drawn—with emphasis on *Middlemarch*. An outline of the nineteenth-century moral philosophy surrounding the intuitionist/utilitarian controversy is given to illustrate Eliot's and Lewes's attempt to reconcile the arguments of the controversy. Although Eliot adhered to Lewes's philosophy, she modified his views by restoring balance to his ethics.

12 CONNORS, PATRICIA ELIZABETH. "A Mythic Analysis of George Eliot's *Adam Bede*." Ph.D. dissertation, University of Detroit, 150 pp.

Discusses the problem of defining the genre of *Adam Bede*. Confronts the question of genre by using a mythic reading and Northrop Frye's methodology from *Anatomy of Criticism*. Allusions to the Arthurian legend, the summer cycle, and the myth of Adam and Eve are drawn. See *Dissertations Abstracts International* 40, no. 12 (1980):6288A.

1978

13 CONWAY, RICHARD. *"Silas Marner* and *Felix Holt*: From Fairy Tale to Feminism." *Studies in the Novel* 10, no. 3 (Fall):295-304.
    Traces parallels in the plots of *Silas Marner* and *Felix Holt, the Radical*. Gives a feminist reading of the novels' names and themes. In *Felix Holt, the Radical*, Eliot takes the Eppie character from *Silas Marner* and dramatizes her freedom in *Felix Holt, the Radical* in the character of Esther Lyon.

14 DAVIS, GABRIELLE A. WITTIG. "Novel Associations: Theodore Fontane and George Eliot within the Context of Nineteenth Century Realism." Ph.D. dissertation, Stanford University, 250 pp.
    Biographical and artistic relationships between Eliot and Theodore Fontane shed new perspective on German realist fiction within the tradition of European realism. Discussion of biographical similarities, aesthetic theories, the authors' approach to the male-female relationship, and their humanistic convictions. See *Dissertations Abstracts International* 39, no. 9 (1979):5491A.

15 ELIOT, GEORGE. *Early Essays*. Norwood, Pa.: Norwood Editions, 71 pp. Orig. pub. London: Westminster Press, 1919.
    Contents include reprints of five essays, a chronology, and index.

16 _____. *The George Eliot Letters, 1840-1870*. Vol. 8. Edited by Gordon S. Haight. New Haven, Conn., and London: Yale University Press, 491 pp.
    Includes letters to Herbert Spencer, her work on *Adam Bede, The Mill on the Floss, Silas Marner, Romola, Felix Holt, the Radical*, and "The Spanish Gypsy," and her life with Lewes in England and Germany. Includes a list of Eliot's correspondents.

17 _____. *The George Eliot Letters, 1871-1881*. Vol. 9. Edited by Gordon S. Haight. New Haven, Conn., and London: Yale University Press, 539 pp.
    Supplements and completes previous editions. Includes new letters to George Combe and Herbert Spencer, letters by George Henry Lewes, Eliot's letters regarding the death of Lewes, her work on *Middlemarch, Daniel Deronda*, and "Theophrastus Such," and her marriage to John Walter Cross. Indexes vol. 1-9.

18 FLEISHMAN, AVROM. "Daniel Charisi: Assessment of *Daniel Deronda* in the History of Ideas." In *Fiction and the Ways of*

1978

Knowing: Essays on British Novels. Austin: University of Texas Press, pp. 86-109.

Analysis of the Jewish part of *Daniel Deronda* in "view of English social values that Eliot creates and of imagining the alternative society that she envisions. For 'Daniel Charisi' ... is a work of systematic social criticism and at the same time a visionary, even 'utopian' novel, acidly etching what is real and, in close juxtaposition, imagining what is possible."

19   FREY, BARBARA GAY. "Love, Sex, and Artists in George Eliot's Works." Ph.D. dissertation, City University of New York, 468 pp.

Considers the relationship of sex, love, and art in the essays, poetry, and fiction of Eliot. As her career progresses, Eliot changes her portrayal of women's art as being inferior to men's art to one of equality, provided each person realistically pursues one's art. "Eliot comes to acknowledge the power of sexuality to help create good art and to bring happiness to the individual." See *Dissertations Abstracts International* 39, no. 4 (1978):2288A.

20   GANIM, VIRGINIA LYNN. "Limitation and Responsibility in the Fiction of Goethe and George Eliot." Ph.D. dissertation, Emory University, 235 pp.

"An exploration of the affinities between Goethe and George Eliot in their presentations of the proper use of, and response to, art; human limitation in the face of the unknown forces of the universe; and the appropriate responses to that limitation indicate a remarkably similar view of the world and its responsibilities." In the areas of the aesthetic, the ethical, and the epistemological, in *Daniel Deronda* and Goethe's *Wilhelm Meister's Apprenticeship*, the authors see the world in similar ways. See *Dissertations Abstracts International* 39, no. 7 (1979):4269A.

21   GEZARI, JANET [K.]. "The Metaphorical Imagination of George Eliot." *ELH* 45, no. 1 (Spring):93-106.

Surveys Eliot's language and readers' response to her metaphors and imagination. Evaluates Eliot's metaphors of vision and of journeys. Attempts to study the metaphor as a mediating device, meant to stir the sympathies of the reader.

1978

22   GOLDSBERRY, DENNIS [MERRILL]. "Goethe and George
     Eliot's *Middlemarch*." *University of South Florida Language Quarterly*
     16, nos. 3-4 (Spring-Summer):39-44, 48.
         Cites Goethe's influence on Eliot. "Both authors start with
     presuppositions and then try to embody or verify them by sensory
     experience. . . . Both thought man was born an egoist . . . that youth
     could grow to unselfish living and their primary intuitions were that
     man found his identity through striving." Compares Dorothea Brooke's
     education and ethical responses to life with those of the Meister in
     Wilhelm Meisters Lehrjahre.

23   GREEN, JANE MERLE. "Creative Ambivalence: George Eliot's
     Narrative Stance." Ph.D. dissertation, State University of New York
     at Buffalo, 285 pp.
         "Explores the tensions of individual relationships, the dynamic
     between author and her audience, and the developmental relationship
     between the author and her work in *Adam Bede, The Mill on the Floss,
     Middlemarch,* and *Daniel Deronda.*" Examines how Eliot
     "simultaneously presents the evolution of social and personal histories
     as the evolution of a set of moral and social imperatives." See
     Dissertations Abstracts International 39, no. 12 (1979):7356A.

24   HAIGHT, GORDON S. "The Heroine of *Middlemarch*." *Victorian
     Newsletter* 54 (Fall):4-8.
         "Mary Garth serves as a control, a standard of life, against which
     Dorothea and Rosamond must be measured." Perceives Mary Garth to
     be the true heroine of the novel.

25   HALEY, BRUCE. "Two Staunch Walkers: Tom Thurnall and Tom
     Tulliver." In *The Healthy Body and Victorian Culture*. Cambridge,
     Mass., and London: Harvard University Press, pp. 180-204.
         Eliot's perceptions on health – mental and physical – are traced
     in *The Mill on the Floss* and *Adam Bede*. Evaluation of Victorian health
     trends such as phrenology and physiological psychology, and Eliot's
     response to them.

26   HARRIS, MASON. "Arthur's Misuse of the Imagination:
     Sentimental Benevolence and Wordsworthian Realism in *Adam
     Bede*." *English Studies in Canada* 4, no. 1 (Spring):41-59.

1978

"Sentimental benevolence" of *Adam Bede* refers to Arthur's attitude toward Hetty Sorrel and refers to the unconscious snobbery of the eighteenth-century upper class.

27   HUTCHINGS, PATRICIA ANN. "From Truism to Truth: George Eliot's Use of the Narrator." Ph.D. dissertation, University of Iowa, 198 pp.
      Studies the role and function of the narrator in all of Eliot's fiction in an attempt to "prove that changes in her use of the narrator stem from a growing skepticism about the possibility of conveying general wisdom in fiction." Eliot was less concerned with the "truisms which generalization can convey than with the truth it cannot." See *Dissertations Abstracts International* 39, no. 6 (1978):3598A.

28   KAYE, ROGER WILLIAM. "Character and Value in George Eliot's Novels." Ph.D. dissertation, Stanford University, 273 pp.
      Argues that Eliot's characters express an "organistic" concept of man. Discussion of Eliot's characters in action, their speech, involvement in schools and reading, the effects of their deeds, and the characters' concept of boredom. Cites examples of Eliot's moral and social alternatives to the despair of isolation and passivity. See *Dissertations Abstracts International* 39, no. 9 (1979):5528A.

29   KENNARD, JEAN E. "Aristocrat Versus Commoner." In *Victims of Convention*. Hamden, Conn.: Archon Books, pp. 46-62.
      The author is "concerned with novels in which the two-suitors convention is successful chiefly because the heroine functions as an everywoman and the main focus of the novel is upon ideas." *Felix Holt, the Radical* sets up a choice for Esther Lyon between the aristocrat, Harold Transome, and Felix Holt, a commoner.

30   _____. "A Wife Who Waddles: The Novels of George Eliot." In *Victims of Convention*. Hamden, Conn.: Archon Books, pp. 108-35.
      Examines the two-suitors convention in *Adam Bede, The Mill on the Floss, Middlemarch*, and *Daniel Deronda*. Finds that much of the critical disappointment with Eliot's endings is a result of the failure of the two-suitor convention.

31   KING, JEANNETTE. "George Eliot: Pathos and Tragedy." In *Tragedy in the Victorian Novel: Theory and Practice in the Novels of*

1978

George Eliot, Thomas Hardy, and Henry James. Cambridge: Cambridge University Press, 182 pp.

Contrasts tragedy's "formal" and "philosophical" influence on Hardy's novels with its "moral" influence on Eliot's. Argues that the novelist "approaches the goals of classical tragedy by conveying universality through a complex of symbolism, relating the individual to nature and history." Examines the "tension between the realistic bias of the Victorian novel and the dramatised, idealised principles of tragic drama." Elements of pathetic tragedy, pathos and the woman's tragedy, and heroic tragedy are studied in *The Mill on the Floss*, "The Spanish Gypsy," *Felix Holt, the Radical*, and *Daniel Deronda*. Eliot's concepts of free will and determinism, tragic responsibility, and realism and symbolism in tragedy are discussed.

32 KNOEPFLMACHER, U.C. "George Eliot." In *Victorian Fiction: A Second Guide to Research*. Edited by George H. Ford. New York: Modern Language Association, pp. 234-73.

Overview of Eliot's life, bibliographies, editions, and letters. Includes general criticism as well as criticism of individual works. Discusses "the woman question," style, ideas, technique, Eliot's place in literary tradition, and her relation to other novelists.

33 LINEHAN, KATHERINE [BAILEY]. "The Struggle for Tolerance: George Eliot's Provincial Past in *The Mill on the Floss*." *Massachusetts English* 5, no. 4:19-27.

Explores social and historical background of *The Mill on the Floss*. The balance between satire and sympathy in Eliot's treatment of the Dodsons is upset by Eliot's own memories of provincial society's treatment of her rejection of the church and her relationship with Lewes.

34 McGUINN, NICHOLAS. "George Eliot and Mary Wollstonecraft." In *The Nineteenth-Century Woman: Her Cultural and Physical World*. Edited by Sara Delamont and Lorna Duffin. London: Croom Helm; New York: Barnes & Noble Books, pp. 188-205.

Discusses article Eliot wrote for the *Leader* 6 (13 October 1855), "Margaret Fuller and Mary Wollstonecraft." Eliot's theories and ideas on philosophy and sociology, with strong emphasis on the rising feminism of her time, are applied to her writings about Wollstonecraft's *A Vindication of the Rights of Woman*.

1978

35 McKENZIE, K.A. *Edith Simcox and George Eliot*. Westport, Conn.: Greenwood Press, 146 pp.

An account of Edith Simcox's journal entitled "Autobiography of a Shirt-Maker," in which Simcox records facets concerning her realtionship with and affection for Eliot.

36 MECKIER, JEROME. "'That Arduous Invention': *Middlemarch* Versus the Modern Satirical Novel." *Ariel* 9, no. 4 (October):31-63.

Compares Eliot's worldview with those of Dickens and Flaubert. "In *Middlemarch*, Eliot satirizes satirists." See also 1987.26.

37 MINTZ, ALAN L. *George Eliot and the Novels of Vocation*. Cambridge, Mass., and London: Harvard University Press, 204 pp.

Thematic approach to Eliot's ideas on social possibilities versus the Puritan doctrine of vocation. Eight sociohistorical themes are applied to *Middlemarch* and *Daniel Deronda*. See also 1975.64.

38 NEW, PETER. "'Moral Tradition' in *The Mill on the Floss*." *English* 27, nos. 128-129 (Summer-Autumn):133-47.

Illustrates Eliot's opposition to the morality of consequence. Eliot's ethic is based on moral choice becoming habit. Defines virtue and applies "virtue" to the characters on Eliot's moral terms.

39 SADOFF, DIANNE F. "Nature's Language: Metaphor in the Text of *Adam Bede*." *Genre* 11, no. 36 (Fall):411-26.

Examines the use of figurative language to create tension between realism and transcendentalism.

40 SANDERS, ANDREW. "'*Romola*'s Waking': George Eliot's Historical Novel." In *The Victorian Historical Novel, 1840-1880*. London: Macmillan Press, pp. 168-96.

Study of Sir Walter Scott's influence on Eliot's approach to the historical novel *Romola*. Analysis of Eliot's detail and exact referencing in effort to "propose a parallel between the progress of the individual toward self-awareness and enlightenment, and the forward movement of the broad mass of humanity in a wider, creative historical process."

41 SEIDENFELD, BARBARA BERMAN. "Vision and Envisioning: Subjectivity in the Novels of George Eliot." Ph.D. dissertation, Union Graduate School-Midwest, 155 pp.

1978

Three different presentations of the way Eliot uses the word *vision* to elucidate her own perception of the interaction between the self and the world. Vision as sense perception and point of view; creative vision; and visions of relationships. Examines how Eliot's realism is basic observation "reflected through the medium of her own nature and in the mirror of her mind." See *Dissertations Abstracts International* 40, no. 1 (1979):277A.

42 SIMPSON, PETER. "Crisis and Recovery: Wordsworth, George Eliot, and *Silas Marner.*" *University of Toronto Quarterly* 48 (Winter):95-114.

Perceives the crisis pattern of *Silas Marner* as a reconstruction of Eliot's childhood recollection of an alienated society. *Silas Marner* is explained as an allegory of the artist's rescue (Silas) by a child (Eppie).

43 SORENSEN, KATHERINE MAREN. "Drama in George Eliot: A Model for Imaginative Expression." Ph.D. dissertation, Yale University, 309 pp.

"Eliot perceived dramatic representation as the central form of artistic expression." Uses biographical studies, journals, and letters to explain the role of dramatic image and form in Eliot's fiction. Contrasts Eliot's characters who possess dramatic imagination. Analyzes the dramatic structures and themes of *Daniel Deronda*. See *Dissertations Abstracts International* 40, no. 1 (1979):278A.

44 SPADY, CAROL HOWE. "The Dynamics of Reader Response in *Middlemarch.*" *Rackham Journal of Literary Studies*, no. 9 (Spring):64-75.

Analysis of Eliot's method of defining the psychological state of *Middlemarch* characters. Eliot uses metaphor to bring text and reader together. Shows how comment is integral to Eliot's purpose to humanize the reader.

45 STONEMAN, PATSY. "George Eliot: *Middlemarch* (1871-1872)." In *The Monster in the Mirror: Studies in Nineteenth-Century Realism.* Edited by D.A. Williams. Oxford: Oxford University Press, pp. 102-30.

"George Eliot's Realism is an attempt at balance between scientific devotion to a true record of things as they are, and the ethical evaluation of those events which arises from subjective consciousness. This attempt at balance characterizes not only a literary theory but a

101

1978

whole philosophy. . . . George Eliot attempts to show both the 'cosmic'
and the 'ethical' processes in her novels, by giving both an objective
view of the laws which govern human society, and a subjective view of
the human value within it."

46 TARR, RODGER L. "Dorothea's 'Resartus' and the Palingenetic
    Impulse of *Middlemarch.*" *Texas Studies in Literature and Language*
    20, no. 1 (Spring):107-18.
        Dates "Theophratus Such" prior to *Middlemarch*. Parallels
    actions between *Middlemarch* and Carlyle's *Sartor Resartus*.

47 THOMSON, PATRICIA. *Victorian Heroine: A Changing Ideal,*
    1837-1873. Westport, Conn.: Greenwood Press, pp. 32-33, 62-64,
    108-10, 140-41. Orig. pub. London: Oxford University Press, 1956.
        Discussion of Eliot and philanthropy for women in
    Middlemarch, education of women in *The Mill on the Floss*, marriage in
    Felix Holt, the Radical, and themes of morality in *Adam Bede*.

48 WEED, ELIZABETH. "The Liquidation of Maggie Tulliver." *Genre*
    11 (Fall): pp. 429-44.
        Feminist analysis of the drowning of Maggie Tulliver in the
    conclusion of *The Mill on the Floss*. Female elements of the book
    disassemble the ordered and conventional logocentric grounding of the
    novel. Symbols of construction and deconstruction are drawn in relation
    to gender and the novel's economy of equivalences. Maggie's drowning
    is a rescue from impasse. Weed applies Eliot's Feuerbachian principles
    to the character of Maggie and recounts and relates five meanings of
    "liquidate." Reprinted: 1986.57.

49 WHITE, KATHERINE ANNE MITCHELL. "Irredeemable
    Egoism in the Novels of George Eliot." Ed.D. dissertation, Ball State
    University, 204 pp.
        "Examines the theme of irredeemable egoism in all seven of
    George Eliot's novels. Irredeemable egoists are those characters who
    do not complete the process of shedding what Eliot identifies in
    Middlemarch as 'the moral stupidity' into which all people are born,
    and they contrast with those major characters in her novels who achieve
    a moral victory over aggression." See *Dissertations Abstracts*
    International 40, no. 3 (1979):1488A.

50 WILT, JUDITH. "Double Reading *Daniel Deronda*." *PMLA* 93, no. 5 (October):1012-13.

In a letter to the editor, comments on Cynthia Chases's "The Decomposition of the Elephants" (*PMLA* 93, no. 2 [March 1978]:215-27) and the insights given in a deconstructionist reading of *Daniel Deronda*. See also 1978.8.

1979

1 ALLEY, HENRY. "The Complete and Incomplete Educations of *The Mill on the Floss*." *Rocky Mountain Review of Language and Literature* 33, no. 4 (Fall):184-201.

Discusses the "incompletenesses and imbalances of education, both in the broad, psychological sense of the word, and the more academic sense." Traces the educations of Maggie and Tom Tulliver and Philip Wakem.

2 _____. "Literature and the Miscast Marriages of *Middlemarch* and *Daniel Deronda*." *Cithara* 19, no. 1 (November):21-25.

Clarifies Eliot's presentation of the difference between literature and experience. The misguided marriages of Lydgate and Dorothea Brooke (*Middlemarch*) and Gwendolen Harleth (*Daniel Deronda*) are examined with regard to what their readings prepared them for and what actually happens in life. "Eliot's use of literature in the education of her characters advances the overall themes of disillusionment and then reverses the process toward the novels' conclusions, suggesting that literature, read with discernment, can lead one out of despair."

3 _____. "Subterranean Intellectual of *Middlemarch*." *Midwest Quarterly* 20 (Summer):347-61.

Examines the underground "scholars" of *Middlemarch* – Casaubon, Lydgate, Farebrother, Mary Garth, and Mr. Brooke – their studies, and the failure or fulfillment of their intellectual pursuits.

4 ARAC, JONATHAN. "Rhetoric and Realism in Nineteenth Century Fiction: Hyperbole in *The Mill on the Floss*." *ELH* 46, no. 4 (Winter):673-92.

Elucidates the complexities of *The Mill on the Floss* by putting the book within the larger history of the realistic novel. The geometrical

1979

definition of hyperbole is used as an attempt to study the novel as having a defined shape and two centers of focus. Gives examples of Eliot's patterns and language in an attempt to apply the theory of hyperbole.

5   ASHTON, ROSEMARY D. "The Intellectual 'Medium' of *Middlemarch*." *Review of English Studies*, n.s. 30, no. 118 (May):154-68.

Traces the influence of Comte, Spinoza, Feuerbach, and Strauss upon Eliot's use of language in *Middlemarch*. "The word 'medium' recurs in *Middlemarch* to denote the mental and social conditions of thought and action. . . . The medium of *Middlemarch* is to be located in the concepts and the language of rationalism, scientific investigation, humanism, and their characteristic preoccupations, determinism and progress, necessity and freedom, and meliorism."

6   BEER, GILLIAN. "Beyond Determinism: George Eliot and Virginia Woolf." In *Women Writing and Writing About Women*. Edited by Mary Jacobus. New York: Barnes & Noble; London: Croom Helm, pp. 80-99.

Discusses plot implications and the modern idea of determinism as reflected in the writings of Eliot and Woolf. Looks at "patterns of intelligibility implied by determinism," how these patterns affected Eliot and Woolf, and a demonstration of their alternatives to these patterns.

7   BELLRINGER, ALAN W. "The Study of Provincial Life in *Middlemarch*." *English* 28, no. 132 (Autumn): 219-47.

Studies provincial qualities in the lives of the characters of *Middlemarch*. "*Middlemarch* can be regarded as structured to record the impact made upon provincial life by a series of exterior forces, economic, political, educational, scientific, religious, and journalistic."

8   BONAPARTE, FELICIA. *The Triptych and the Cross: The Central Myths of George Eliot's Poetic Imagination*. New York: New York University Press, 264 pp.

Examines the epic and poetic form of Eliot's novels. Traces the use of Bacchic, Christian, Greek, and Roman myths and symbols in *Romola*.

1979

9   BURDICK, NORMAN RICHARD. "The Incarnate Idea: Character and Purpose in George Eliot's Fiction." Ph.D. dissertation, University of Wisconsin – Madison, 372 pp.

Defines the development of Eliot's use of four character types that embody her moral ideas. The "strong man" (Adam Bede), the "young squire" (Arthur Donnithorne, Godfrey Cass), the "loving woman" (Romola, Maggie Tulliver), and the vain "water-nixie" (Hetty Sorrel, Rosamond Vincy) are discussed in terms of their effects on the novels, their spiritual deaths, and their parallels to the psychological theory of human character. See *Dissertations Abstracts International* 40, no. 7 (1980):4049A.

10 BYATT, A.S. Introduction to *The Mill on the Floss*. Harmondsworth, Eng.: Penguin Books, pp. 7-40.

Cites parallels and differences in the author's and Maggie's early life and the emotional brother-sister relationship. Examines Eliot's accuracy and sense of language regarding locale as well as her focus on local history. Discusses science, history, and Feuerbachian philosophy as relevant to the combined facets of the tragi-comedy to the fate-ruled tragedy.

11 CASERIO, ROBERT L[AWRENCE], Jr. "The Featuring of Act as 'the Rescue': Story in Dickens and George Eliot." In *Plot, Story, and the Novel: From Dickens and Poe to the Modern Period*. Princeton, N.J.: Princeton University Press, pp. 91-132.

"The relation of narrative reason and its moral discriminations to significant and willful human action is investigated. . . ." Contrasts acts of rescue written by Eliot and Dickens and finds that Eliot "uses narrative reason to arrive at meaning and the representation of action and yet she then humbles narrative reason by using it also to portray the evanescence of meaning, the nominal and yet essentially indefinable nature of action. For Eliot, the rescue is finally not practicable." Parallels are drawn between *Felix Holt, the Radical* and *Bleak House*.

12 ____. "*Felix Holt* and *Bleak House*." In *Plot, Story and the Novel: From Dickens and Poe to the Modern Period*. Princeton, N.J.: Princeton University Press.

Structural contrast of *Felix Holt, the Radical* and Dickens's *Bleak House*. Analysis of Dickens's sense of plot and Eliot's internalization of action. *Felix Holt, the Radical* exhibits similarities to

1979

Bleak House, which are illustrated by plot summaries. Reprinted in part: 1986.8.

13 CLAYTON, JAY. "Visionary Power and Narrative Form: Wordsworth and *Adam Bede*." *ELH* 46, no. 4 (Winter): 645-72.
    Theoretical and interpretive analysis of the Wordsworthian influence in *Adam Bede*. *Adam Bede* demonstrates the conflict and outcome that occurs between visionary powers and narrative form. "George Eliot's narrative begins with a 'hard' unpitying strength; the intervention of the visionary power comes as a crisis in this first narrative order; yet, ultimately, a new order is established, one which emphasizes consciousness and human feeling over the stern logic of consequences.

14 COLLINS, K[ENNY] K[AYLE]. "Sources of Some Unidentified Serial Offprints in The George Eliot-George Henry Lewes Library." *Bibliographical Society of America, Papers* 73 (October):468-73.
    A list of thirty-two previously unidentified serial offprints, their sources now supplied from the George Eliot-George Henry Lewes Library collection.

15 DAWSON, CARL. *Victorian Noon: English Literature in 1850*. Baltimore, Md., and London: Johns Hopkins University Press, pp. 158, 171-73, 177, passim.
    Descriptive study of English literature in the year 1850. Reviews literary models, the public role of the novelist, and the use of memory and myth. Passages on Eliot describe her writing and that of Charlotte Brontë and Francis Newman, as well as her philosophy on fiction and painting.

16 DeJONG, MARY LOU GOSSELINK. "The Rhetoric of the Romancer and the Realist: A Comparative Study of Nathaniel Hawthorne and George Eliot." Ph.D. dissertation, University of South Carolina, 345 pp.
    Compares the rhetorical stances of the romantic fiction of Hawthorne and the realist fiction of Eliot. Both authors deal with how man copes with temptation, guilt, and sorrow. "Hawthorne focuses on the effect of evil upon the individual consciousness." Eliot depicts her characters as members of a social environment for whom concerns are ethical and psychological. See *Dissertations Abstracts International* 40, no. 7 (1980): 4016A.

1979

17 DESSNER, LAWRENCE JAY. "Autobiographical Matrix of *Silas Marner*." *Studies in the Novel* 11, no. 3 (Fall):251-82.
     Traces autobiographical elements within the text of *Silas Marner*. Cites criticism relevant to the autobiographical themes of the novel.

18 EAGLETON, MARY, and PIERCE, DAVID. "Aspects of Class in George Eliot's Fiction." In *Attitudes to Class in the English Novel: From Walter Scott to David Storey*. London: Thames & Hudson, pp. 53-68.
     Eliot's concept of society, in particular the English middle and working class, are examined in *Adam Bede* and *Felix Holt, the Radical*.

19 ELIOT, GEORGE. *George Eliot's Middlemarch Notebooks: A Transcription*. Edited by John Clark Pratt and Victor A. Neufeldt. Berkeley: University of California Press, 346 pp.
     Reproduces Eliot's two notebooks (Folger and Berg) derived from her literary and historical readings and preparations for *Middlemarch* between 1868 and 1871. Introduction clarifies the issues of biography, dating, entries, and the evolution of the novel. Includes a checklist of Eliot's readings.

20 ELKINS, MARY JANE. "Definition and Control: The Exercise of Power in the Novels of George Eliot." Ph.D. dissertation, Southern Illinois University at Carbondale, 239 pp.
     Eliot illustrates the power struggles of her characters with a technique called "definition of situation." "The character who defines the situation and who convinces others to accept his definition is the character who controls the situation." Studies how Eliot develops and changes her ideas on definition-making is studied in *Adam Bede, Felix Holt, the Radical, Middlemarch*, and *Daniel Deronda*. See *Dissertations Abstracts International* 40, no. 6 (1979): 3312A.

21 FAJANS, ELIZABETH. "Melodrama in Victorian Fiction: Studies in Charles Dickens, Charlotte Brontë, George Eliot." Ph.D. dissertation, Rutgers University, 183 pp.
     Examines the characteristics of melodrama and its applications in the realistic fiction of Dickens, Brontë, and Eliot. Melodrama responds to the "realistic framework that is constructed out of a provided social environment." Within the novel, melodrama is used to accentuate, alleviate, or change everyday experiences. *Daniel Deronda*

1979

uses melodramatic vision to alter conventional social realities. See *Dissertations Abstracts International* 40, no. 7 (1980):4051A.

22 FISCHER, SANDRA K. "Eliot's *Daniel Deronda*." *Explicator* 37, no. 3 (Spring):21-22.
    Eliot uses fairy-tale elements to "set up expectations in her characters and in the reader ... to emphasize contrasts of character and structure, and to reinforce her philosophy that life never follows the anticipated pathway."

23 FITZPATRICK, TERENCE DANIEL. "Alienation and Mediation in the Novels of George Eliot." Ph.D. dissertation, Rutgers University, 299 pp.
    Concentrates on *The Mill on the Floss*, *Middlemarch*, and *Daniel Deronda* to illustrate Eliot's movement toward a rejection of English society. Eliot depicts the alienated individual in *The Mill on the Floss* to study the destructive effects of social change on the family. In *Middlemarch*, she tests the concept of marriage by subjecting it to the forces of English society. *Daniel Deronda* concludes with the alienated individual emigrating from English society to help build a new society that Eliot hopes will be superior to its English antecedents. See *Dissertations Abstracts International* 40, no. 1 (1979):266A.

24 FURST, LILIAN R. *Contours of European Romanticism*. Lincoln: University of Nebraska Press, pp. 20-36, passim.
    Studies the narrative stance and romantic irony in *Middlemarch*.

25 GILBERT, SANDRA M., and GUBAR, SUSAN. "George Eliot as the Angel of Destruction." In *The Madwoman in the Attic*. New Haven and London: Yale University Press, pp. 478-535
    Analysis of Eliot's resolution of contradictions between herself and her characters and the tensions between head and heart. Discusses Eliot's attraction to American writers Margaret Fuller and Harriet Beecher Stowe and their shared anxieties of the power of authorship. *Scenes of Clerical Life* illustrates Eliot's fascination with the angel of destruction and the "contradiction between feminine renunciation countenanced by the narrator [and] a female (even feminist) vengeance exacted by the author." How *Adam Bede*, *The Mill on the Floss*, *Middlemarch*, and *Daniel Deronda* suggest that heterosexual relationships are "a struggle between the transcendent male and immanent female."

26 ____. "Made Keen by Loss: George Eliot's Veiled Vision." In *The Madwoman in the Attic*. New Haven and London: Yale University Press, pp. 443-77.

Eliot's novella, "The Lifted Veil," shows that she is a part of a "strong female tradition," as suggested by her self-conscious relatedness to other writers, her critique of male literary conventions, her interest in clairvoyance and telepathy, her imagery of confinement, her schizophrenic sense of fragmentation, and her self-hatred. "Eliot transforms what she experiences as a loss – her alienation from the human community – into a gain: since she is an outsider, a fallen female, viewing respectable society . . . her unique perspective gains by its obliqueness. . . ."

27 GRANT, JUDITH [ANN] SKELTON. "Italians with White Mice in *Middlemarch* and *Little Dorrit*." *English Language Notes* 16, no. 3 (March):232-34.

Cites the passages regarding "Italians with white mice" in *Middlemarch* and Dickens's *Little Dorrit*. Gives meaning to the symbolism, wherein such people were often poor, young, foreign, street-folk in need of charity. See also 1984.4.

28 HAKAMY, ABDULWAHAB ALI. "The Struggle Between Traditionalism and Modernism: A Study in the Novels of George Eliot and Najīb Mahfūz." Ph.D. dissertation, University of Michigan, 239 pp.

Parallels the works of Najīb Mahfūz, written before the 1952 Egyptian revolution, and those of Eliot. Both authors depict the individual's confrontation with family and society. Characters undergo moral growth and are influenced by the authors' beliefs in determinism. See *Dissertations Abstracts International* 40, no. 2 (1979):837A.

29 HALL, ROLAND. "Words from *Middlemarch* Not Noticed in *OED*." *Notes & Queries* 26 (August):301-4.

Alphabetical list of word-uses found in *Middlemarch* but not in the *Oxford English Dictionary* edition of that period. Nonce-compounds, which are characteristic of Eliot's style, are not included in this list.

30 HERTZ, NEIL. "Recognizing Casaubon." *Glyph*, vol. 6. Johns Hopkins University Press, pp. 24-41.

Examination of Casaubon of *Middlemarch* and his personification as a quasi-allegorical figure. Discussion of the

1979

representation of character as text or clusters of signs. Evaluates passages where it is Eliot, not Casaubon, "around whom are clustered the signs of egotism and of writing." Reprinted: 1985.28; 1986.28; 1987.16.

31 HOLLOWAY, JOHN. "Narrative Process in *Middlemarch*." In *Narrative and Structure: Exploratory Essays*. Cambridge: Cambridge University Press, pp. 38-52.

Identifies several kinds of continuity within *Middlemarch*: proximate continuity, proximate discontinuity, indirect continuity, and initiative-response continuity.

32 HOWE, IRVING. "George Eliot and the Jews." *Partisan Review* 46, no. 3:359-75.

Examines Eliot's approach to Zionism, the Jewish issues in *Daniel Deronda*, and why she sought to deal with Jews as subject matter. *Daniel Deronda*, in dealing with anti-Semitism, also deals with the weight of power.

33 _____. "George Eliot in Her Letters." In *Celebrations and Attacks: Thirty Years of Literary and Cultural Commentary*. New York: Horizon Press, pp. 127-31.

Overview of Eliot's letters, which provide insight into the nineteenth-century intellectual life. Examines Eliot's commentary on the disintegration of orthodox Christian belief, her views on literature, and her social views.

34 IRWIN, MICHAEL. *Picturing: Description and Illusion in the Nineteenth-Century Novel*. London: George Allen & Unwin, 161 pp.

Technical and detailed analysis of nineteenth-century novelists' use of pictorials and descriptions. Analysis of Eliot's descriptive writing about facial expressions, gestures, clothing and adornments, rooms and houses, and towns.

35 JEFFERS, THOMAS L. "Myths and Morals in *The Mill on the Floss*." *Midwest Quarterly* 20 (Summer):332-46.

Discusses the romantic tradition in *The Mill on the Floss* and its vision of childhood as Eden. Eliot "creates a credible childhood world" in which children "exhibit a humanity still uncorrupted by experience. ... *The Mill on the Floss* suggests a myth that human nature once was whole but now is divided into parts."

1979

36 KENNEDY, ALAN. "George Eliot: The Invisible Fabrick and the Clothes of Time." In *Meaning and Signs in Fiction*. New York: St. Martin's Press, pp. 105-27.

"Eliot's two most important themes are an analysis of the nature of action (and therefore also of passion) and the complicating fact that men live by interpreting signs that are ambiguous and cannot contain all that they wish to say. . . . Her earlier works are explorations into the implications of her belief that the complete human individual is fulfilled only by means of action and her recognition that such action is often frustrated by the very circumstances which seem to demand it."

37 KULERMAN, RUTH MOSS. "Theme and Structure in George Eliot's Early Fiction." Ph.D. dissertation, City University of New York, 479 pp.

Discusses Eliot's treatment of love in her early fiction. *Scenes of Clerical Life*, *Adam Bede*, and *The Mill on the Floss* contain elements of eroticism within the subtexts. Analyzes through the psychosexual theories of Freud, Fromm, Roheim, and Reik how Eliot deals with the dark side of female sexuality. See *Dissertations Abstracts International* 40, no. 2 (1979):871A.

38 LEVINE, GEORGE [L.]. "Repression and Vocation in George Eliot: A Review Essay." *Women and Literature* 2, no. 7 (Spring):3-13.

Examines the issues of repression and vocation in Eliot's novels and how they are approached in Laura Emery's *George Eliot's Creative Conflict* (Berkeley, 1976) and Alan Mintz's *George Eliot and the Novel of Vocation* (Cambridge, 1978). See also 1976.21; 1978.37.

39 LINDAU, BERTHA L. "Feminism in the English Novel: George Eliot, Virginia Woolf, Doris Lessing." Ph.D. dissertation, University of South Carolina, 457 pp.

Analysis of the emergence of a feminist hero in *The Mill on the Floss* and *Daniel Deronda*, Woolf's *To the Lighthouse*, and Lessing's *The Summer Before the Dark*. Both Maggie Tulliver and Gwendolen Harleth are similarly damaged by their upbringing. Their poor self-images cause them to make devastating choices in life. Shows that the authors' high regard for their female characters illustrates their concern for feminism. See *Dissertations Abstracts International* 40, no. 3 (1979):1483A.

1979

40 McMURTY, JO. "Jews in Fiction: Fagin Versus Daniel Deronda." In *Victorian Life and Victorian Fiction: A Companion for the American Reader*. Hamden, Conn.: Archon Books, pp. 79-81.
Presents fictional stereotypes of Jews. Dickens's Fagin in *Oliver Twist*, and Svengali from Du Maurier's *Trilby*, are offered as contrast to Eliot's attempt to change the Jewish stereotype in *Daniel Deronda*.

41 _____. "Political Background in George Eliot's *Middlemarch*." In *Victorian Life and Victorian Fiction: A Companion for the American Reader*. Hamden, Conn.: Archon Books, pp. 103-4.
Outlines the political background of *Middlemarch*. Both Mr. Brooke and Will Ladislaw are active in politics and their commentaries reflect on current politics of the country.

42 _____. "The Power of Scandal: Eliot and Hardy." In *Victorian Life and Victorian Fiction: A Companion for the American Reader*. Hamden, Conn.: Archon Books, pp. 226-27.
Traces the plots of *The Mill on the Floss* and Hardy's *Far From the Madding Crowd*, wherein both heroines are conscious of public opinions regarding sexual scandal and guilt.

43 _____. "Sympathetic Views of Dissenters: Eliot." In *Victorian Life and Victorian Fiction: A Companion for the American Reader*. Hamden, Conn.: Archon Books, pp. 77-78.
Refers to Eliot's presentation of the conflict between Dissenters and the Church of England in *Adam Bede* and *Felix Holt, the Radical*.

44 MAGILL, FRANK N., ed. *Magill's Bibliography of Literary Criticism*. Vol. 1. Englewood Cliffs, N.J.: Salem Press, pp. 581-91.
Bibliography of scholarly criticisms of *Adam Bede*, *Daniel Deronda*, *Felix Holt, the Radical*, *Middlemarch*, *The Mill on the Floss*, *Romola*, and *Silas Marner*, with an emphasis on works published in the 1960s and 1970s. Citations are listed alphabetically by author's last name.

45 MARIANI, GIGLIOLA SACERDOTI. "Il sionismo di Moses Hess e George Eliot." *Nuova antologia* (Rome) 537, no. 2130 (April-June):339-49.

46 MILLER, J. HILLIS. *The Form of Victorian Fiction: Thackeray, Dickens, Trollope, George Eliot, Meredith, and Hardy*. Cleveland,

Ohio: Case Western Reserve University, Arete Press, pp. 80-85, 95, 96, 113-23. Orig. pub. 1968.

Analyzes *Adam Bede* and *Middlemarch* for Victorian conventions of time, realism, and interpersonal relations.

47 MORRIS, HARRIET KRAVITZ. "Authorial Control of Sympathy for the Social Offender in Selected Novels by Elizabeth Gaskell and George Eliot." Ph.D. dissertation, University of Toronto (Canada).

Examination of philosophical, literary, and religious bases of the Victorian idea of sympathy. In the early fiction of Gaskell and Eliot, the authorial control of sympathy for the social offender is determined by their different social positions. In *Felix Holt, the Radical* and *Adam Bede*, the social offender "conforms to the best inclinations of the ideal community which shape and sustain the individual moral consciousness." Discusses the authorial control of sympathy for the fallen woman character, the murderer, and perpetrators of violent crime. See *Dissertations Abstracts International* 40, no. 12 (1980):6293A.

48 NAWALANIC, LILLIAN ANTOINETTE. "George Eliot's Ecological Consciousness in *Middlemarch*." Ph.D. dissertation, University of Houston, 273 pp.

In *Middlemarch*, Eliot depicts man's interdependencies on every facet of life – social, political, emotional, cognitive, economic, and biological. The novel is examined as an ecologically conscious work wherein Eliot uses ecologic language. Bulstrode is examined in the context of a "paradigm of human ecology stressing the output function." The various marriages are studied using a "Contingency Model of Organizational Behavior which emphasizes environmental, individual and group processes." See *Dissertations Abstracts International* 40, no. 7 (1980):4057A.

49 O'NEAL, ELEANOR MARIE. "George Eliot's Novels: Confronting the Fathers." Ph.D. dissertation, University of California at Berkeley, 308 pp.

Traces patterns of fictional events, character types, imagery, and myths to explain Eliot's theories on the duality of masculinity and femininity. Examined chronologically, the novels demonstrate Eliot's struggle to resolve the conflicts she associates with patriarchal and matriarchal values. See *Dissertations Abstracts International* 40, no. 7 (1980):4058A.

1979

50 PACE, TIMOTHY. "Narrative Anxieties: George Eliot's Early Novels." Ph.D. dissertation, Harvard University.
    Cited but not abstracted in *Dissertation Abstracts International* (1979).

51 PHELPS, GILBERT. *A Reader's Guide to Fifty British Novels, 1600-1900*. London: Heinemann Educational Books; New York: Barnes & Noble, pp. 358-72, 420-32.
    Brief biographical account; plot summaries of *The Mill on the Floss* and *Middlemarch* with critical commentary. Comparisons are drawn with Anthony Trollope and Elizabeth Gaskell.

52 PUTZELL [-KORAB], SARA MOORE. "The Search for a Higher Rule: Spiritual Progress in the Novels of George Eliot." *Journal of the American Academy of Religion* 47, no. 3 (September):389-407.
    "Read in the context of Hegel's *Phenomenology of Spirit* (1807), George Eliot's novels depict individual spiritual progress toward full self-consciousness through an individual's conceptual relation to the objects of his faith."

53 SAID, EDWARD W. "Zionism From the Standpoint of Its Victims." *Social Text* 1, no. 1 (Winter):7-58.
    Uses *Daniel Deronda* to present a figurative example of Zionism. Zionism is presented, in the novel, as a general condition of homelessness. "Eliot uses the plight of Jews to make a universal statement about the nineteenth century's need for a home, given the spiritual and psychological restlessness reflected in her characters' almost ontological physical restlessness."

54 SIKORSKI, HENRY. "Catastrophe of *The Mill on the Floss*." *Notes & Queries* 26 (August):304
    The final drowning scene in *The Mill on the Floss* is found to be physically possible. Given the water current and the factor of wind velocity, the floating machinery is driven downstream at a rate fast enough to overtake the Tullivers' boat.

55 STUBBS, PATRICIA. "The Well-Regulated Heroine." In *Women and Fiction: Feminism and the Novel, 1880-1920*. Sussex, Eng.: Harvester Press; New York: Barnes & Noble, pp. 26-50.
    In *Daniel Deronda*, Eliot examines the marriage of Gwendolen and Grandcourt and its destructive effects on Gwendolen. She explores

the sexual and spiritual failure in the Dorothea-Casaubon marriage in *Middlemarch*.

56 TANNER, TONY. "Law and the River." In *Adultery in the Novel: Contract and Transgression*. Baltimore, Md., and London: Johns Hopkins University Press, pp. 66-72.

Examines the evolving morphology of the oppositions within *The Mill on the Floss*. The oppositions are symbolically linked to the river, the mill, and nature–particularly human nature. The tension between familial and social bonds and desire; between culture, law, and nature; and between "obligations of property and the importunities of passion" center on Maggie Tulliver's and Stephen Guest's relationship. Suggests that Tom and Maggie's relationship is incestuous and uses language and symbols from the final chapter to prove this point.

57 THOMPSON, DAVID OWEN. "Fiction and the Forms of Community: Strauss, Feuerbach, and George Eliot." Ph.D. dissertation, Yale University, 243 pp.

The form of community, for Eliot, exists in language. Demonstrates how Eliot tested and criticized the theories of German philosophers David Friedrich Strauss and Ludwig Feuerbach. In *Adam Bede*, the narrator uses Straussian historical standards to analyze the individual's illusions. *Middlemarch* and *Daniel Deronda* analyze the "webs of interpretation that characters weave for themselves." See *Dissertations Abstracts International* 40, no. 11 (1980):5881A.

58 WHEELER, MICHAEL. "The Spectacles of Books: *Middlemarch*." In *The Art of Allusion in Victorian Fiction*. London: Macmillan Press; New York: Barnes & Noble Books, pp. 78-99.

Studies the use and function of literary and biblical allusion. Allusion, in *Middlemarch*, is examined as both a technique and a theme. The textual allusion of shorthand notation and allusion in relation to the characters of Casaubon and Dorothea are examined in detail.

59 WITEMEYER, HUGH. "George Eliot and Jean-Jacques Rousseau." *Comparative Literature Studies* 16, no. 2 (June):121-30.

Discusses Rousseau's influence on Eliot. Rousseau was a "liberating influence in her early intellectual development and a vital presence in the liberal-progressive milieu of her maturity." Eliot saw Rousseau as a precursor to Wordsworth and an example of the

1979

nineteenth-century romantic naturalist. He directly influenced *Daniel Deronda* and "The Lifted Veil."

60 ____. *George Eliot and the Visual Arts*. New Haven, Conn., and London: Yale University Press, 238 pp.

Discusses Eliot's use of and knowledge of pictorial traditions in her fiction. Examines Eliot's word-painting and her fiction's identification with English, Dutch, and Flemish genre paintings, portraiture, landscape painting, and sacred and heroic history painting. Explores Eliot's emphasis on true naturalistic representation as a mode of vision – both spiritual and moral. Analyzes the illustrations by Frederic Leighton in the first edition of *Romola*.

61 WOOLF, VIRGINIA. "George Eliot." In *Women and Writing*. Edited by Michèle Barrett. New York and London: Harcourt Brace Jovanovich, pp. 150-60.

Identifies Eliot as a woman writer who overcame obstacles of sex, health, and contemporary conventions to seek and share knowledge and freedom.

62 ZIMMERMAN, BONNIE [SUE]. "*Felix Holt* and the True Power of Womanhood." *ELH* 46, no. 3 (Fall):432-51.

Felix Holt, the Radical treats, by analogy, the "problem of woman's true power." The contrast between Esther Lyon and Mrs. Transome is similar to political distinctions within the novel. *Felix Holt, the Radical* is Eliot's transition from individual expression of female oppression to social and sexual politics on a larger scale.

1980

1 ADAMS, KATHLEEN. *Those of Us Who Loved Her: The Men in George Eliot's Life*. N.p.: George Eliot Fellowship, 187 pp.

Examines the men who played a role in Eliot's life – Robert Evans, Isaac Evans, Charles Bray, Dr. Robert Brabant, Francois D'Albert Durade, John Chapman, Herbert Spencer, George Henry Lewes, Lewes's sons, John Blackwood, and John Walter Cross.

2 AIKEN, RALPH. "Oliphant, Gaskell and Eliot as Comedians." *Victorians Institute Journal* 9:49-56.

1980

Evaluates and compares Margaret Oliphant, Elizabeth Gaskell and Eliot's comedic elements. Finds Eliot frustrating to readers of comedy in that she relies on irony and black comedy in *Middlemarch*.

3   ASHTON,   ROSEMARY   D.   "Combative,   Amative, Philoprogenitive." *Times Literary Supplement* (London), 19 December, p. 1439.
    Review of the retrospective George Eliot centenary exhibition at the British Library includes manuscript holdings, paintings, and illustrations by Edward Henry Corbould and Samuel Laurence, and a representation of Eliot's letters.

4   _____. "George Eliot and Goethe (1854-76)." In *The German Idea: Four English Writers and the Reception of German Thought, 1800-1860*. Cambridge: Cambridge University Press, pp. 166-73.
    Analysis of Johann Wolfgang von Goethe's influence on Eliot's ideas of sympathy and renunciation. Discusses her article on *Wilhelm Meister's Apprenticeship* in *The Leader* (July 1855), entitled "The Morality of Wilhelm Meister."

5   _____. "George Eliot, Translator of Strauss (1844-6)." In *The German Idea: Four English Writers and the Reception of German Thought, 1800-1860*. Cambridge: Cambridge University Press, pp. 147-55.
    Discusses Eliot's translation of David Friedrich Strauss's *The Life of Jesus* (London, 1846) and her subsequent contribution to the introduction of German thought to England.

6   _____. "More Translations: Spinoza and Feuerbach (1849-54)." In *The German Idea: Four English Writers and the Reception of German Thought, 1800-1860*. Cambridge: Cambridge University Press, pp. 155-66.
    Examines Spinoza's influence on Eliot as a result of her translations of *Tractatus Theologico-Politicus* (1670) and *Ethics* (London, 1948). Spinoza was instrumental to her "conversion to disbelief" and pantheism. Discusses Feuerbach's influence on Eliot's belief in the religion of humanity as a result of her translation of *The Essence of Christianity* (London, 1854).

1980

7   _____. "The Pros and Cons of the German Genius." In *The German Idea: Four English Writers and the Reception of German Thought, 1800-1860*. Cambridge: Cambridge University Press, pp. 173-77.

Examines Eliot's admiration for Heinrich Heine. In her article for *Westminster Review* (January 1856), "German Wit: Heinrich Heine," she examines humor in German literature.

8   BAKER, WILLIAM. "A New George Eliot Manuscript." In *George Eliot: Centenary Essays and An Unpublished Fragment*. Edited by Anne Smith. Totowa, N.J.: Barnes & Noble, pp. 9-20.

Description of and printing of ten pages of previously unpublished material from Eliot's notebook. Outlines what was to be a work dealing with the Napoleonic Wars.

9   BEATY, JEROME. "George Eliot Studies for 1978." In *Dickens Studies Annual: Essays on Victorian Fiction*. Vol. 8. Edited by Michael Timko, Fred Kaplan, and Edward Guiliano. New York: AMS Press, pp. 333-47.

Critically evaluates and reviews essays, dissertations, and monographs written about Eliot in 1978.

10   BEER, GILLIAN. "Plot and the Analogy with Science in Later Nineteenth-Century Novelists." In *Comparative Criticism: A Yearbook*. Vol. 2. Edited by Elinor [S.] Shaffer. Cambridge: Cambridge University Press, pp. 131-49.

Examines systems of literary metaphor used in *Middlemarch* to incorporate new developments in nineteenth-century science. Discusses scientific ideas available to novelists, particularly as found in the works of Emile Zola.

11   BLAKE, KATHLEEN. "Armgart – George Eliot on the Woman Artist." *Victorian Poetry* 18 (Spring):75-80.

In her poem "Armgart," Eliot deals with the conflict of the woman artist who contemplates forgoing her vocation for love. "The poem is resolute in supporting Armgart against the threats posed by men and motherhood."

12   BOLTON, FRANÇOISE. "George Eliot hier et aujourd'hui." *Études anglaises* (Paris) 33, no. 3 (July-September):257-67.

1980

13   BUTWIN, JOSEPH. "The Pacification of the Crowd: From 'Janet's Repentence' to *Felix Holt*." *Nineteenth-Century Fiction* 35, no. 3 (December):349-71.

Discusses the communal action of crowds in *Felix Holt, the Radical, Romola*, and "Janet's Repentence." Explains how this action symbolizes Eliot's ambivalence toward political action. Analysis of religious processionals and political demonstrations as being intrusive into the rural and intimate locality because they rob the smaller unit of its communal intimacy.

14   CALDWELL, PATRICE JOAN. "Historical Romance: The Contribution of Scott, Bulwer-Lytton, and George Eliot." Ph.D. dissertation, University of California, Los Angeles, 290 pp.

An examination of the historical romance's literary, historical and philosophical antecedents in England. Eliot's novels indicate her commitment to realism and a real setting. An analysis of Eliot's and Edward Bulwer-Lytton's criticism of Scott's formula for historical romance. See *Dissertations Abstracts International* 41, no. 8 (1981):3588A.

15   CARROLL, DAVID. "'Janet's Repentence' and the Myth of the Organic." *Nineteenth-Century Fiction* 35, no. 3 (December):331-48.

Attempts to define the relationship between Eliot's organic ideas and the form of her fiction by examining examples of organic metaphor in "Janet's Repentence," from *Scenes of Clerical Life*. In the story, Eliot sets her ideas in the form of a myth – both organic and dialectical – in which she adapts and dramatizes the "triangle of romantic love to express the process of growth in the individual and society."

16   CHASE, LANCE DAVIS. "Preaching without Book: The Rhetoric of Religion in the Novels of George Eliot." Ph.D. dissertation, Marquette University, 212 pp.

"Examines George Eliot's use in her fiction of 'telling,' including voice and point of view, and 'showing,' or the direct presentation of religious experience." Provides an explanation of her successful attempts at presenting religious ambiguities. A summary of Eliot's techniques – multiple voices, irony, use of transvaluation – is discussed. See *Dissertations Abstracts International* 41, no. 12 (1981):5105A.

1980

17 CHURCHILL, KENNETH. "Italy and the English Novel in the Mid-Century." In *Italy and English Literature, 1764-1930*. Totowa, N.J.: Barnes & Noble, pp. 129-46.

Surveys Eliot's treatment of Italy in *Romola* and *Middlemarch*. The Renaissance setting of *Romola* undercuts the novel's moral intent and contributes to its failure. Italy, as depicted in *Middlemarch*, is not merely background, however, but a creative presence.

18 COLLINS, K[ENNY] K[AYLE]. "George Eliot and Herbert Spencer: An Unnoted Reference in *The Study of Sociology*." *English Language Notes* 17, no. 3 (March):199-203.

Notes Herbert Spencer's reference to George Eliot in chapter 15 of his *The Study of Sociology* (International Scientific Series, London, 1873).

19 _____. "Questions of Method: Some Unpublished Late Essays." *Nineteenth-Century Fiction* 35, no.3 (December):385-405.

Unpublished late essays of Eliot illuminate her thoughts on social evolution of the 1870s. Eliot argues that cultural facts originate within human limitations and these limitations account for similarities in language, dress, and mythology. Eliot also confirms the artist's social responsibility to portray real human beings and ideal moral types.

20 COOPER, HELEN. "Mrs. Browning and Miss Evans." *Nineteenth-Century Fiction* 35, no. 3 (December): 257-59.

An epigraph, using quotations from the letters and writings of Elizabeth Barrett Browning and Eliot. Illustrates Eliot as a woman listening and speaking to other women.

21 COSTIC, LINDA ANNETTE SEIDEL. "Education in the Novels of Charlotte Brontë, Elizabeth Gaskell, and George Eliot." Ph.D. dissertation, University of Delaware, 231 pp.

Studies the theme of education in the novels of Brontë, Gaskell, and Eliot. Critical of Victorian educational practices, the three novelists use education in the delineation of character. Eliot attacks the educational system because it was deficient in areas of women's education and failed to widen the sympathies of men. See *Dissertations Abstracts International* 41, no. 3 (1980):1062A.

1980

22 DENEAU, DANIEL P. "Chronology in *The Mill on the Floss*." Appendix B in *The Mill on the Floss*. Edited by Gordon S. Haight. Oxford: Clarendon Press, pp. 468-72.

Book-by-book evaluation of the time scheme of *The Mill on the Floss*.

23 DOODY, MARGARET ANNE. "George Eliot and the Eighteenth Century Novel." *Nineteenth-Century Fiction* 35, no. 3 (December):260-91.

"Examines Eliot against the backdrop of the eighteenth century novel. How Eliot, mediating between the extremes of Henry Fielding and Samuel Richardson, followed models first devised by a host of literary women." The influence of Sarah Scott, Mary Hays, Sarah Fielding, Charlotte Smith, and Agnes Maria Bennett on Eliot's characters, images, conflicts and style, particularly the use of "style indirect libre" in *Middlemarch*.

24 GALLAGHER, CATHERINE. "The Failure of Realism: *Felix Holt*." *Nineteenth-Century Fiction* 35, no. 3 (December):372-84.

Examines how the political climate of the 1860s contributed to the realism of *Felix Holt, the Radical*. "With its emphasis on radical politics and on the working class's demands for the franchise, this novel connects the author's skepticism about democracy to her reactivated doubts about facts and values." Felix and the plot surrounding him contradict the inductive metonymic assumptions of the rest of the novel.

25 GARRETT, PETER K. "George Eliot: Equivalent Centers." In *The Victorian Multiplot Novel: Studies in Dialogical Form*. New Haven and London: Yale University Press, pp. 135-79.

Identifies the range of problems and possibilities inherent in the inclusiveness of Eliot's multiplot novels–*Daniel Deronda* and *Middlemarch*. The variety of analogies, and differences and similarities between situations and characters, make "interpretive choice of a single center an act of arbitrary projection." Examines Eliot's multiple narration in order to understand how well it applies to her theory of organic form.

26 GEZARI, JANET K. "*Romola* and the Myth of Apocalypse." In *George Eliot: Centenary Essays and an Unpublished Fragment*. Edited by Anne Smith. Totowa, N.J.: Barnes & Noble, pp. 77-102.

1980

Illustrates historical events in the plot of *Romola* to better understand the novel's themes. The theme of imaginative vision is given particular attention.

27 GILBERT, KATHLEEN. "Rosamond and Lady Blessington: Another *Middlemarch* Anachronism." *Notes & Queries* 27 (December):527-28.

Researches the fact that the keepsake–a watered-silk publication–given to Rosamond Vincy by Ned Plymdale in *Middlemarch*, is an anachronism. Also the mention of Lady Blessington by Rosamond is anachronistic.

28 GINSBURG, MICHAL PELED. "Pseudonym, Epigraphs, and Narrative Voice: *Middlemarch* and the Problems of Authorship." *ELH* 47, no. 3 (Fall):542-58.

Examines how the question of authorship is evident in Eliot's use of a penname as related to the problems of being a woman author in the nineteenth century. Shows "how certain techniques of narrative voice operate in *Middlemarch* a parallel movement, that of calling into question the status of a subject, an 'I', as the origin of an utterance."

29 GOLDBERG, S.L. "Morality and Literature; with Some Reflections on *Daniel Deronda*." *Critical Review*, no. 22:3-20.

Discusses two kinds of moral thought and judgment–that of the morality of action and modes of conduct and that of the morality of life. Examines themes of life-morality in *Daniel Deronda*.

30 GORDON, JAN B. "Origins, *Middlemarch*, Endings: George Eliot's Crisis of the Antecedent." In *George Eliot: Centenary Essays and an Unpublished Fragment*. Edited by Anne Smith. Totowa, N.J.: Barnes & Noble, pp. 124-51

Analyzes the theme of origin and ending in *Middlemarch*. Discusses how the theme of origin ("Prelude") and ending ("Finale") is reflected in the novel's structure. Reprinted: 1987.13.

31 GREGOR, IAN. "Reading a Story: Sequence, Pace, and Recollection." In *Reading the Victorian Novel: Detail Into Form*. Edited by Ian Gregor. New York: Barnes & Noble Books, pp. 92-110.

Considers the elements involved in the reading process in Hardy's *Far From the Madding Crowd* and Eliot's *The Mill on the Floss*.

1980

Analyzes sequence, pace, and memory in the problematic ending. The novel's ending juxtaposes the past and present.

32   HAIGHT, GORDON S., ed. Introduction to *The Mill on the Floss*. Oxford, Eng.: Clarendon Press, pp. xiii-xliv.
     Describes Eliot's progress in writing *The Mill on the Floss*; description of the manuscript, its publication, and various editions.

33   HARDY, BARBARA; MILLER, J. HILLIS; and POIRIER, RICHARD. "*Middlemarch*, Chapter 85: Three Commentaries." *Nineteenth Century Fiction* 35, no. 3 (December):432-53.
     Hardy uses the Bunyan quotation from *Pilgrim's Progress* to expound on the theme of moral consciousness, the dual function of the motto, and its appropriateness to the narrative tone and to Bulstrode's consciousness. Miller concentrates on Eliot's technique of "parable" and the "adequacy of similitude and synecdoche." Discusses the self-referential rhetoric of the chapter and how it accounts for its mode of narration and ethical judgments. Poirier finds the chapter to be a commentary on judgment, intuition and intelligence. Reprinted in part: 1982.25. Reprinted: 1986.26.

34   HERRON, JERRY SIM. "Reading George Eliot." Ph.D. dissertation, Indiana University, 331 pp.
     Attempts to develop a vocabulary for discussing Eliot, based on the historical materialism of Marx and to apply this vocabulary to a criticism of *Silas Marner*, *Felix Holt, the Radical*, and *Romola*. Eliot's fiction constitutes a sort of "demographic *bildungsroman*, which traces the progressive development of certain value forms as the characters whose lives are defined by those forms grow up into a world more and more like her own, and apparently more resistant to coherent interpretation." See *Dissertations Abstracts International* 41, no. 9 (1981):4041A.

35   HIGDON, DAVID LEON. "A Bibliography of George Eliot Criticism, 1971-1977." *Bulletin of Bibliography* 37, no. 2 (April-June):90-103.
     Bibliography of criticism between 1971 and 1977, arranged alphabetically by author and divided into two sections – general studies and individual works.

1980

36 IRWIN, MICHAEL. "Readings of Melodrama." In *Reading the Victorian Novel: Detail into Form*. Edited by Ian Gregor. New York: Barnes & Noble Books, pp. 15-31.

Examines the relationship between the realistic and melodramatic elements of *Middlemarch, The Mill on the Floss*, and various other Victorian novels.

37 JENKYNS, RICHARD. "George Eliot and the Greeks." In *The Victorians and Ancient Greece*. Cambridge, Mass.: Harvard University Press, pp. 112-32.

Traces the influence of classic Greek literature on Eliot's attempt to demonstrate the "tragedy of everyday unromantic suffering." Examines Greek references, themes (such as Aeschylean tragedy and the perils of erudition), symbolic patterns, and motifs in Eliot's fiction.

38 JONES, LAWRENCE. "George Eliot and Pastoral Tragicomedy in Hardy's *Far From the Madding Crowd*." *Studies in Philology* 77 (Fall):402-25.

Explains the influence of George Eliot on Hardy's *Far From the Madding Crowd*. Studies the impact Eliot had on Hardy's style, nature and structure of the fictional world, use of the omniscient point of view, and the use of *Adam Bede* as the model for a pastoral tragicomedy.

39 JUMEAU, ALAIN. "*Scenes of Clerical Life*: George Eliot sur les chemins de la 'conversion.'" *Études anglaises* (Paris) 33, no. 3 (July-September):268-81.

40 LEE, A. ROBERT. "*The Mill on the Floss*: 'Memory' and the Reading Experience." In *Reading the Victorian Novel: Detail into Form*. Edited by Ian Gregor. New York: Barnes & Noble Books, pp. 72-91.

Describes how Eliot "implicates her reader in a quite unique idiom of memory. ..." The various levels of memory within the novel enable the reader to collaborate in the reading experience. Examines the novel "as geography, as society, and as family" and Eliot's method of progressing forward by consulting the past.

41 LERNER, LAURENCE. "Posterity's Fickle Ways with Marian Evans." *Times Higher Education Supplement* (London), 19 December, p. 7.

Eliot's need for love and her intellect are described in this review of her centenary tribute which questions Eliot's stature as a novelist. *Middlemarch*'s stature as the greatest English novel is still secure.

42 LEVINE, GEORGE [L.]. "George Eliot's Hypothesis of Reality." *Nineteenth-Century Fiction* 35, no. 1 (June):1-28.

Examines Eliot's pursuit of an ethical and intellectual ideal in her personal life and fictional characters. "She believed that submission of the self to the voices of external reality was a condition of intellectual power ... reality remains incommensurate with the desires of an aspiring self, but that personality is an obstruction to perception."

43 ____. "The Hero as Dilettante: *Middlemarch* and *Nostromo*." In *George Eliot: Centenary Essays and an Unpublished Fragment*. Edited by Anne Smith. Totowa, N.J.: Barnes & Noble, pp. 152-80.

Eliot's *Middlemarch* and Conrad's *Nostromo* "are the most ambitious enterprises of the pseudonymous and late-blooming authors; separated by 32 years, they are both encyclopedic histories and imaginative articulations of the late-century scientific vision. ... While *Middlemarch* attempts to see the ideal in the real and charges each moment with the significances of multiple perspectives, *Nostromo* sees the real in the ideal while multiplying perspectives beyond the possibility of significance." Reprinted: 1981.37.

44 McCARRON, ROBERT. "Evil and Eliot's Religion of Humanity: Grandcourt in *Daniel Deronda*." *Ariel* 11, no. 1 (January):71-88.

Analysis of the character and role of Grandcourt. Grandcourt represents Eliot's "ambivalent response to the question of human evil."

45 McGOWAN, JOHN P. "The Turn of George Eliot's Realism." *Nineteenth-Century Fiction* 35, no. 2 (September):171-92.

Discusses the complexities of fiction's referential abilities and the fact that "George Eliot's realism involves the refusal to recognize that literary language has no referent. ... Her realism is pre-occupied with establishing the literary work's relation to the world and with its power to denote, describe and represent things and events in the world." Examines Eliot's shift in realism from *The Mill on the Floss* to *Middlemarch*.

1980

46   MANN, KAREN B. "George Eliot and Wordsworth: The Power of Sound and the Power of Mind." *Studies in English Literature* 20, no. 4 (Autumn):675-94.

     Discussion of Eliot's and Wordsworth's conception of "mind" and how their differences separate the qualities of the mind of poet and novelist. Examines metaphors of sound and music in Eliot's transference of this metaphor in her poem "The Legend of Jubal" to that of her fiction.

47   MARTIN, GRAHAM. "*The Mill on the Floss* and the Unreliable Narrator." In *George Eliot: Centenary Essays and an Unpublished Fragment*. Edited by Anne Smith. Totowa, N.J.: Barnes & Noble, pp. 36-54.

     Compares the "discontinuities between the authorial meta-language and the narrated fiction. . . ." The narrator has two conflicting roles within the novel, which are evidence of suppressed silence – an important facet of the novel's structure.

48   MEIKLE, SUSAN. "Fruit and Seed: The Finale to *Middlemarch*." In *George Eliot: Centenary Essays and an Unpublished Fragment*. Edited by Anne Smith. Totowa, N.J.: Barnes & Noble, pp. 181-95.

     Analyzes phrase and word changes in three versions of Eliot's finale to *Middlemarch* and examines critical social events during 1872 and 1874 that served to alter Eliot's stance on the woman question.

49   MIDLER, MARCIA STONE. "George Eliot's Rebels: Portraits of the Artist as a Woman." *Women's Studies* 7, no. 3:97-108.

     Assesses Eliot's restless female artist characters who, like Eliot, resist the confines of domesticity and seek emotional release from "unwomanly feelings."

50   ____. "The 'He and She of It': Self-Division as Shaping Force in George Eliot's Fiction." Ph.D. dissertation, Rutgers University, 349 pp.

     "Eliot's novels are marked by the emotional and creative disjunction between public and private selves." Describes "fictional tension between plot patterns that reflect female imaginative identification, and narrative which serves to disguise that perspective." See *Dissertations Abstracts International* 41, no. 4 (1980):1615A.

1980

51 MILLET, STANTON. "The Union of 'Miss Brooke' and *Middlemarch*: A Study of the Manuscript." *Journal of English and Germanic Philology* 79, no. 1 (January):32-57.

Indicates textual revisions in *Middlemarch* that demonstrate Eliot's two related themes. The first theme is concerned with people's attempts to reshape "their thought and deed in noble agreement." The second theme is feminist in nature and relates to Dorothea Brooke's search for vocation.

52 NACHLAS, JENNIFER REBECCA. "Moral Problems and Social Integration in the Later Novels of George Eliot." Ph.D. dissertation, University of Toronto (Canada).

Presents Eliot's approach to the moral problems shared by her characters and reflected as a social problem within the novels' setting. The central moral problem in *Romola* concerns authority and "conscious obedience." Types of power and its applications are the moral problems in *Felix Holt, the Radical*. Choice is the central moral problem of *Middlemarch*, which involves decisions about marriage, career, and money. In *Daniel Deronda*, the moral problem concerns individual ability to feel faith. See *Dissertations Abstracts International* 41, no. 6 (1980):2617A.

53 NAMAN, ANNE ARESTY. "George Eliot: Prejudiced Sympathy." In *The Jew in the Victorian Novel: Some Relationships Between Prejudice and Art*. AMS Studies in the Nineteenth Century. New York: AMS Press, pp. 161-207.

Analyzes the psychology of prejudice in the formation of the Jewish characters in *Daniel Deronda*. "George Eliot presents a variety of Jewish people, and in order to understand the relationship between the individual Jew and his group, she establishes a comparative network within which the Jews may be compared with one another and with the English."

54 PALLISER, CHARLES. "*Adam Bede* and 'the Story of the Past.'" In *George Eliot: Centenary Essays and an Unpublished Fragment*. Edited by Anne Smith. Totowa, N.J.: Barnes & Noble, pp. 55-76.

"In *Adam Bede*, George Eliot sets out to examine the nature of fiction and its peculiar kind of access to the truth, asking what the differences are between the way we read fiction and the way we 'read' actual experience, and in what sense ... a novel can claim to offer its readers advice on how to conduct their lives. Since *Adam Bede* is a

1980

historical novel this issue is more specifically related to the question of how fiction's method of insight into the truth about the past compares with that of the discipline of history."

55   PELL, NANCY ANNE. "'A Flight From Home': Displacement as Feminist Critique in George Eliot's Expatriate Fiction." Ph.D. dissertation, State University of New York at Buffalo, 258 pp.

Examines *Romola*, "The Spanish Gypsy," and Eliot's use of foreign settings to "express critical perceptions of patriarchal power." Using geographical displacement, Eliot developed daughter-characters who could struggle against the father-figure and, thus, Eliot could indirectly criticize English culture. See *Dissertations Abstracts International* 41, no. 9 (1981): 4047A.

56   PESKIN, S.G. "Music in *Middlemarch*." *English Studies in Africa* 23, no. 2 (September):75-81.

Eliot's "references to music belong to a cluster of images which centre on motifs from literature, painting and myth, and which assert the ascendancy of feeling and imagination over scientific truths."

57   PETERSON, CARL. "Heroine as Reader in the Nineteenth-Century Novel: Emma Bovary and Maggie Tulliver." *Comparative Literature Studies* 17, no. 2 (June, pt. 1):168-83.

Compares similarities between Flaubert's *Madame Bovary* and Eliot's *The Mill on the Floss*. In both novels, the heroines are readers and their reading is a prime motivating force which directly shapes their lives and fates." Both Eliot and Flaubert deal with issues concerning women, the status of the artist, and the problems of moral choice in the Victorian era.

58   PRESTON, JOHN. "The Community of the Novel: *Silas Marner*." In *Comparative Criticism: A Yearbook*. Vol. 2. Edited by Elinor [S.] Shaffer. Cambridge: Cambridge University Press, pp. 109-30.

Silas Marner is found to be about "community and self-hood" and the relationships within a society. "It is a novel about a story" in that the novel attempts to be an "utterance" for a complex society in the way that the story was a voice for a simpler community.

59   PUTZELL [-KORAB], SARA MOORE. "George Eliot's Location of Value in History." *Renascence* 32, no. 3 (Spring):167-77.

1980

Examines the function of feeling – as a guide to moral action and as a locus of value – in Eliot's fiction. Like Hegel, Eliot writes about people and society as parts of an evolving world "such that history is a locus of moral value."

60 RICKS, CHRISTOPHER. "It Was Her Books to Which She Gave Birth." *Listener* 104 (December 11):783-86.
    Discussion of Eliot's childlessness and the idea that her novels and characters, especially the young people, made up for her own childlessness.

61 SCHELLY, JUDITH MAY. "A Like Unlike: Brother and Sister in the Works of Wordsworth, Byron, George Eliot, Emily Brontë, and Dickens." Ph.D. dissertation, University of California at Berkeley, 246 pp.
    Surveys the brother-sister relationship. In the fiction of the above-mentioned authors, the characters desire unity with their sibling as a "mirror-image of self." *The Mill on the Floss* demonstrates the changes on the brother-sister relationship caused by maturity and social imperatives. The anthropological model of Claude Lévi-Strauss and the psychological model of Jacques Lacan are used to illuminate the authors' attempts to deal with the incest taboo and psychic development. See *Dissertations Abstracts International* 42, no. 1 (1981):205A.

62 SHOWALTER, ELAINE. "The Greening of Sister George." *Nineteenth-Century Fiction* 35, no. 3 (December): 292-311.
    Analyzes feminist critics' and women writers' perceptions and reactions to Eliot's novels. Includes commentary and reworkings of Eliot's plots by Virginia Woolf, Katherine Mansfield, Simone de Beauvoir, Margaret Drabble, Gail Godwin, P.D. James, and Lee R. Edwards.

63 SMITH, ANNE, ed. *George Eliot: Centenary Essays and an Unpublished Fragment.* Totowa, N.J.: Barnes & Noble, 217 pp.
    Each article annotated within this section.

64 STANGE, G. ROBERT. "The Voices of the Essayist." *Nineteenth-Century Fiction* 35, no. 3 (December): 312-30.
    Studies Eliot's use of the moral and literary, or critical, essay. Contrasts her essays against the background of the growth of the form

in the seventeenth and eighteenth centuries, and its decline during Eliot's lifetime. Examines Eliot's early essays for her handling of the authorial voice, her opinions, and signs of preliminary studies for her later fiction. "The Impressions of Theophrastus Such," written after finishing her last novel, is meant to revive the genre of the moral essay.

65 STONE, DONALD D[AVID]. "George Eliot: The Romantic Legacy." In *The Romantic Impulse in Victorian Fiction*. Cambridge, Mass., and London: Harvard University Press, pp. 173-248.

Examines how Romantic traditions created difficulties for Eliot as a woman novelist. Traces Wordsworthian themes but emphasizes the fact that Wordsworth was not the impetus for Eliot's writings. Reviews Eliot's essays for her "indebtedness to Romantic theories concerning the aims and methods of artistic creativity, the nature of genius, and the importance of inspiration. . . . The Romantic focus in the essays, as in the novels, is on feeling, feeling as the means and end of art and life."

66 THOMSON, FRED C., ed. Introduction to *Felix Holt, the Radical*. Oxford: Clarendon Press, pp. xiii-xlii.

Discusses the evolution of ideas in formulating *Felix Holt, the Radical*. Reviews political history, social reforms, and influences on Eliot. Includes emendations, treatment of accidentals, and a list of editions between 1866 and 1878.

67 VANCE, NORMAN. "Law, Religion and the Unity of *Felix Holt*." In *George Eliot: Centenary Essays and an Unpublished Fragment*. Edited by Anne Smith. Totowa, N.J.: Barnes & Noble, pp. 103-23.

Compares parliamentary reform of the 1830s and 1860s and its significance in *Felix Holt, the Radical*. The novel is a depiction of the changes in English society and the rise of the middle class as a result of the Industrial Revolution. The novel is about political and social change. The legal plot is a "metaphor for the underlying Law of human sympathy and moral order which is the only possible source of social stability. The themes of moral and political warrant and legitimacy which convey the novelist's radical insight stem from this central image of Law and link the public and private worlds of the novel."

68 VOGELER, MARTHA S. "George Eliot and the Positivists." *Nineteenth-Century Fiction* 35, no. 3 (December):406-31.

Traces the extent of Eliot's affiliation with the Positivists by studying the work of Auguste Comte and other Comtists. Finds that

1980

Eliot believed in Comte's Religion of Humanity, but she ignored most of its politics.

69   VONVILLAS, BARBARA ANNE. "George Eliot and Feminism." Ph.D. dissertation, University of Rhode Island, 247 pp.
Defines Eliot's feminism as a "constant determination to present fictional situations which in themselves suggest the necessity for reform." The essays reflect a strong protest against male and female cultural impositions. The development of her control of her feminist view in her fiction is studied in three stages. See *Dissertations Abstracts International* 41, no. 8 (1981):3597A.

70   WADE, ROSALIND. "George Eliot's Wedding." *Contemporary Review* 236 (May):266-69.
Description of and commentary on Eliot's relationship with and marriage to John Walter Cross in May 1880. References to her twenty-five-year relationship with George Henry Lewes provide analysis of Eliot's male relationships.

71   WALEY, DANIEL. "The Department of Manuscript's George Eliot Holdings." *British Library Journal* 6, no. 2 (Autumn):123-29.
Description of the twenty-four volumes of Eliot's autograph manuscripts held at the British Museum.

72   WILT, JUDITH. "George Eliot: The Garment of Fear." In *Ghosts of the Gothic: Austen, Eliot & Lawrence*. Princeton, N.J.: Princeton University Press, pp. 173-230.
Survey of gothicism discusses and examines how Eliot was influenced by conventions in Gothic novels. Identifies psychological, historical, political, and theological roots of Gothic narrative and how its themes and structure were used by Eliot in "The Lifted Veil," *Daniel Deronda*, *Adam Bede*, *Middlemarch*, *Silas Marner*, and *Romola*. Discusses differences in eighteenth- and nineteenth-century Gothic motifs and the heretic/orthodox relationships between Austen, Eliot, and Lawrence. For Eliot, vision proceeds from terror, and imagination is triggered by dread.

73   WRIGHT, TERENCE. "Critical Appproaches to George Eliot." In *George Eliot: Centenary Essays and an Unpublished Fragment*. Edited by Anne Smith. Totowa, N.J.: Barnes & Noble, pp. 21-35.

1980

Discusses examples of current Eliot criticism – political, feminist, historical, intellectual, and psychological.

74   ZIMMERMAN, BONNIE [SUE]. "Gwendolen Harleth and 'The Girl of the Period.'" In *George Eliot: Centenary Essays and an Unpublished Fragment*. Edited by Anne Smith. Totowa, N.J.: Barnes & Noble, pp. 196-217.

Finds the characterization of Gwendolen Harleth of *Daniel Deronda* to be the culmination of Eliot's theory on the role of women. In Gwendolen, Eliot "created her most rebellious and egoistic heroine, her most dreadful punishment, and her most rigorous renunciation to illustrate how serious had become the problem of women's needs and duties."

75   _____. "'The Mother's History' in George Eliot's Life, Literature and Political Ideology." In *The Lost Tradition: Mothers and Daughters in Literature*. Edited by Cathy N. Davidson and E.M. Broner. New York: Frederick Unger Publishing, pp. 81-94.

Eliot, in portraying motherless heroines and heroines who were not mothers, sought a meaning for motherhood in both her novels and personal life. Applies the following fictional pattern to Eliot's own life: "women who step beyond the social and biological limitations of womankind, who desire to transcend the ordinary lot of woman, who defy sexual standards, who rebel rather than submit – these women are visited with the curse of sterility. Those women who do not rebel . . . become the radiating center of a quasi-mystical family circle. . . . George Eliot's heroines cannot be mothers because society provides no realistic model for healthy motherhood."

1981

1   BAKER, WILLIAM. *The Libraries of George Eliot and George Henry Lewes*. English Literary Studies. Edited by Samuel L. Macey. Victoria, British Columbia, Canada: University of Victoria, 146 pp.

Listing of the book collection of Eliot and Lewes. Includes a subject breakdown of items, alphabetical author categorization of works sold in the Foster Sale of 1923, and an alphabetical list of 1,051 items from the original libraries.

2   BUCKLEY, JEROME H[AMILTON]. "George Eliot's Double Life: *The Mill on the Floss* as a *Bildungsroman.*" In *From Smollett to James: Studies in the Novel and Other Essays Presented to Edgar Johnson.* Edited by Samuel I. Mintz, Alice Chandler and Christopher Mulvey. Charlottesville: University Press of Virginia, pp. 211-36.

Examines the elements of a *bildungsroman* as they apply to *The Mill on the Floss.* "A chronicle of adolescence, of the pains of growing up and of the trials to be faced before reaching physical maturity and some sort of integration of personality. Here education by emotional experience as much as by formal schooling is a central issue; first love and misplaced affection is a familiar theme. . . ."

3   BURCH, BETH. "Eliot's *Adam Bede.*" *Explicator* 40, no. 1 (Fall):27-28.

Points out "Eliot's blending of sexual with classical imagery" in Arthur Donnithorne's seduction of Hetty Sorrel. Literal symbolism of the woods and pink handkerchief further confirm the seduction.

4   ____. "A Folk Source and Analogue for *Adam Bede.* "*American Notes and Queries* 19, nos. 7-8 (March-April):136-38.

Finds that Eliot used analogical elements from the fairy tale "Little Red Riding Hood" to delineate characters and the thematic structure of *Adam Bede.*

5   BUZAN, MARY MARGARET. "Tragedy and Parable in George Eliot's Novels." Ph.D. dissertation, University of Texas at Austin, 271 pp.

Application of several definitions of parable and tragedy to the plots and subplots of *The Mill on the Floss, Silas Marner, Felix Holt, the Radical,* and *Daniel Deronda.* Parable and tragedy are used to describe Eliot's treatment of the self-identification process. See *Dissertations Abstracts International* 42, no. 4 (1981):1643A.

6   CAMPBELL, THOMAS J. "From Country to Town: The Growth of Abstract Consciousness in *The Mill on the Floss.*" *Research Studies of Washington State University* 49, no. 2 (June):107-15.

Eliot's shift from a rural to an urban theme, in *The Mill on the Floss,* suggests several parallel changes – how the individual is related to his community; the breakdown of social hierarchies; new theories regarding work; the growth of education; the secularization of religion;

1981

roles for women; and a change in consciousness from concrete to abstract thought.

7 CARLISLE, JANICE. *"Adam Bede*: 'The Art of Vision.'" In *The Sense of an Audience: Dickens, Thackeray, and George Eliot at Mid-Century*. Athens: University of Georgia Press, pp. 187-213.

Traces how Eliot created *Adam Bede* out of the influences of Wordsworth and the earlier poetic traditions. In *Adam Bede*, Eliot recaptures a sense of former times when creating a tale about infanticide.Wordsworth's poem "The Thorn" was Eliot's model for the novel.

8 _____. "After *Adam Bede*: Severing Relations." In *The Sense of an Audience: Dickens, Thackeray, and George Eliot at Mid-Century*. Athens: University of Georgia Press, pp. 214-26.

Confirms the author/narrator's relationship with characters of *Middlemarch* and *Daniel Deronda*. *Daniel Deronda* epitomizes the purpose of Eliot's fiction in that it "coincided with social factors that undermined the relation between novelist and public, the source and object of the mid-century faith in the bonds wrought by imagination."

9 _____. *"Scenes of Clerical Life*: The First Experiment." In *The Sense of an Audience: Dickens, Thackeray, and George Eliot at Mid-Century*. Athens: University of Georgia Press, pp. 166-86.

Studies Eliot's development of a narrative technique in *Scenes of Clerical Life*, in which she creates characters who produce her desired effects upon the audience. Throughout the book, the narrator shows a growing personal involvement with the characters he is speaking about. In doing so, Eliot creates imaginative ties between the reader and the characters by implementing narration in the present tense.

10 CORTESE, ROMANA. "George Eliot and Dante." Ph.D. dissertation, University of Wisconsin – Madison, 227 pp.

Uses Eliot's letters and notebooks to ascertain her knowledge of Dante and how she used Dante to develop symbolic patterns that have bearing on the theme and structure of *Romola, Felix Holt, the Radical, Middlemarch*, and *Daniel Deronda*. Traces passages and themes to Dante's *Divine Comedy*. See *Dissertations Abstracts International* 42, no. 7 (1982):3162A.

1981

11 CRAIB, IAN. "*Criticism and Ideology*: Theory and Experience."
    Contemporary Literature 22, no. 4 (Fall):489-509.
        In reviewing Eagleton's *Criticism and Ideology*, Craib analyzes
    Eagleton's study of Eliot and general social analysis. Finds "that the
    social context of her work is described in terms of a nineteenth-century
    bourgeois ideology becoming increasingly dependent upon organicist
    concepts of society as capitalism assumed increasingly organic
    corporate forms. ... There was no attempt to come to grips with the
    economic and political complexities of the period, let alone the way
    these formed the social relationships."

12 DALE, PETER [ALLAN]. "Symbolic Representation and the
    Means of Revolution in *Daniel Deronda*." *Victorian Newsletter* 59
    (Spring):25-30.
        Examines what "Eliot considered to be the philosophical status
    of symbols." Expands Eliot's concept of symbolic representation as
    myth and as linguistic form.

13 DAVID, DEIRDRE. "Deronda and the Jews." In *Fictions of
    Resolution in Three Victorian Novels: North and South, Our Mutual
    Friend, Daniel Deronda*. New York: Columbia University Press, pp.
    147-75.
        Daniel Deronda is about the discovery and acceptance of a
    Jewish identity. "Eliot mediates between representation and desire for
    difference. ...As Deronda matures, his critical examination of his
    culture and his self-consciousness in regard to his origins is associated
    by Eliot ... with writing and with texts and ... is self-consciously
    concerned with interpretation of social and psychological actuality by
    language." For Daniel to identify his Jewish heritage means an end to
    his doubts and psychological uneasiness.

14 _____. *Fictions of Resolution in Three Victorian Novels: North and
    South, Our Mutual Friend, Daniel Deronda*. New York: Columbia
    University Press, 209 pp.
        Historical, social, psychological, and literary analysis of *Daniel
    Deronda* suggest that the "tension between representation of social
    actuality and desire for difference is mythically resolved." Eliot creates
    fiction of resolution for the problems of social injustices; a middle
    ground where "politics, commerce, art and morality might meet and
    enrich each other." Uses Freud's theories of culture, discontent, and
    female sexuality.

1981

15 _____. "Gwendolen Harleth as Heroine and Metaphor." In *Fictions of Resolution in Three Victorian Novels: North and South, Our Mutual Friend, Daniel Deronda*. New York: Columbia University Press, pp. 176-206.

Gwendolen Harleth, in *Daniel Deronda*, is both metaphor and heroine as she deals with "four symptoms of neurotic conflict – a fierce psychological imperialism, an obsession with performance, a fear of adult sexuality, and recurrent fits of spiritual dread." These elements of Gwendolen's disturbed psyche are analogous to the elements of a disturbed society. For Gwendolen – and the society for which she is a metaphor – to perceive her problems is "to have symbolically identified the origins of dread and guilt and means isolation and abandonment."

16 _____. "Social Realism and Moral Correction." In *Fictions of Resolution in Three Victorian Novels: North and South, Our Mutual Friend, Daniel Deronda*. New York: Columbia University Press, pp. 135-146.

Analyzes *North and South, Our Mutual Friend*, and *Daniel Deronda* in order to make clear the relationship between specific social groups and fiction. *Daniel Deronda* is split because Eliot is "unable to reconcile her fine study in psychological and social realism with the strange, difficult and sometimes virtually unreadable Deronda narrative of Jewish identity. . . . In *Daniel Deronda*, there is no positive connection between the family and moral regeneration."

17 DAVIS, G[ABRIELLE] A. WITTIG. "Ruskin's *Modern Painters* and George Eliot's Concept of Realism." *English Language Notes* 18, no. 3 (March):194-201.

Discusses John Ruskin's *Modern Painters* III and its influence on Eliot's description of realism. Eliot uses Ruskin's two major concepts of truth and beauty to define realism and aesthetic theory. Eliot's synthetic concept of realism links the perceiving subject to the intentional object.

18 DODD, VALERIE A. "A George Eliot Notebook." In *Studies in Bibliography*. Vol. 34. Charlottesville: University of Virginia Press, pp. 258-62.

Description of an Eliot notebook (No. GE 890 ELI-8) in the collection of the Nuneaton Library, Warwickshire, England. Reveals Eliot's interest in Comte, Locke, and Greek philosophy.

19 DOYLE, MARY ELLEN. *The Sympathetic Response: George Eliot's Fictional Rhetoric*. East Brunswick, N.J., and London: Associated University Presses, 183 pp.

Rhetorical analysis of Eliot's treatment of sympathy and understanding in *Adam Bede, The Mill on the Floss, Felix Holt, the Radical, Middlemarch*, and *Daniel Deronda*. Examines Eliot's success and failure in achieving the internal norms for distance in each novel.

20 ELIOT, GEORGE. *George Eliot: A Writer's Notebook, 1854-1879, and Uncollected Writings*. Edited by Joseph Wiesenfarth. Charlottesville: University of Virginia Press, 342 pp.

Reprints Eliot's recorded research for *Adam Bede, Felix Holt, the Radical*, "The Spanish Gypsy," *Romola, Middlemarch*, and *Daniel Deronda*. Brings together Eliot's articles relevant to entries in the notebook. Includes sixteen illustrations, notes, and textual notes.

21 FISHER, PHILIP. *Making Up Society: The Novels of George Eliot*. Pittsburgh: University of Pittsburgh Press, 244 pp.

Traces changes in Eliot's novels based on her feeling of a loss of trust in community as the basis of moral life. Thesis is that Eliot moved from "writing social novels to making up social fictions."

22 GRAHAM, PETER W. "George Eliot." In *Critical Survey of Short Fiction*. Edited by Frank N. Magill. Vol. 4. Englewood Cliffs, N.J.: Salem Press, pp. 1333-37.

How Eliot influenced mid-Victorian readers with fictional accounts of ethical and social problems. Analysis of short fiction–*Scenes of Clerical Life*, "The Lifted Veil," and "Brother Jacob"–wherein the common man is portrayed within the complexities of seemingly simple lives.

23 GREENSTEIN, SUSAN M. "A Question of Vocation: From *Romola* to *Middlemarch*." *Nineteenth-Century Fiction* 35, no. 4 (March):487-505.

Examines Eliot's development and use of women's vocational crises as a theme in *Romola* and *Middlemarch*. *Romola* deals with women's fates and choices and sets the stage for the creation of *Middlemarch*'s Dorothea Brooke.

24 HAMMOND, PAUL. "George Eliot's Ersatz Christianity." *Theology* 84, no. 699 (May):190-96.

1981

Clarifies Eliot's "intellectual and moral case against Christianity" by assessing her translations of Strauss and Feuerbach and her essays.

25 HOLLOWAY, ANNA REBECCA. "Henry James and the Intellectuals: Relativism and Form in G. Eliot, R. Browning, W. Pater, and H. James." Ph.D. dissertation, Kent State University, 269 pp.

Analyzes the relationship between the ideas and writing techniques of Eliot, James, Browning, and Pater in an attempt to demonstrate the conflict between the authors' "relativism and their intellectual absolutism." James's focus on character development allows him to portray the "development of consciousnessin detail. Eliot, Browning and Pater believe that the evolution of behavior and viewpoints from social and psychological conditions is the basis for understanding people." See *Dissertations Abstracts International* 42, no. 4 (1981):1646A.

26 HOMANS, MARGARET. "Eliot, Wordsworth, and Scenes of the Sister's Instruction." *Critical Inquiry* 8, no. 2 (Winter):223-41.

"Argues that gender difference is the basis of Eliot's ambivalent response to Wordsworth's instructions ... the literalness of her transposition of Wordsworthian themes–her effort to be a docile student on the model of Wordsworth's implied sister–that constitutes her subversion of them. ..." Applies this theory to *The Mill on the Floss*. See also 1986.30.

27 HORR, CATHERINE HALL. "George Eliot's Theory of the Novel, 1857-1880." Ph.D. dissertation, Ohio University, 278 pp.

Identifies Eliot's theory of the novel and traces changes and development of that theory. The categories of Eliot's theory are author as teacher; sympathy; a need for and types of unity; the narrative role; appropriate characterization; the importance of research; development of a writing style; the use of humor and wit; and the use of realism. See *Dissertations Abstracts International* 42, no. 8 (1982):3610A.

28 HOWELS, CORAL ANN. "Dreams and Visions in George Eliot's Fiction." *AUMLA* 56 (November):167-82.

Discusses Eliot's interest in dreams, visions, and dreamlike experiences in "The Lifted Veil," *The Mill on the Floss*, *Romola*, and *Daniel Deronda*. Argues that "dreams chronicle important crises in

1981

George Eliot's thinking, registering radical changes in her attitude towards modes of knowledge available to human consciousness. . . ."

29 JACOBUS, MARY. "The Question of Language: Men of Maxims and *The Mill on the Floss*." *Critical Inquiry* 8, no. 2 (Winter):207-22.

Applies theories of feminine linguistic practice to *The Mill on the Floss* to establish how the feminine is determined by discourse. Feminist criticism, the politics of women's writing, and the writings of Luce Irigaray are examined. Reprinted: 1982.40; 1986.33.

30 JAHN, KAREN FROST. "Providence in the Victorian Novel: *Bleak House, Middlemarch*, and *The Mayor of Casterbridge* Examined for Their Aesthetic Realization of Providence." Ph.D. dissertation, University of Detroit, 276 pp.

Reviews the use of imagery, narration, and coincidence by Eliot, Dickens, and Hardy in an attempt empirically to define the concept of Providence. Eliot, in *Middlemarch*, explores various ways of responding to experience. The author "creates a mythos of expanding perception as providential" and uses coincidence to reward and punish those who overcome or cling to egoism. See *Dissertations Abstracts International* 47, no. 2 (1986):537A.

31 JONES, LAWRENCE. "Imagery and the 'Idiosyncratic Mode of Regard': Eliot, Hardy, and Lawrence." *Ariel* 12, no. 1 (January):29-49.

Compares the shared imagery but different response Eliot, Hardy, and Lawrence give to their basic assumption of the post-Darwinian idea that there is a "disjunction between human consciousness and a natural universe quite indifferent to it."

32 JOSEPH, GERHARD. "The *Antigone* as Cultual Touchstone: Matthew Arnold, Hegel, George Eliot, Virginia Woolf, and Margaret Drabble." *PMLA* 96, no. 1 (January):22-35.

"George Eliot accepts the modernity of Antigone's character as a moral pioneer but finds the play's action without much application to Victorian reality."

33 KLIENEBERGER, H.R. "George Eliot and Gottfried Keller." In *The Novel in England and Germany*. London: Oswald Wolff, pp. 87-107.

1981

Discusses influence of David Friedrich Strauss and Ludwig Feuerbach on the writing of Eliot and Gottfried Keller. Comparative study of Eliot's and Keller's handling of religion, the *bildungsroman*, social realism, and human sympathy.

34 KNOEPFLMACHER, U.C. "Unveiling Men: Power and Masculinity in George Eliot's Fiction." In *Men by Women*. Women and Literature Series, vol. 2, edited by Janet Todd. New York and London: Holmes & Meier Publishers, pp. 130-46.

Argues that "Eliot's handling of male characters aims less at probing the masculine than at liberating a stifled or veiled female self; through projecting and impersonating masculinity, Eliot wants to tame, subdue and feminize it."

35 KOWALESKI, ELIZABETH ANN. "The Dark Night of Her Soul: The Effects of Anglican Evangelicalism on the Careers of Charlotte Elizabeth Tonna and George Eliot." Ph.D. dissertation, Columbia University, 312 pp.

Discusses the "formative impact of Anglican Evangelicalism" in the careers of Tonna and Eliot. Examines how Eliot's theories on politics and women were based on the Evangelical movement. See *Dissertations Abstracts International* 44, no. 9 (1984):2773A.

36 LEVINE, GEORGE L. "George Eliot, Conrad, and the Invisible World." In *The Realistic Imagination: English Fiction from Frankenstein to Lady Chatterly*. Chicago and London: University of Chicago Press, pp. 252-90.

Focuses on "the struggle to avoid the inevitable conventionality of language in pursuit of the unattainable unmediated reality. Realism, as a literary method, can in these terms be defined as a self-conscious effort to make literature appear to be describing . . . reality itself." The transformation of realism in *The Mayor of Casterbridge*, *Middlemarch*, and *Nostromo* is considered with regard to Victorian scientific thought, social reforms, economic changes, and colonial expansion.

37 ____. "The Hero as Dilettante: *Middlemarch* and *Nostromo*." In *The Realistic Imagination: English Fiction from Frankenstein to Lady Chatterly*. Chicago and London: University of Chicago Press, pp. 291-316.

Reprint of 1980.43.

38 ____. "The Scientific Texture of *Middlemarch*." In *The Realistic Imagination: English Fiction from Frankenstein to Lady Chatterly*. Chicago and London: University of Chicago Press, pp. 66-89.

 Middlemarch is an illustration of man's moral need for scientific vision. Discussion of how science made sense of life in the Victorian debate over evolution and consciousness in nature. "By virtue of rigorous secularity Eliot attempts, in a way comparable to that of Feuerbach, to resacralize a world from which God has been dismissed." Discusses the widespread fragmentation in the beginning of the novel and its later attempt to find order in reality and epistemology. Reprinted: 1986.39.

39 LITVAK, JOSEPH DAVID. "Poetry in the Novel: The Poetics of Disunity in George Eliot." Ph.D. dissertation, Yale University, 374 pp.

 "Abstract not available." See *Dissertations Abstracts International* 43, no. 7 (1983):2342A.

40 LONGFORD, ELIZABETH H. "George Eliot, 1819-1880." In *Eminent Victorian Women*. London: Weidenfeld & Nicolson, pp. 61-84.

 Describes Eliot's life story in light of nineteenth-century society's rules and conventions. How Eliot overcame social ostracism for her personal lifestyle to receive adulation for her novels.

41 McCORMACK, KATHLEEN. "Characters' Reading and Changing Reality in the Novels of George Eliot." Ph.D. dissertation, University of Miami, 309 pp.

 By using reading to develop character and depict changes in social reality, Eliot sets up patterns of ironic connections. Her response to cultural changes, as reflected in her characters' reading, makes clear her seeming ambivalence toward printed matter. See *Dissertations Abstracts International* 42, no. 12 (1982):5129A.

42 ____. "George Eliot: Wollstonecraft's 'Judicious Person with Some Turn for Humour.'" *English Language Notes* 19, no. 1 (September):44-46.

 Discusses Mary Wollstonecraft's essay "A Vindication of the Rights of Women" and its influence on Eliot's novels and essay "Silly Novels by Lady Novelists."

1981

43   McLAVERTY, JAMES. "Comtean Fetishism in *Silas Marner.*"
      Nineteenth-Century Fiction 36, no. 3 (December):318-36.
          Analyzes the contrast between Silas Marner and Godfrey Cass
      with regard to Comte's theory of fetishism. According to Comte,
      fetishism was the first stage of man's progress. Silas retains the life of
      feeling; Godfrey lacks it because of his corrupt background. Eliot, in
      creating Silas and Godfrey, attempts to illustrate how feelings can
      change man and his world.

44   MANN, KAREN B. "George Eliot's Language of Nature:
      Production and Consumption." *ELH* 48, no. 1 (Spring):190-216.
          Interprets Eliot's humor, in particular the structure of the
      anecdote concerning Godfrey Cass of *Adam Bede*. Studies Eliot's use of
      word-play and natural language as the "source of energy and order in
      her novels."

45   MARTIN, JEAN-PAUL. "Les *Atrocités* de George Eliot." *Critique*
      (Paris) 37, no. 405-406 (February-March):221-31.

46   MATUS, JILL LAZAR. "Accommodating the Actual: Determinism
      and Modes of Writing in the Novels of George Eliot." Ph.D.
      dissertation, University of Toronto (Canada).
          Examines Eliot's views on determinism and compares her views
      with those of nineteenth-century philosophers. Studies Eliot's
      determinism as it is expressed in a mode of writing that tends toward
      the metonymic pole of language. In this style, Eliot uses metaphor
      rather than simile; relies on sequence and chronology; and uses
      conditional structures and antithesis. Focus is on the balance of
      metaphoric and metonymic elements in *Daniel Deronda*, *Adam Bede*,
      and *Silas Marner*. See *Dissertations Abstracts International* 42, no. 10
      (1982):4459A.

47   MIDDLETON, CATHERINE A. "Roots and Rootlessness: An
      Exploration of the Concept in the Life and Novels of George Eliot."
      In *Humanistic Geography and Literature: Essays on the Experience of
      Place*. Edited by Douglas C.D. Pocock. London: Croom Helm;
      Totowa, N.J.: Barnes & Noble, pp. 101-20.
          Considers the idea of rootedness and rootlessness in Eliot's life
      and literary techniques. Temporal settings and geographical detail in
      Eliot's novels find that people need an "organic centre."

1981

48   MILLER, D.A. "George Eliot: The Wisdom of Balancing Claims."
      In *Narrative and Its Discontents: Problems of Closure in the
      Traditional Novel*. Princeton, N.J.: Princeton University Press, pp.
      107-94.
          Assesses the narratable and closure in *Middlemarch*. Eliot
      positions the text "within a controlling perspective of narrative closure,
      which would restore the world to a state of transparency, once and for
      all released from errancy and and equivocation." Eliot, as well as Jane
      Austen and Stendhal, triangulates the scope of the novel ...
      psychoanalytically as the normal, neurotic and perverse; ideologically as
      the conservative, liberal and libertarian."

49   MILLER, NANCY K. "Emphasis Added: Plots and Plausibilities in
      Women's Fiction." *PMLA* 96, no. 1 (January):36-48.
          Discusses the issue of women's relationship to the production of
      prose fiction. Mme. de Lafayette's *La Princesse de Clèves* and Eliot's
      The Mill on the Floss suggest the "possiblity of deciphering a female
      erotics that structures the plots of women's fiction, plots that reject the
      narrative logic of the dominant discourse."

50   MITCHELL, SALLY. "Sexual Attitudes in the Middle-Class Novel,
      1835-1860." In *The Fallen Angel: Chastity, Class, and Women's
      Reading, 1835-1880*. Bowling Green, Ohio: Bowling Green
      University Press, pp. 45-72.
          Develops contrasts between *Adam Bede* and Edward Bulwer-
      Lytton's *Alice; or, The Mysteries* (1838). Examines treatment of sexual
      activity and of the unchaste woman in literature.

51   NEWTON, JUDITH LOWDER. "*The Mill on the Floss*." In *Women,
      Power, and Subversion: Social Strategies in British Fiction, 1778-1860*.
      Athens: University of Georgia Press, pp. 125-57.
          Study of Maggie Tulliver and her power to change the
      community of St. Ogg's. Finds the novel to be a critique of women's
      dependency but because of Eliot's ideology of love and sacrifice,
      Maggie is denied self-enhancing power.

52   NEWTON, K.M. "*Daniel Deronda* and Circumcision." *Essays in
      Criticism* 31, no. 4 (October):313-27.
          Discusses circumcision of Jews and non-Jews in the Victorian
      era to substantiate Deronda's lack of knowing of his Judaism, despite

1981

the fact that he was circumcised. The fact of circumcision "casts an ironical light on Deronda's Jewishness."

53 ____. *George Eliot, Romantic Humanist: A Study of the Philosophical Structure of Her Novels*. Totowa, N.J.: Barnes & Noble, 222 pp.

Perceives Eliot as an "advanced Romantic" who relied on her personal ideas of memory, continuity, and idealism and "who sympathizes almost entirely with the aims and values of the organicist Romantics. . . ." Eliot's aims as a philosophical novelist were to attack the egoistic and nihilistic philosophies and to support a humanist philosophy. Discusses her philosophical relationships with Lewes and Feuerbach.

54 PINION, F.B. *A George Eliot Companion: Literary Achievement and Modern Significance*. Totowa, N.J.: Barnes & Noble, 277 pp.

Studies the development of Eliot, including relevant history, essays and reviews, her three phases of fiction, later essays, her influence on Thomas Hardy, her notes on "The Spanish Gypsy" and tragedy, and a key to places and people of Eliot's fiction. Includes a glossary, maps, and plates.

55 PUJALS, ESTEBAN. "La novelista inglesa George Eliot (1819-1880): Un centenario memorable." *Arbor* (Madrid) 108, no. 424 (April):57-65.

56 ____. "Una gran novelista inglesia: George Eliot (1819-1880)." *Revista de la Universidad Complutense de Madrid* 1:42-53.

57 RICKS, C[HRISTOPHER]. "Pink Toads in *Lord Jim*." *Essays in Criticism* 31, no. 2 (April):142-44.

Discusses the use, in Conrad's *Lord Jim* and Eliot's "Janet's Repentence," of "pink toads" to describe delirium tremens (dt's). Eliot was the source for Conrad's use of the term "pink toads."

58 SANDERS, ANDREW. "George Eliot: An Exhibition." *History Today* 31 (April):50.

Describes the British Library's centenary commemorative exhibition of Eliot's literary manuscripts, which took place 11 December 1980-26 April 1981.

59   TORGOVNICK, MARIANNA. "George Eliot and the 'Finale' of
     Middlemarch." In *Closure in the Novel*. Princeton, N.J.: Princeton
     University Press, pp. 20-36.
         The "Finale" of *Middlemarch* reflects Eliot's desire to be both a
     popular and intellectual novelist. The purpose of the "Finale" is that of
     an after-history – a popular method, but one in which Eliot attempts to
     justify her reasons for writing an after-history. "Eliot's ending is an
     epilogue, circular in pattern, overview in technique, which assumes a
     complementary relationship between author and reader during
     closure."

60   VIERA, CARROLL. "'In the Zoo' and *The Mill on the Floss*."
     American Notes and Queries 20, nos. 1-2, (September-October):53-
     54.
         The polar bear from *The Mill on the Floss* provides an
     analogous symbol in Jean Stafford's story "In the Zoo" (New York,
     1944).

61   WIESENFARTH, JOSEPH, ed. *George Eliot: A Writer's Notebook
     1854-1879, and Uncollected Writings*. Charlottesville: University of
     Virginia Press, 342 pp.
         Emphasizes Eliot's habit of research, her interest in the
     condition of women and her knowledge of foreign languages. Reveals
     that she felt that her best poetry was satirical in style.

62   WILT, JUDITH. "Steamboat Surfacing: Scott and the English
     Novelists." *Nineteenth-Century Fiction* 35, no. 4 (March):459-86.
         Considers Walter Scott's influence on Eliot. Eliot made use of
     the Scott characterization and his manner of preserving anonymity.

63   WRIGHT, T.R. "George Eliot and Positivism: A Reassessment."
     Modern Language Review 76, no. 2 (Spring):257-72.
         Reviews Eliot's relationship with other Positivists and her "study
     and annotation of Comte's works" in *Daniel Deronda*. Her interest in
     Comte's philosophical attempt at the reconciliation of objective and
     subjective method is a predominant theme in *Daniel Deronda*.

1982

1   ADAM, IAN. "The Ambivalence of *The Mill on the Floss*." In *George Eliot: A Centenary Tribute*. Edited by Gordon S. Haight and Rosemary T. VanArsdel. Totowa, N.J.: Barnes & Noble, pp. 122-36.

Analysis of the final drowning scene. "*The Mill on the Floss* emphasizes the psychological and ethical side of Wordsworthian doctrine: it deals with the assumption that Nature will never betray the heart that loves her. . . . The novel is a record of its persistent betrayal of the loving heart, which by an act of faith seeks evidence of . . . purpose and fails to find it. The novelist shares Maggie's faith, and no more than her, will she finally abandon it. She reaffirms it strongly at the novel's end where Nature answers Maggie's prayer with the flood that reunites brother and sister and, incidentally, punishes the apostates of St. Ogg's."

2   ANDERSON, R[OLAND] F. "'Things Wisely Ordered': John Blackwood, George Eliot and the Publication of *Romola*." *Publishing History* 11:5-39.

An account of Eliot's decision to publish *Romola* with George Smith of the firm Smith, Elder instead of her previous publisher, John Blackwood.

3   apROBERTS, RUTH. "*Middlemarch* and the New Humanity." In *George Eliot: A Centenary Tribute*. Edited by Gordon S. Haight and Rosemary T. VanArsdel. Totowa, N.J.: Barnes & Noble, pp. 38-46.

Discusses social concerns in the Victorian novel, particularly in *Middlemarch*. "In its panorama of society we see man functioning and interacting in his conventions or institutions – church, land-holding and inheritance, marriage, medicine, scholarship, politics, and labour."

4   AUERBACH, NINA. *Woman and the Demon: The Life of a Victorian Myth*. Cambridge, Mass., and London: Harvard University Press, pp. 53-56, 118-24, 143-44, 174-78.

Reconstructs three myths of the Victorian woman – angel/demon, fallen woman, and old maid. Applies Eliot's essay "Silly Novels by Lady Novelists" and her fiction to the theory that "woman rules her own perpetual activity while man recedes into a passive watcher." Examines Eliot's spinsterhood and her use of the language of demonism. Particular attention is given to the character Hetty Sorrel, the fallen woman of *Adam Bede*.

1982

5 BAKER, WILLIAM. "George Eliot's Shakespeare Folio at the Folger Library." *George Eliot-George Henry Lewes Newsletter,* no. 1 (September):6-7.
  Description of Eliot's copy of William Shakespeare's *Comedies, Histories, and Tragedies* (4th ed.), Knight edition, now in the Folger Shakespeare Library.

6 ____, ed. *George Eliot-George Henry Lewes Newsletter.* Gorway, Eng.: West Midlands College, no pp.
  Published twice yearly for research, notes, queries, and comments on Eliot or George Henry Lewes.

7 BELSEY, CATHERINE. "Re-Reading *The Great Tradition.*" In *Re-Reading English.* Edited by Peter Widdowson. London and New York: Methuen & Co., pp. 121-35.
  Proposes an alternative, feminist rereading of *Daniel Deronda* and F.R. Leavis's *The Great Tradition* (1962). Shows how critical reading of criticisms enlightens the texts.

8 BERLIN, MIRIAM H. "George Eliot and the Russians." In *George Eliot: A Centenary Tribute.* Edited by Gordon S. Haight and Rosemary T. VanArsdel. Totowa, N.J.: Barnes & Noble, pp. 90-106.
  Discusses the enthusiastic reception of Eliot's work in Russia in the 1860s and 1870s as contrasted with its indifferent reception in France.

9 BRADBROOK, MURIEL C. "Barbara Bodichon, George Eliot and the Limits of Feminism." In *Women and Literature, 1779-1982: The Collected Papers of Muriel Bradbrook.* Vol. 2. Sussex, Eng.: Harvester Press; New York: Barnes & Noble, pp. 49-65.
  Description of the relationship between Barbara Bodichon and Eliot, as well as a discussion of feminism and women's literature.

10 CARAES, COLETTE. "La peur dans *Daniel Deronda* de George Eliot." *Cahiers victoriens & edouardiens* (Montpellier) 15, (April):63-70.

11 CHIN, SHEON-JOO. "The Rite of Passage in the Novels of Eliot and Dickens—the Case of *Middlemarch* and *Great Expectations.*" *Journal of the English Language and Literature* (Chungchong) 21:143-53.
  In Korean.

1982

12   COOPER, LETTICE. "George Eliot." In *British Writers*. Vol. 5. Edited by Ian Scott-Kilvert. New York: Charles Scribner's Sons, pp. 187-201.

Biography of Eliot; description of her relationship with Lewes. Analysis of her personal life; how it influenced her writing. How the elements of woman, family, rural life, and humanity are vital to Eliot's plots.

13   COSSLETT, TESS. "George Eliot." In *The 'Scientific Movement' and Victorian Literature*. Sussex: Harvester Press; New York: St. Martin's Press, pp. 74-100.

Examines elements of the Victorian scientific worldview in *Middlemarch* – scientific themes of gradualism, evolution, geology, entymology, biological metaphors, and principles and processes of research.

14   COTTOM, DANIEL. "The Romance of George Eliot's Realism." *Genre* 15, no. 4 (Winter):357-77.

Analyzes the figure of synechdoche as it is used to describe the relationship of the individual to society and the formation of the individual's social discipline. The author "defines the particularly Victorian meaning of the conflict of realism and romance throughout Eliot's work. In Eliot's conception, then, Realism transcends Romance. It transcends Romance as liberal intellectuals such as Eliot transcend society in general: by interpreting it, understanding it, and so gaining the power to patronize it."

15   DANIELS, ELIZABETH A. "A Meredithian Glance at Gwendolen Harleth." In *George Eliot: A Centenary Tribute*. Edited by Gordon S. Haight and Rosemary T. VanArsdel. Totowa, N.J.: Barnes & Noble, pp. 28-37.

Compares Eliot's views on women in *Middlemarch* and *Daniel Deronda* with those of George Meredith in *The Egoist* (1879) and *Diana of the Crossways* (1885). "Both believed that women must rise to flourish at the same intellectual level as men and must learn to be realists, counteracting the inanity and passivity of Philistinism and sentimentalism which were at the heart of Victorian custom."

16   DEEGAN, THOMAS. "George Henry Lewes's Collaboration with George Eliot on Her Translation of Spinoza's *Ethics*." *George Eliot-George Henry Lewes Newsletter*, no. 1 (September):1-3.

1982

Discusses Lewes's contribution to Eliot's translation of Spinoza's *Ethics*. Lewes wrote an introduction, acted as editor, and Eliot used his word renditions and style.

17   FRY, RUTH ECKMANN. "The Victorian Image of the German Revolution, 1806-1871, as Reflected in the Writings of Carlyle, Matthew Arnold, and George Eliot." Ph.D. dissertation, Georgia State University, 530 pp.
     Evaluates Anglo-German relations in the nineteenth century. Analyzes the German revolution and Eliot, Arnold, and Carlyle's linguistic and literary familiarity with German literature. *Middlemarch* reflects Eliot's reevaluation of her belief in scientific progress following the war of 1870-1871. See *Dissertations Abstracts International* 44, no. 5 (1983):1464A.

18   GOLDBERG, S.L. "'Poetry' as Moral Thinking: *The Mill on the Floss*." *Critical Review*, no. 24:55-79.
     "A universal doubleness in the way we think about moral issues, a doubleness that is an essential characteristic of 'poetry,' and makes it a special and indispensible medium of moral thinking" is studied in relation to *The Mill on the Floss*.

19   GOLDMAN, PAUL. "A New Portrait of George Eliot?" *British Library Journal* 8, no. 2 (Autumn):174-81.
     Evaluates drawn and painted portraits as well as written descriptions of Eliot's appearance. Critical attention given to a drawing in colored chalks done by Sir Frederic Burton between 1864 and 1865.

20   GRAY, B.M. "Pseudoscience and George Eliot's 'The Lifted Veil.'" *Nineteenth-Century Fiction* 36, no. 4 (March):407-23.
     Traces Eliot's sources and influences in the creation of "The Lifted Veil," particularly noting her research and fictional development of phrenology, clairvoyance, revivification experimentation, and mesmerism.

21   GUBAR, SUSAN. "'The Blank Page' and the Issues of Female Creativity." In *Writing and Sexual Difference*. Edited by Elizabeth Abel. Sussex, Eng.: Harvester Press, pp. 73-93.
     Finds that Eliot's female characters waste their creativity on efforts that are self-destructive. Hetty Sorrel wastes her life by dreaming of an unattainable future self-identity.

1982

22 HAIGHT, GORDON S. "George Eliot and Watts's 'Clytie.'" *Yale University Library Gazette* 56, no. 3-4 (April):65-69.
    An account of sculptor George Frederic Watts's gift of a bust, "Clytie: A Water Nymph," to Eliot. Includes her response in a letter of thanks to the artist.

23 _____. "George Eliot's Bastards." In *George Eliot: A Centenary Tribute*. Edited by Gordon S. Haight and Rosemary T. VanArsdel. Totowa, N.J.: Barnes & Noble, pp. 1-10.
    Examines the theme of paternity and illegitimacy in Eliot's novels and in her personal friendship with Charles Bray.

24 HAIGHT, GORDAN S., and VanARSDEL, ROSEMARY T., eds. *George Eliot: A Centenary Tribute*. Totowa, N.J.: Barnes & Noble, 166 pp.
    Each article annotated within this section.

25 HARDY, BARBARA. "Chapter 85 of *Middlemarch*: A Commentary." In *Particularities: Readings in George Eliot*. London: Peter Owen, pp. 174-80.
    Reprint of 1980.33.

26 _____. "George Eliot on Imagination." In *Particularities: Readings in George Eliot*. London: Peter Owen, pp. 181-204.
    Discusses Eliot's art of representing imaginative processes. Uses Eliot's letters, essays, poems, and novels to postulate Eliot's ideas and theories on imagination and truth.

27 _____. "Implication and Incompleteness in *Middlemarch*." In *Particularities: Readings in George Eliot*. London: Peter Owen, pp. 15-36.
    Considers the novel's lack of balance and completeness. In its treatment of sexuality it is unevenly restricted.

28 _____. "*Middlemarch* and the Passions." In *Particularities: Readings in George Eliot*. London: Peter Owen, pp. 86-103.
    "In *Middlemarch* Eliot uses statements about the passions as well as passionate enactment, needing words that classify psychological experience as well as words that stay faithfully and subtly close to the movement of feeling, in inner life and outer expression. . . . In each

analysis George Eliot attends to the place of the passions in the psychic unity of character." Reprint of 1975.34.

29 _____. "*Middlemarch*: Public and Private Worlds." In *Particularities: Readings in George Eliot*. London: Peter Owen, pp. 104-25.
Reprint of 1976.28.

30 _____. "*The Mill on the Floss*." In *Particularities: Readings in George Eliot*. London: Peter Owen, pp. 58-74.
Examines pragmatism, use of the personal experience of religious conversion, the transformation of Eliot's sexual crisis, and the resort to solution by fantasy in *The Mill on the Floss*.

31 _____. "Objects and Environments." In *Particularities: Readings in George Eliot*. London: Peter Owen, pp. 147-73.
Studies Eliot's presentation of objects as relevant to the realism of her fiction. Eliot is "concerned with the interaction of people and the inanimate world, with speculation about social and economic influences, and with the individual's imagination, aspiration, relationships, sense of society, and sense of self."

32 _____. *Particularities: Readings in George Eliot*. London: Peter Owen, 204 pp.
Collection of Hardy's essays and lectures on Eliot, individually annotated in this section.

33 _____. "The Reticent Narrator." In *Particularities: Readings in George Eliot*. London: Peter Owen, pp. 126-46.
Perceives Eliot's narrators as voices rather than as fictitious persons. The narrators have a "flexible language for rumination, judgment, reminiscence, humor, satire, irony, and sympathy."

34 _____. "Rituals and Feeling." In *Particularities: Readings in George Eliot*. London: Peter Owen, pp. 75-85.
Reprint of 1973.28.

35 _____. "The Surface of the Novel: Chapter 30 in *Middlemarch*." In *Particularities: Readings in George Eliot*. London: Peter Owen, pp. 37-57.

1982

Interprets the details of chapter 30 as representations of the "continuous surface of the novel." There are elements of crisis of action and decision, as well as symbolism.

36 HAWES, DONALD. "Chance in *Silas Marner*." *English* 31, no. 14 (Autumn):213-18.
Cites discrepancies between Eliot's moralizing and philosophizing in *Silas Marner*. Examines her use of the element of chance amongst her characters, who have a strong belief in Providence.

37 HEILMAN, ROBERT B. "'Stealthy Convergence' in *Middlemarch*." In *George Eliot: A Centenary Tribute*. Edited by Gordon S. Haight and Rosemary T. VanArsdel. Totowa, N.J.: Barnes & Noble, pp. 47-54.
Distinguishes Eliot's techniques for convergence and transition between multiple strands of action in *Middlemarch*.

38 HOUSLEY, ROBYN WARHOL. "The Engaging Narrator: Gaskell, Stowe, Eliot, and 'You.'" Ph.D. dissertation, Stanford University, 235 pp.
Describes differences between two types of intrusive narrators – the distancing narrator and the engaging narrator. Analysis of Gaskell, Stowe, and Eliot's use of the engaging narrator. "All three use direct address to stir the reader's egoistic emotions and memories, and then ask the reader to imitate themselves and empathize with their characters, who often undergo parallel sentimental educations." See *Dissertations Abstracts International* 43, no. 4 (1982):1152A.

39 HULCOOP, JOHN F. "'This Petty Medium': In the Middle of *Middlemarch*." In *George Eliot: A Centenary Tribute*. Edited by Gordon S. Haight and Rosemary T. VanArsdel. Totowa, N.J.: Barnes & Noble, pp. 153-66.
Discusses the focus of *Middlemarch* on the middle class. "*Middlemarch* articulates the awakening consciousness of the corporate power of the bourgeoisie."

40 JACOBUS, MARY. "The Question of Language: Men of Maxims and *The Mill on the Floss*." In *Writing and Sexual Difference*. Edited by Elizabeth Abel. Sussex, Eng.: Harvester Press, pp. 37-52.
Reprint of 1981.29.

1982

41 KORG, JACOB. "How George Eliot's People Think." In *George Eliot: A Centenary Tribute*. Edited by Gordon S. Haight and Rosemary T. VanArsdel. Totowa, N.J.: Barnes & Noble, pp. 82-89.

Explains Eliot's analyses of thinking and the processes of the mind. Examines stream of consciousness, immediate perception and memory, and the simple dialectic of the mind.

42 LAWSON, TOM OLIVER. "Samuel Richardson's *Sir Charles Grandison* and Its Influence on Jane Austen's *Persuasion* and George Eliot's *The Mill on the Floss*." Ph.D. dissertation, University of Arkansas, 335 pp.

Analysis of the influence of Richardson's *Sir Charles Grandison* upon the characters, plots, symbols, themes, devices, and techniques used by Austen and Eliot. See *Dissertations Abstracts International* 43, no. 10 (1983):3325A.

43 LEAVIS, F.R. "Gwendolen Harleth." In *The Critic as Anti-Philosopher: Essays and Papers*. Edited by G. Singh. Athens: University of Georgia Press, pp. 65-75.

Perceives Gwendolen Harleth of *Daniel Deronda* to be the representation of the creative greatness of Eliot. Analysis of Eliot's characterization of Gwendolen.

44 LERNER, LAURENCE. "George Eliot." In *From Dickens to Hardy*. New Pelican Guide to English Literature, vol. 6, edited by Boris Ford. Harmondsworth, Eng.: Penguin Books, pp. 264-84.

Analyzes chapter 20 of *Middlemarch* as a general introduction to Eliot's work–the use of the omniscient narrator, the relation between image and fact, and the dialectic of culture and the individual.

45 ____. "Literature and Money." In *The Literary Imagination: Essays on Literature and Society*. Sussex, Eng.: Harvester Press; Totowa, N.J.: Barnes & Noble, pp. 39-59.

Reprint of 1975.50

46 LEVINE, HERBERT J. "The Marriage of Allegory and Realism in *Daniel Deronda*." *Genre* 15, no. 4 (Winter):421-45.

Studies the intersection of the two narrative modes of *Daniel Deronda*–realism and allegory.

1982

47 LINDLEY, D.N. "Clio and Three Historical Novels." In *Dickens Studies Annual: Essays on Victorian Fiction*. Edited by Michael Timko, Fred Kaplan, and Edward Guiliano. New York: AMS Press, pp. 77-90.

   Dickens's *A Tale of Two Cities*, Eliot's *Romola*, and Thackeray's *The History of Henry Esmond* are studied as historical novels. Applies aspects of historical novels – a sense of conveying the "recovered" rather than the "felt" past. Eliot's "sophisticated" view of history is analyzed as well as the influence of Comte and Saint-Simon upon her perspectives of history.

48 McCOBB, ANTHONY. *George Eliot's Knowledge of German Life and Letters*. Edited by Dr. James Hogg. Salzburg Studies in English Literature, 102:2. Salzburg: Institut für Anglistik und Amerikanistik, 394 pp.

   Collates published and unpublished material related to Eliot's knowledge of German life and letters. Chronologically surveys Eliot's interest in German culture. Includes a list of critical studies of German influence on Eliot's art.

49 McDONNELL, JANE. "'Perfect Goodness' or 'The Wilder Life': *The Mill on the Floss* as Bildungsroman." *Genre* 15, no. 4 (Winter):379-402.

   Demonstrates Eliot's failure to carry out the *bildungsroman* genre in *The Mill on the Floss* by concluding with mythic elements of the fairy tale, romance and Romantic poetry. Examines the failure of the *bildungsroman* genre as it relates to women writers of the nineteenth century.

50 McMASTER, JULIET. "George Eliot's Language of the Sense." In *George Eliot: A Centenary Tribute*. Edited by Gordon S. Haight and Rosemary T. VanArsdel. Totowa, N.J.: Barnes & Noble, pp. 11-27.

   Discusses the sensuous language of Eliot: "the degree and quality of her characters' sensory perceptions frequently becomes a means of characterisation." Cites passages in which Eliot's language moves from the sensuous registering of experience to the sensual indulgence of the experience.

51 MANN, KAREN B. "Self, Shell, and World: George Eliot's Language of Space." *Genre* 15, no. 4 (Winter):447-75.

1982

"Analysis of Eliot's recurrent metaphor of the seashell and its relevance to the language of space in Eliot's novels argues that George Eliot's realism embodies her allegiance not only to the physical facts of the three-dimensional world, but to the inescapable centripetal force of the human mind. For Eliot, the ideal structure must acknowledge both realities. Her characteristic settings and spatial metaphors embody this effort to accommodate self and world."

52 MARKIN, ALLAN. "George Eliot and Education." Ph.D. dissertation, University of Calgary (Canada).
Cited but not abstracted in *Dissertation Abstracts International* (1982).

53 MAROTTA, KENNY [RALPH]. "Introduction: George Eliot and Genre." *Genre* 15, no. 4 (Winter):353-56.
Considers Eliot's "experimentation in genres" and her "self-consciousness in the use of genre."

54 _____. "*Middlemarch*: The 'Home Epic.'" *Genre* 15, no. 4 (Winter):403-20.
"Argues that the language of epic ambition, employed by narrator and characters as well, aptly describes the marital struggles displayed in the novel, an aptness emphasized by the ironic irrelevance of Lydgate's notions of 'romance' to the reality of competition in the novel's marriages. In emphasizing this aspect of human relations Eliot asserts the inescapability of ambition in modern life."

55 MAYER, HANS. "The Bourgeois Way of Life as an Alternative." In *Outsiders: A Study in Life and Letters*. Translated by Denis M. Sweet. Cambridge, Mass., and London: MIT Press, pp. 77-96.
Identifies the course of Eliot's life as a social alternative to Victorian morals. Her life is seen as a "double failure: that of famous conformity and that of famous scandal."

56 MINTZ, MERI-JANE ROCHELSON. "George Eliot and Metaphor: Creating a Narrator in the Mid-Nineteenth Century Novel." Ph.D. dissertation, University of Chicago.
Cited but not abstracted in *Dissertation Abstracts International* (1982).

1982

57   NADEL, IRA BRUCE. "George Eliot and Her Biographers." In
     George Eliot: A Centenary Tribute. Edited by Gordon S. Haight and
     Rosemary T. VanArsdel. Totowa, N.J.: Barnes & Noble, pp. 107-21.
          "Analysis of biographical strategies and approaches adopted by
     various writers in their treatment of George Eliot's life." The variety of
     biographical treatments to Eliot's life parallels the problems in the
     history and theory of biography.

58   NAHM, MI-KYUNG. "Human Relationships in George Eliot's
     Middlemarch." *Journal of the English Language and Literature*
     (Chungchong) 28:457-73.
          In Korean.

59   PAXTON, NANCY L. "Evolution and the Mother in the Novels of
     George Eliot." Ph.D. dissertation, Rutgers University, 621 pp.
          Critical and biographical treatment of Eliot's response to
     feminism and the issue of motherhood. Details Eliot's reactions to the
     theories of evolution as espoused by Auguste Comte and Herbert
     Spencer. In *Romola* and *Felix Holt, the Radical*, Eliot demonstrates her
     interest in matriarchal and patriarchal law in her efforts to "exalt the
     mother's role." See *Dissertations Abstracts International* 43, no. 10
     (1983):3326A.

60   PELL, NANCY [ANNE]. "The Fathers' Daughters in *Daniel
     Deronda*." *Nineteenth-Century Fiction* 36, no. 4 (March):424-51.
          Daniel Deronda explores the difficulties of the daughter,
     Gwendolen Harleth, "in achieving cultural and social legitimacy within
     an unresponsive, if not actually menacing, patriarchal society. The
     appearance of numerous women, rather than a solitary heroine, may
     attest to George Eliot's growing awareness of the necessity of
     addressing women's wrongs, though she is not yet an enthusiastic
     advocate of women's rights." Discussion of spatial imagery and
     metaphors. Review of the theme of inheritance and family relations.

61   PINION, F.B. *A George Eliot Miscellany: A Supplement to Her
     Novels*. London: Macmillan Press, 194 pp.
          Chronological selections from Eliot's prenovel essays and
     reviews, stories, writings relative to her publications, four poems, late
     essays, and evaluations of her world. Readings supplement and
     establish relationships between Eliot's works.

1982

62 PUTZELL-KORAB, SARA M[OORE]. *The Evolving Consciousness: An Hegelian Reading of the Novels of George Eliot.* Edited by Dr. James Hogg. Salzburg, Austria: Institut für Anglistik und Amerikanistik, Universität Salzburg, 143 pp.

Compares the intellectual and moral development of Eliot's characters with the "evolution of self-consciousness in Hegel's *The Phenomenology of Spirit* (1807) to show the need for considering Hegel as part of the philosophic context for Eliot's human nature. ... Demonstrates the inadequacy of conventional dualistic terminology for comprehending Eliot; establishes the terms of Hegel's phenomenology as more appropriate; exemplifies how Hegel's terms make Eliot's vision more comprehensible."

63 _____. "Role of the Prophet: The Rationality of *Daniel Deronda*'s Idealist Mission." *Nineteenth-Century Fiction* 37, no. 2 (September):170-87.

Daniel Deronda is about the process by which an individual discovers his work and identity within his community. It describes "the ideal relation between the community and the individual in which the latter comprehends and advances the communal consciousness." The character Deronda searches for his work, which will allow him to act rationally for a universal good. His discovery that his "ideal task is to preserve his Jewish heritage" is Eliot's presentation of a "rational idealism based in a rationalist literature and consistent with contemporary nationalist movements inspired by German idealism."

64 QUALLS, BARRY V. "Speaking Through Parable: George Eliot." In *The Secular Pilgrims of Victorian Fiction: The Novel as Book of Life.* Cambridge: Cambridge University Press, pp. 139-88.

"Each novel, as it focuses on the myths, fictions, histories – on the art – that human beings require to live, is a meditation intended to make its readers share the process of seeing that foundation in memory of action and choice. ... An examination of those themes, situations, and narrative devices that constitute George Eliot's meditation on nineteenth-century English life." Reprinted: 1986.51.

65 ROBERTSON, LINDA KATHRYN. "George Eliot's Ideas on Education." Ph.D. dissertation, University of Arkansas, 220 pp.

Assesses Eliot's theories on education with reference to her fiction, essays, and letters. Eliot was adamant in advocating schooling suitable to individual needs. However she did not believe in equal educational opportunity for all. She believed in the "ideal education as being a lifelong process of learning." See *Dissertations Abstracts International* 43, no. 10 (1983):3327A.

66   ROSENBERG, BRIAN. "George Eliot and the Victorian 'Historic Imagination.'" *Victorian Newsletter* 61 (Spring):1-4.
   Study of an entry in Eliot's notebook written between 1872 and 1879 and entitled "Historic Imagination" provides insight into Eliot's and the Victorian writers' preoccupation with the incorporation of history into art. Provides sources for Eliot's relation to nineteenth-century English historiography (i.e., Carlyle and Ruskin).

67   SADOFF, DIANNE F. "George Eliot: 'A Sort of Father.'" In *Monsters of Affection: Dickens, Eliot and Brontë on Fatherhood.* Baltimore and London: Johns Hopkins University Press, pp. 65-118.
   Contemplates the idea of fatherhood and applies Freud's theory of primal fantasy. Finds that the authors wrote to liberate themselves from their fathers and to confront authority. Reviews scenes of seduction in "Amos Barton," *Silas Marner,* and *Felix Holt, the Radical*; the law and the father; the trauma of writing *Romola*; and gender and narrative authority as it is applied to Eliot.

68   SANDLER, FLORENCE. "The Unity of *Felix Holt.*" In *George Eliot: A Centenary Tribute.* Edited by Gordon S. Haight and Rosemary T. VanArsdel. Totowa, N.J.: Barnes & Noble, pp. 136-52.
   Argues for the architectonic unity of *Felix Holt, the Radical* on three issues: "the centrality of Esther and the significance of her final decision; the role of Rufus Lyon; and the nature of the radicalism of Felix Holt."

69   SHEETS, ROBIN [LAUTERBACH]. "*Felix Holt*: Language, the Bible, and the Problematic of Meaning." *Nineteenth-Century Fiction* 37, no. 2 (September):146-69.
   "*Felix Holt* analyzes the problematic nature of human communication by exposing the ill-will and incompetence of the speaker-authors, by showing the limited understanding of their listener-readers, and by demonstrating the uncertain meanings of the language-texts. George Eliot's careful attention to the way people read and speak helps to elucidate her own anxieties about authorship; to explain the significance of many minor characters and incidents; and to unify the

two strains of narrative that scholars have traditionally seen as separate – the political plot and Mrs. Transome's personal tragedy."

70   STILL, JUDITH. "Rousseau in *Daniel Deronda*." *Revue de littérature comparée* (Paris) 56, no. 1 (January-March):61-77.
     Examines Eliot and Jean-Jacques Rousseau's handling of the "psychological law governing the efficacy of the code of beneficence. *Daniel Deronda*, like the Rousseau texts, focuses closely on the inner changes wrought in two people when one offers counsel and moral guidance to the other, and also on the pernicious efforts when such help is lacking. Processes of educative influence and example are explored in equal depth and with equal passion by Rousseau and Eliot."

71   VOGELER, MARTHA S. "'The Choir Invisible': The Poetics of Humanist Piety." In *George Eliot: A Centenary Tribute*. Edited by Gordon S. Haight and Rosemary T. VanArsdel. Totowa, N.J.: Barnes & Noble, pp. 64-81.
     Discusses the inspiration for Eliot's poem, "O May I Join the Choir Invisible." Examines its analogies and reception.

72   WASSERMAN, RENATA R. MAUTNER. "Narrative Logic and the Form of Tradition in *The Mill on the Floss*." *Studies in the Novel* 14, no. 3 (Fall):266-79.
     "The contradictions in *The Mill on the Floss* run their course into an ending that transposes motivation from the realm of will and causality within the work to that of a chance or of a will outside the work. It is an ending which, by appealing to what is conventional in the novels of the period, evades the unconventional questions raised in the book and the unconventional answers that would have been logical. The ending saves the appearances but it does it in such an exaggeratedly 'literary' way that it calls attention to what lies unsaid within it."

73   WIESENFARTH, JOSEPH. "*Antique Gems* from *Romola* to *Daniel Deronda*." In *George Eliot: A Centenary Tribute*. Edited by Gordon S. Haight and Rosemary T. VanArsdel. Totowa, N.J.: Barnes & Noble, pp. 55-63.
     Charles William King's *Antique Gems: Their Origin, Uses, and Values as Interpreters of Ancient History* (1860) was a source for Eliot's use of gems and stones in her novels to emphasize monetary and mystic values, beauty and vanity themes, and issues regarding health.

1982

74 ___. "The Greeks, the Germans, and George Eliot." In *Browning Institute Studies*. Vol. 10. Edited by Gerhard Joseph and William S. Peterson. New York: Browning Institute and City University of New York, pp. 91-104.

Examines, in detail, chapter 19 of *Middlemarch* for Eliot's application of the Greek myths and her interpretation of antiquity and German thought.

75 ___. "*Middlemarch*: The Language of Art." *PMLA* 97, no. 3 (May):363-77.

Discusses the importance of a language of art in the imagery, aesthetic theory, and iconography of *Middlemarch*. Dorothea Brooke, characterized by imagery of the arts, is oppressed by her Puritanic sensibilities, the classical art of Rome, and her marriage to Casaubon. Eliot uses the myths of Theseus, Ariadne, and Dionysus to dramatize the relationships between Dorothea, Casaubon, and Ladislaw.

76 WILSON, KATHARINA M. "The Key to All Mythologies – A Possible Source of Inspiration." *Victorian Newsletter* 61 (Spring):27-28.

Attempts to prove that the source for the name of the character Casaubon (of *Middlemarch*) stems from the French scholar Isaac Casaubon from the *Dittionario novo hebraico molto copioso dechirato in tre lingua of* David de Pomis (Apud Joannem de Gara: Venetiis, 1587).

77 WRIGHT, T.R. "From Bumps to Morals: The Phrenological Background to George Eliot's Moral Framework." *Review of English Studies*, n.s. 33, no. 129 (February):35-46.

Considers "the phrenological foundations of her moral theory." Eliot's role in the development of phrenological discoveries and their role in her novels is examined as well as the "claim that Comte's cerebral theory provides a key to George Eliot's moral framework."

1983

1 ASHTON, ROSEMARY [D.]. *George Eliot*. Past Masters Series. Oxford: Oxford University Press, 105 pp.

Examines the development of Eliot – her emergence from her life as Mary Ann Evans; the influence of Dutch realism and English provincial life on her work; the elements of historical romance and Wordsworthian fable in her writing; and the importance of natural history, politics, and tragedy in her work. Analyzes brother-sister theme, the influence of Comte, her use of symbolic myth, and her use of narrator.

2 _____. "Two Velvet Peaches." *London Review of Books* 5, no. 3 (17 February-2 March):13.

Considers Eliot's treatment of sexuality in *The Mill on the Floss*, *Silas Marner, Adam Bede, Middlemarch*, and *Daniel Deronda*. Finds that it is her handling of sexual relationships that allows Eliot to analyze the moral nature of people within their complex social networks.

3 AUERBACH, EMILY. "The Domesticated Maestro: George Eliot's Klesmer." *Papers on Language and Literature* no. 19 (Summer):280-92.

Discusses Eliot's use of the character Julius Klesmer in *Daniel Deronda* to satirize the Victorian literary stereotype of the romantic musician. Klesmer is also a parody of German art. His domestication and placement in a realistic background satirizes the philistinism and xenophobia of English provincials and that society's hypocritical treatment of artists. Some attention given to Klesmer's model.

4 BEER, GILLIAN. "Responses: George Eliot and Thomas Hardy." In *Darwin's Plots: Evolutionary Narrative in Darwin, George Eliot, and Nineteenth Century Fiction*. London: Routledge & Kegan Paul, pp. 149-258.

Studies how Eliot and Hardy were influenced by the writings of Darwin. Illuminates similarities between *Daniel Deronda* and *Middlemarch* and Darwin's *Descent of Man and Selection in Relation to Sex* (1871) and *The Origin of Species* (1859). Both Eliot and Darwin dealt with the problems of relations and origins, Eliot using these ideas as both theme and structure in her fiction.

5 BLAKE, KATHLEEN. "Elizabeth Barrett Browning (and George Eliot): Art Versus Love." In *Love and the Woman Question in Victorian Literature: The Art of Self-Postponement*. Sussex, Eng.: Harvester Press; Totowa, N.J.: Barnes & Noble, pp. 171-201.

Compares female creativity and Victorian women writers' predilection to be wary of love. "The centrality of the conflict, for women, between art and love is indicated by the stress given it in works by Elizabeth Barrett Browning and George Eliot, even though these writers were able to resolve the conflict in their own lives."

6 _____. "*Middlemarch*: Vocation, Love and the Woman Question." In *Love and the Woman Question in Victorian Literature: The Art of Self-Postponement*. Sussex, Eng.: Harvester Press; Totowa, N.J.: Barnes & Noble, pp. 26-55.
　　Examines Eliot's treatment of Dorothea Brooke's wait for love. Perceives *Middlemarch* as a feminist work and discusses Dorothea's marriage to Casaubon as a strategy for deferring adult sexual experience.

7 BOMSTEIN, BETTY S. "The Frame around the Self: Description and Narration in Novels by Jane Austen, Charlotte Brontë, George Eliot, and Charles Dickens." Ph.D. dissertation, Columbia University, 259 pp.
　　Documents the authors' attack on Victorian novels, which depended on cultural hegemony. All four authors reject the experiences their societies promoted – those of seeing oneself "within the controlled, knowable ahistorical boundaries of a picture frame or descriptive passage." See *Dissertations Abstracts International* 44, no. 12 (1984):3691A.

8 CAMPBELL, ELIZABETH ANNE. "Disposable Containers: Metonymy in the Novel." Ph.D. dissertation, University of Virginia, 264 pp.
　　"Through analyses of *Emma*, *Middlemarch*, and *Sons and Lovers* . . . shows how each work stands out as a literary sign of the times: how the estate, society in reform, character, and finally even metaphor serve as metonymic containers for the respective author's vision of society and for the novel's generic development." See *Dissertations Abstracts International* 44, no. 11 (1984):3386A.

9 CARON, JAMES. "Rhetoric of Magic in *Daniel Deronda*." *Studies in the Novel* 15, no. 1 (Spring):1-9.
　　Examines the organic construction of *Daniel Deronda* by Eliot "delineating a pattern of diction, imagery, and dramatic scenes . . . called the rhetoric of magic." Eliot uses magical concepts from romance and folklore to describe the "psychology of interpersonal relationships as well as attitudes toward shaping individual destiny and the destiny of humanity."

10   CARPENTER, MARY WILSON. "The Landscape of Time: George Eliot and Apocalyptic Structure of History." Ph.D. dissertation, Brown University, 296 pp.

Eliot's early letters and her fiction identify her knowledge of the Apocalypse both as dramatic poetry and as history. In *Romola*, the heroine's spiritual search is developed within divisions of prophetic history that cross the chronological narrative. In *Middlemarch*, the apocalyptic scheme is satirized. The theme of the apocalypse is romanticized in *Daniel Deronda*. "Eliot's 'Legend of Jubal' (1874) consists of poems arranged into a form that reconstructs John Keble's apocalyptic fiction of time, *The Christian Year*." See *Dissertations Abstracts International* 44, no. 9 (1984):2762A.

11   CARROLL, DAVID. "George Eliot: The Sybil of Mercia." *Studies in the Novel* 15, no. 1 (Spring):10-25.

Examines the idea of George Eliot as a Victorian sibyl. Studies how Eliot became popular despite her beliefs about religion, her relationships, her sexual ambiguity, and her moral comments.

12   CARTER, MARGARET LARRABEE. "George Eliot's Early Fiction: The Movement from Alienation to Integration." Ph.D. dissertation, University of Illinois at Urbana-Champaign, 294 pp.

Eliot's early fiction depicts how moral progress depends on harmonious integration of self with family and community. "The movement from alienation to integration in *Scenes of Clerical Life*, *Adam Bede*, *The Mill on the Floss*, and *Silas Marner* is examined through the narrative techniques." Eliot's five stages of moral growth are "alienation, crisis of disenchantment, confession to wise counsellor, recognition of communal allegiance, and integration into familial and communal life." See *Dissertations Abstracts International* 45, no. 1 (1984):188A.

13   CLARK-BEATTIE, ROSEMARY EILEEN. "The Problem of Language in George Eliot's Later Novels." Ph.D. dissertation, University of Toronto (Canada).

Compares the 'systole-diastole' movement of realism with the 'idealism' of *Felix Holt, the Radical* and *Daniel Deronda*. For each, the narrative action is a series of signs that defines the characters. By examining the characters' relations the reader may discover something about the relation of the character's inner self to the world. In both texts, the metaphysical and epistemological implications of 'ideal'

1983

language and the development of idealism are traced. See *Dissertations Abstracts International* 44, no. 3 (1983):758A.

14   COHEN, SUSAN R[EGINA]. "'A History and a Metamorphosis': Continuity and Discontinuity in *Silas Marner*." *Texas Studies in Literature and Language* 25, no. 3 (Fall):410-26.
      Identifies how the character Silas Marner illustrates the hardships of discontinuity and disintegration. "Eliot identifies in Silas's life, and in the responses it elicits from other characters, a basic human impulse to fill in blanks, deny gaps, create continuities – to convert inexplicable metamorphoses into rationally understandable history."

15   COLLINS, K[ENNY] K[AYLE]. "Sources of Remaining Unidentified Serial Offprints in the George Eliot-George Henry Lewes Library." *Papers of the Bibliographical Society of America* 77, no. 4:486-89.
      A list of nine previously unidentified serial offprints and their sources. Includes six "tracts" and an index of periodicals cited.

16   COLLISTER, PETER. "Portraits of 'Audacious Youth': George Eliot and Mrs. Humphry Ward." *English Studies* 64, no. 4 (August):296-317.
      Cites Eliot's influence on the novels of Mrs. Ward. Both *The Mill on the Floss* and *Daniel Deronda* influenced Mrs. Ward's change from writing about young men to themes concerning the aesthetic, moral, and intellectual development of women. Draws parallels between Eliot's novels and Ward's *Marcella* (London: Smith, Elder, 1894) and *Sir George Tressady* (London, 1896).

17   DAVIS, PHILIP. "Margaret Oliphant and George Eliot." In *Memory and Writing from Wordsworth to Lawrence*. Liverpool English Texts and Studies, 21. Totowa, N.J.: Barnes & Noble, pp. 273-331.
      Studies the relation between the writer's mind, memory, and writing by comparing the works and processes of Eliot, Wordsworth, Thomas Hardy, Margaret Oliphant, Dickens, and D.H. Lawrence.

18   DIEDRICK, JAMES. "Eliot's Debt to Keller: *Silas Marner* and *Die drei gerechten Kammacher*." *Comparative Literature Studies* 20 (Winter):376-87.
      Parallels in plots, characters, philosophies, and aesthetics between *Silas Marner* and Gottfried Keller's *Die drei gerechten*

Kammacher. Keller's work influenced Eliot's use of the fairy-tale motif and a fictional ending bordering on the grotesque.

19   ERMARTH, ELIZABETH DEEDS. "George Eliot's Invisible Community." In *Realism and Consensus in the English Novel.* Princeton, N.J.: Princeton University Press, pp. 222-56.
     Discusses the identity between things and ideas, the unifying collective narrative consciousness in *Adam Bede* and *Middlemarch*, and the power of memory. Using "realistic" as a descriptive term, Ermarth examines the special powers of realistic conventions and their limitations. Eliot's communities, their language and codes, are central to an individual's consciousness. Her narratives reflect her treatment of the conflicting valid claims.

20   FLEISHMAN, AVROM. "The Fictions of Autobiographical Fiction: *The Mill on the Floss* Conversion to Tragedy." In *Figures of Autobiography: The Language of Self-Writing in Victorian and Modern England.* Berkeley and Los Angeles: University of California Press, pp. 235-56.
     "*The Mill on the Floss* is not only a characteristic autobiographical novel but marks a crucial turning in the use of traditional forms and figures in fictional self-conception." The language of conversion and the imagery of the river's movement toward annihilation are central to Eliot's vision of human life, her own in particular. "She is at one with the defeated heroine and with the survivors of the past – both united in feeling with her family and irrevocably apart."

21   FOLTINEK, HERBERT. "George Eliot und der Unwissende Erzähler." *Germanische-Romanische Monatsschrift* (Heidelberg) 33, no. 2:167-78.

22   FORSTER, JEAN-PAUL. "Beyond Reticence: The Power Politics Relationship in George Eliot." *Études de lettres* (Lausanne) 6, no. 1 (January-March):13-29.
     Examines the narrative functions of dialogue in *Daniel Deronda*. Perceives Eliot's novels as tragedies of egoism. "George Eliot's characters depend on others for their happiness, and their need of others leaves them, for all their fear and restraint, unprotected against other people's designs on them."

1983

23   . "George Eliot: The Language and Drama of Reticence." *English Studies* 64, no. 5 (October):433-46.

    Evaluates the theme and structural importance of reticence in Eliot's later novels, particularly *Middlemarch*. Defines reticence and explores Eliot's use of the language of attitudes, gestures, and irony. For Eliot, reticence comes from one's desire to protect oneself rather than to spare others by one's restraint.

24 FOURNIER, SUZANNE JOAN. "The Nostalgia of Modern Fiction: Loss of Home in George Eliot, Henry James, and William Faulkner." Ph.D. dissertation, University of Notre Dame, 235 pp.

    Discusses how the works of Eliot, James, and Faulkner illustrate the experience of loss of home and the desire to return to self and society. *The Mill on the Floss* and *Middlemarch* portray the effects of loss of home and the desire to return on the heroines Maggie Tulliver and Dorothea Brooke. See *Dissertations Abstracts International* 44, no. 6 (1983):1780A.

25 GOODE, JOHN. "'The Affections Clad with Knowledge': Woman's Duty and the Public Life." *Literature and History* 9, no. 1 (Spring):38-51.

    Assumes that, for Eliot, writing novels was a compromise between "vocations of intellectual leadership and womanhood." Examines sexual politics in *Romola, The Mill on the Floss*, and *Daniel Deronda*.

26 GRAVER, SUZANNE [L.]. "Modeling Natural History: George Eliot's Framings of the Present." *Studies in the Novel* 15, no. 1 (Spring):26-34.

    Studies the two historical periods Eliot worked within and the patterns she used in framing the beginnings and endings of her novels. The images evident in the beginnings and endings of the novels "reflect thematic progressions correlative to the changing nature of community."

27 GUTH, BARBARA. "Philip: The Tragedy of *The Mill on the Floss*." *Studies in the Novel* 15, no. 4 (Winter):356-63.

    "The character of Philip, whose reaction to tragedy reveals the influence of Wordsworth on Eliot, most nearly expresses the narrator's view of life, anticipates the character of Dorothea in *Middlemarch*, and illustrates the ways in which the ending fails as a tragedy. . . . Philip is a

1983

male counterpart of Maggie in that his handicap and his exceptional nature separate him from the male-dominated, mercantile society around him. He enables Eliot to explore the tragedy of those, who because of their position outside society, perceive the world differently. . . ."

28 HANLON, BETTINA LOUISE. "Supporting Characters and Rural Communities in the Novels of George Eliot and Thomas Hardy." Ph.D. dissertation, Ohio State University, 352 pp.

Studies the novels of Eliot and Hardy that are set in one village and which demonstrate how supporting characters add to the depiction of main characters and their rural settings. The supporting characters of *Adam Bede*, *The Mill on the Floss*, and *Silas Marner* represent communal values and provincial thought, and provide commentary on the main characters' attempts to maintain or procure their places in the community. See *Dissertations Abstracts International* 44, no. 9 (1984):2772A.

29 HARRIS, LAURIE LANZEN, and FITZGERALD, SHEILA, eds. *Nineteenth-Century Literature Criticism*. Vol. 4. Detroit: Gale Research, pp. 92-154.

Compendium of reviews, analyses, and critiques of Eliot by Charles Dickens, David Carroll, Ian Gregor, Barbara Hardy, Henry James, F.R. Leavis, George Levine, V.S. Pritchett, Edith Simcox, Stephen Leslie, Virginia Woolfe, and others.

30 HARRIS, MASON. "Infanticide and Respectability: Hetty Sorrel as Abandoned Child in *Adam Bede*." *English Studies in Canada* 9, no. 2 (June):177-96.

Examines Hetty Sorrel's relationship to the Poysers to better understand her role as a member of the Hayslope community who is dubbed the fallen woman. Hetty is perceived as a confused child whose sexual indiscretion is in contrast with the Puritan values of the Poysers and Eliot.

31 HELSINGER, ELIZABETH K.; SHEETS, ROBIN LAUTERBACH; and VEEDER, WILLIAM. "The Woman Question, Literary Issues, 1837-1883." *The Woman Question: Society and Literature in Britain and America, 1837-1883*. Vol. 3. New York and London: Garland Publishing, pp. 72-78, 92-93, passim.

1983

Compares both male and female Victorian responses to the literary handling of the "Woman Question." Evaluates the response to Eliot as a novelist and as a critic of women's literature.

32 HIRSCH, MARIANNE. "Spiritual Bildung: The Beautiful Soul as Paradigm." In *The Voyage In: Fictions of Female Development*. Edited by Elizabeth Abel, Marianne Hirsch, and Elizabeth Langland. Hanover, N.H.: University Press of New England, pp. 23-48.

Surveys fictional representations of female development and "integrates gender with genre and identifies distinctly female versions of the *Bildungsroman*." In novels by Eliot, Kate Chopin, and Theodore Fontane, the spiritual growth resulting from religion culminates in death. For Maggie Tulliver, in *The Mill on the Floss*, limited social possibilities and religious salvation are *self*-destructive.

33 HOCHMAN, BARUCH. "George Eliot: Maternal Ichor, Crying Need." In *The Test of Character: From the Victorian Novel to the Modern*. East Brunswick, N.J.: Associated University Presses, pp. 50-71.

Considers the ramifications of the moral, artistic, and psychological issues between parents and children in *Middlemarch*, *Silas Marner*, and *Adam Bede*.

34 HOGGE, DAVID ASHE. "Male-Male Bonding: A Study of *Adam Bede*, *The Mayor of Casterbridge*, and *Sons and Lovers*." Ph.D. dissertation, University of Kentucky, 201 pp.

"In George Eliot's *Adam Bede*, Hardy's *The Mayor of Casterbridge*, and Lawrence's *Sons and Lovers*, the male-male bond – accentuated by a wrestling match between two men – develops from an individual's inner struggle. Physically embroiled with another male friend, man actualizes his true identity, bonding with another man and affirming his new moral, political and sexual awareness. Self-realized, man then bonds with woman. The two relationships represent a microcosmic community of men and women." See *Dissertations Abstracts International* 45, no. 1 (1984):191A.

35 KNAPP, SHOSHANA. "Tolstoj's Reading of George Eliot: Visions and Revisions." *Slavic and East European Journal* 27 (Fall):318-26.

Examines Tolstoy's reading of and respect for Eliot. Knapp rereads Eliot from a Tolstoyan point of view to examine the "aesthetic program of the earliest George Eliot." Compares political, economic, and sexual views of *Felix Holt, the Radical* and Tolstoy's *What Then Must We Do?* Includes mention of correspondence between Eliot and Tolstoy.

36   KUCICH, JOHN. "George Eliot and Objects: Meaning as Matter in *The Mill on the Floss*." In *Dickens Studies Annual: Essays on Victorian Fiction.* Vol. 12. Edited by Michael Timko, Fred Kaplan, and Edward Giuliano. New York: AMS Press, pp. 319-40.

The fusion of commercial with natural objects, in *The Mill on the Floss*, "which subject the entire landscape to the functional use of man, begin very subtly to suggest George Eliot's fundamental perception about material things: the perception that a world of autonomous objects does not exist, and that such a condition is inherently claustrophobic." Analyzes the symbolic elements that illustrate this claustrophobia.

37   LEAVIS, Q.D. "A Note on Literary Indebtedness: Dickens, George Eliot, Henry James." In *Collected Essays: The American Novel and Reflections on the European Novel.* Vol. 2. Edited by G. Singh. Cambridge: Cambridge University Press, pp. 151-57. Orig. pub. in *Hudson Review* 8, no. 3 (Autumn, 1955):423-28.

Analyzes passages from *Middlemarch*, Dickens's *Little Dorrit*, and James's *Portrait of a Lady* for evidence of literary indebtedness. The use of Rome as symbolism and setting is common to the three novels.

38   ____. *"Silas Marner."* In *Collected Essays: The Englishness of the English Novel.* Vol. 1. Edited by G. Singh. Cambridge: Cambridge University Press, pp. 275-302.

Finds that *Silas Marner* "embodies George Eliot's ideas about the novel at their maturest." Reviews elements of Greek tragedy and the Wordsworthian doctrine of familial ties.

39   LEE, OK. "The Relationship Between the Individual and Society as Represented in *Silas Marner.*" *Journal of the English Language and Literature* (Chungchong) 26:70-100.

In Korean.

1983

40 LEVAY, JOHN. "Maggie as Muse: The Philip-Maggie Relationship in *The Mill on the Floss*." *English Studies in Canada* 9, no. 1 (March):69-79.

Explains how the "muse theme persists as a sort of undercurrent throughout Maggie's story, and tends to surface in the Philip episodes."

41 LISLE, BONNIE JEAN. "History and Ending in George Eliot's Fiction." Ph.D. dissertation, University of California, Los Angeles, 284 pp.

Eliot's fiction is about history and is history in itself. Discusses how Eliot balances continuity and closure in her conclusions. Emphasizes her attempt to work on the narrative structure of the evolution of history, to which she applied the theories of Comte and Spencer. See *Dissertations Abstracts International* 45, no. 1 (1984):192A.

42 McCORMACK, KATHLEEN. "The Sybil and the Hyena: George Eliot's Wollstonecraftian Feminism." *Dalhousie Review* 63, no. 4 (Winter):602-14.

Discusses how Wollstonecraft's *A Vindication of the Rights of Women* (1792) influenced Eliot's novels, especially in themes regarding the connection between education and adultery.

43 MALCOLM, DAVID. "*Adam Bede* and the Unions: 'A ... Proletarian Novel.'" *Zeitschrift für Anglistik und Amerikanistik* (Leipzig) 31, no. 1:5-16.

"Demonstrates a working-class presence, largely dissenting from the status quo, in *Adam Bede*." Examines how facts regarding Methodism and artisanship give the action of the novel contemporary and radical overtones.

44 MANN, KAREN B. *The Language That Makes George Eliot's Fiction*. Baltimore, Md., and London: Johns Hopkins University Press, 237 pp.

Reviews "specific kinds of language not only as evocative of a particular sensory reality but also as constitutive of the elements usually considered to pre-dominate in mimetic prose fiction." Discusses relations between setting and character when expressed through spatial and gustatory language. The language of sound and sexuality contribute to the organizing principles of Eliot's plots. Considers language of drama and point of view. See also: 1980.46; 1981.44.

1983

45   MARKS, SYLVIA KASEY. "A Brief Glance at George Eliot's 'The
      Spanish Gypsy.'" *Victorian Poetry* 21, no. 2 (Summer):184-90.
          Eliot's dramatic poem, "The Spanish Gypsy," was influenced by
      Titian's painting of the Annunciation. Draws a parallel between the
      poem's devices and themes and those of her fiction: the dilemmas of
      heroes and heroines denote change. The "state of illusion is followed by
      a crisis which shatters" the character's misperceptions. Characters move
      from being spiritually blind to gaining insight.

46   MARTIN, CAROL A. "No Angel in the House: Victorian Mothers
      and Daughters in George Eliot and Elizabeth Gaskell." *Midwest
      Quarterly* 24 (Spring):297-314.
          Explores Eliot's and Gaskell's treatment of Victorian women.
      Finds a woman novelist's perceptions regarding mothers and daughters
      to be more realistic than depictions by male novelists. Eliot and Gaskell
      depict troubled and tempestuous mother/daughter relationships, where
      their male counterparts idealize women and their roles. In Gaskell's
      and Eliot's novels, the mother is often dead, weak, or ineffective and in
      need of more assistance than she is able to offer to her daughter.

47   MECKIER, JEROME. "Hidden Rivalries in Victorian Fiction: The
      Case of the Two Esthers." In *The Changing World of Charles
      Dickens*. Edited by Robert Giddings. London: Vision Press; Totowa,
      N.J.: Barnes & Noble, pp. 216-38.
          Finds *Felix Holt, the Radical* to be a systematic revision of
      Dickens's *Bleak House*. Cites parallels in the novels, such as the use of
      hidden parentage and a long legal battle. See also 1987.27.

48   MOLSTAD, DAVID. "Dantean Purgatorial Metaphor in *Daniel
      Deronda*." *Papers on Language and Literature* 19, no. 2 (Spring):183-
      98.
          In *Daniel Deronda*, Eliot draws heavily on Dante's *Divine
      Comedy*. How the Dantean elements underlie the purgatorial metaphor
      in six scenes relating to Gwendolen's marriage and regeneration. The
      Dantean purgatorial metaphor is Eliot's mode of dealing with
      Gwendolen's struggle in coming to terms with herself and her motives.
      The parallels with the *Divine Comedy* place the Gwendolen part of the
      story in a context having temporal depth and emphasizing the long
      history of human hopes and errors.

1983

49 MOLZAHN, LAURA JEANNE. "The Novel as Speech Act: A Liguistic/Psychological Perspective on the Novel." Ph.D. dissertation, Northwestern University, 252 pp.

Uses speech-act theory and H.P. Grice's notion of implication to determine a method of forming determinate meanings for novels. Examines the interaction of the establishment of a value system and character identification in *Adam Bede*. Uses Freud's theory of literature to analyze the claim that the author's speech act creates sympathies and establishes values. See *Dissertations Abstracts International* 44, no. 3 (1983):761A.

50 MUNDHENK, ROSEMARY. "Patterns of Irresolution in Eliot's *The Mill on the Floss*." *Journal of Narrative Technique* 13, no. 1 (Winter):20-30.

Examines the final drowning scene of *The Mill on the Floss* and finds that this scene "repeats the pattern of Maggie's decisions throughout the entire novel. From childhood, Maggie has vacillated between extremes. Often, she impulsively makes a resolution . . . only to discover the human impossiblity of living according to that decision. Her strong will is repeatedly at war with her feelings. This is her human predicament."

51 NEUFELDT, VICTOR A. "Madonna and the Gypsy." *Studies in the Novel* 15, no. 1 (Spring):44-54.

Both *Romola* and "The Spanish Gypsy" marked turning points in Eliot's career. "*Romola* ends with the heroine finding fulfillment in the role of a madonna." The heroine of "The Spanish Gypsy" is depicted as a woman who is an angel/goddess, who finds only frustration. The progression of these characters elucidates Eliot's understanding that "the claims of public duty and responsibility must not be satisfied at the expense of personal fulfillment and happiness."

52 POOLE, ADRIAN. "Hidden Affinities in *Daniel Deronda*." *Essays in Criticism* 33, no. 4 (October):294-311.

Reviews a variety of scenes that rely on drama. Examines elements of sights, sounds, movements, attitudes and expressions as well as the collaboration of different forms of art to create affinities and to demonstrate Eliot's use of allusion.

1983

53 PRICE, MARTIN. "The Nature of Decision." In *Forms of Life: Character and Moral Imagination in the Novel*. New Haven and London: Yale University Press, pp. 147-75.

   Discusses Eliot's concern with moral experience and how the emergence of her realism is a "study of how a man's virtues are implicated in and in some measure promote his errors. . . . Eliot is concerned with the medium in which morality lives: the ways in which our choice may be limited by circumstances or even made for us by the structure of the situation in which we find ourselves." Reprinted: 1986.50.

54 PYKETT, LYN. "Typology and the End(s) of History in *Daniel Deronda*." *Literature and History* 9, no. 1 (Spring):62-73

   Analysis of the problem of the dual structure of *Daniel Deronda*, which "embeds a quasi-Arnoldian analysis of an alienated, barbaric culture of forms within a highly stylised, complex fictional structure which incorporates myth, legend, epic and typology. By means of its adoption of typology *Daniel Deronda* thus moves from the "*chronos*" of the historical novel to the "*kairos* of metahistory."

55 RINGLER, ELLIN. "*Middlemarch*: A Feminist Perspective." *Studies in the Novel* 15, no. 1 (Spring):55-61.

   Supports feminist criticisms against *Middlemarch*, yet points out strengths in the novel – Eliot's presentation of dominance and her voice against women's educational limitations.

56 ROCHELSON, MERI-JANE. "Weaver of Raveloe: Metaphor as Narrative Persuasion in *Silas Marner*." *Studies in the Novel* 15, no. 1 (Spring):35-43.

   Discusses the creation of the narrator of *Silas Marner* based on Eliot's metaphors, which come from Aristotle's idea of the "ethos of a speaker." Analyzes three perspectives of metaphor as narrative persuasion. Metaphorically describes the theme of "universal interconnectedness" as Silas, the weaver, who ties the threads of the community together.

57 ROSE, PHYLLIS. "George Eliot and George Henry Lewes." In *Parallel Lives: Five Victorian Marriages*. New York: Alfred A. Knopf, pp. 193-237.

1983

Description and analysis of Eliot and Lewes's personal relationship. For Eliot, being in love with a man who was unable to marry her was a test of her personal ethics and morals.

58 ROSOWSKI, SUSAN J. "The Novel of Awakening." In *The Voyage In: Fictions of Female Development.* Edited by Elizabeth Abel, Marianne Hirsch, and Elizabeth Langland. Hanover, N.H.: University Press of New England, pp. 49-68.
 Identifies a "female variation of the classic male form." Rosowski discovers the essence of female *Bildung* in a moment of simultaneous awakening to inner aspirations and social limitations. She traces this pattern in Flaubert's *Madame Bovary*, Chopin's *The Awakening*, Eliot's *Middlemarch*, and other nineteenth-century novels. In *Middlemarch*, Dorothea Brooke experiences two stages of awakening.

59 SOKOLSKY, ANITA RUTH. "A Dark Inscription: Questions of Representation in *Daniel Deronda*." Ph.D. dissertation, Cornell University, 181 pp.
 "Explores the problematic nature of representation in *Daniel Deronda*." Argues that it is the "novel's desire to subsume its ambitious narrative and psychological experimentation to a coherent spiritual vision in which the novel works to restrain and authorize a stable moral interpretation of itself." See *Dissertations Abstracts International* 44, no. 9 (1984):2776A.

60 VANARSDEL, ROSEMARY T. "George Eliot Centenary Year." *Studies in the Novel* 15, no. 1 (Spring):74-76.
 Overview of tributes, writings, exhibitions, and conferences dedicated to George Eliot on the centenary of her death (1980).

61 WIESENFARTH, JOSEPH. "George Eliot." In *Dictionary of Literary Biography*. Vol. 21. Detroit: Gale Research, pp. 145-70.
 Biography of Eliot. Notes how her husband, John Walter Cross, contributed to the decline in her popularity following her death because he removed from her journal pages that described her relationship with George Henry Lewes. Traces the development of and publication details of her works and the effect of her "immoral" relationship on the Victorian reader.

1984

62   WILLIAMS, DAVID. *Mr. George Eliot: A Biography of George Henry Lewes*. New York: Franklin Watts, 289 pp.

Biography of George Henry Lewes, with whom Eliot lived for more than twenty-five years. Lewes is given credit for providing Eliot encouragement and incentive to write her novels. Discusses Lewes's career as a journalist, novelist, and biographer, and his contributions to English literary history.

63   WITEMEYER, HUGH. "George Eliot's *Romola* and Bulwer Lytton's *Rienzi*." *Studies in the Novel* 15, no. 1 (Spring):62-73.

Demonstrates how Bulwer Lytton's *Rienzi: The Last of the Tribunes* (1835) – its theory and use of the historical romance – influenced Eliot's organization of her vision of the historical process before writing *Romola*. Compares setting and characters of *Romola* and *Rienzi*.

1984

1   ADAMS, HARRIET FARWELL. "Dorothea and 'Miss Brooke' in *Middlemarch*." *Nineteenth-Century Fiction* 39, no. 1 (June):69-90.

Analysis of the character development of Dorothea Brooke from Eliot's original conception of her and as Mrs. Casaubon. Parallels are drawn to St. Theresa. Examines issues of marriage and one's capacity for tragedy as maturational stages.

2   ALLEY, HENRY. "*Romola* and the Preservation of Household Gods." *Cithara* 23, no. 2 (May):25-35.

Examines the iconographic symbols of "how a young woman nurtures age, how she may derive and apply messages from the past, and how she may transcend a strong family *hubris*" in *Romola*.

3   BAKER, TRACEY ALISON. "The Figure of the Nurse: Struggles for Wholeness in the Novels of Jane Austen, Anne, Charlotte and Emily Brontë, and George Eliot." Ph.D. dissertation, Purdue University, 173 pp.

Analyzes nurses and nursing to better understand the struggle for wholeness in the novels of the Brontës, Austen, and Eliot. Each novelist uses nursing to aid her characters in learning how to adapt to society and attain an identity of wholeness. The nursing relationships

1984

allow the heroines to grow while under stress. See *Dissertations Abstracts International* 46, no. 2 (1985):427A.

4   BATES, RICHARD. "The Italian with White Mice in *Middlemarch*." *Notes and Queries* 229 [n.s. 31, no. 4] (December):497.

Source of Eliot's use of the phrase "you might just as well marry an Italian with white mice," by Mrs. Cadwaller, refers to Count Fosco in Wilkie Collins's *The Woman in White*. Count Fosco was an eccentric character who kept white mice about him. See also 1979.27.

5   BENNETT, JAMES R. "Scenic Structure of Judgement in *Middlemarch*." In *Essays and Studies*. Collected by Raymond Chapman. London: John Murray; Atlantic Highlands, N.J.: Humanities Press, pp. 62-74.

Analyzes Eliot's use of inductive knowledge to derive standards of good and evil from experience. Uses a method based on the organization of individual scenes to "understand characters' relative moral stupidity or intelligence."

6   BERKELEY, LINDA EILEEN. "George Eliot: Towards a Complex Realism." Ph.D. dissertation, Columbia University, 571 pp.

Considers Eliot's representation of reality in the context of the political relationship between women in nineteenth-century English novels and in the context of Eliot's personal position in Victorian England. Examines Eliot's development as a novelist and how she overcame the prevailing mental oppression of society to create, in her novels, "the possibility of possibility itself." See *Dissertations Abstracts International* 47, no. 6 (1986):2166A.

7   BODE, RITA GISELA. "Art as Method: A Study of George Eliot's Novels." Ph.D. dissertation, University of Toronto (Canada).

Analysis of art as a method of both the artist and her characters in Eliot's fiction. Art as method allows Eliot to explore the limits of sexual stereotyping. Compares "the place Eliot gives to human nature in relation to art and nature; the nature and effects of art and anti-art; the dual aspects of imitation and inspiration; and the perceptions of the narrator and the artist." See *Dissertations Abstracts International* 45, no. 9 (1985):2881A.

1984

8   BRODY, SELMA [B.]. "Origins of George Eliot's 'Pier-Glass' Image." *English Language Notes* 22, no. 2 (December):55-58.

Alludes to the "pier-glass" metaphor in *Middlemarch* and traces its source to Eliot's relationship with natural scientist John Tyndall. Tyndall was known for his work in meteorological optics and the pier-glass effect.

9   BUSHNELL, JOHN P. "Maggie Tulliver's 'Stored-Up Force': A Re-Reading of *The Mill on the Floss*." *Studies in the Novel* 16, no. 4 (Winter):378-95.

Re-creates the ending of *The Mill on the Floss* to portray Maggie Tulliver as a strong character who faces conflict and the struggle for survival. Refutes prior criticisms that find Maggie to be escaping from the real world.

10   CARPENTER, MARY WILSON. "The Apocalypse of the Old Testament: *Daniel Deronda* and the Interpretation of Interpretation." *PMLA* 99, no. 1 (January):56-71.

"George Eliot's 'Oriental Memoranda' notebook documents her interest in current histories of the Jews and suggests a context of universal history based on critical interpretation of the *Book of Daniel*. This exegetical 'key' to interpretation reveals both the significance of Eliot's separation of the plot into two strands and the apocalyptic symbolism that links those strands together in a universal history of humanity in exile."

11   CHASE, KAREN. *Eros and Psyche: The Representative of Personality in Charlotte Brontë, Charles Dickens and George Eliot*. New York and London: Methuen & Co., pp. 136-87.

Examines, in *Middlemarch*, the representation and expression of personality in a realist mode, "in which moral reason displays its own elaborate figures of mind and structures of feeling."

12   DALESKI, H.M. "*The Mill on the Floss*: The Dividing of the Seasons." In *The Divided Heroine: A Recurrent Pattern in Six English Novels*. New York and London: Holmes & Meier, pp. 47-68.

Identifies the pattern of self-division and disintegration in the love triangle of *The Mill on the Floss*. The ultimate fate of Maggie is a result of her inability to reconcile the opposing forces within herself.

1984

13   DeMARIA, JOANNE THIELEN. "The Yale George Eliot Letters:
     A Correction." *Notes & Queries* 229 [n.s. 31, no. 1] (March):69.
         Researches the definition of "truck" as used by Disraeli in *Sybil*.
     In *The George Eliot Letters*, Haight refers to Eliot's explanation of the
     Truck System.

14   EDRICH, EVA K. "Women in the Novels of George Sand, Emily
     Brontë, George Eliot, and Marie Von Ebner-Eschenbach: To
     Mitigate the Harshness of All Fatalities." Ph.D. dissertation,
     University of Denver, 226 pp.
         Discusses the adherence to traditional values in novels by Sand,
     Eliot, Brontë, and Ebner-Eschenbach, despite their criticisms of church
     and society. All four authors share the common theme of believing
     women can overcome their confinements and help others escape from
     similar existences. It is a sign of women's moral superiority that their
     tasks of "duty and power" can alleviate what misfortunes may befall all
     people. See *Dissertations Abstracts International* 45, no. 6 (1984):1744A.

15   EDWARDS, LEE R. "Heroes into Heroines: The Limits of Comedy
     in *Emma, Jane Eyre* and *Middlemarch*." In *Psyche as Hero: Female
     Heroism and Fictional Form*. Middletown, Conn.: Wesleyan
     University Press, pp. 62-103.
         "Examines the fulfillment or frustration of heroic possibilities of
     plot and character" as these possibilities relate to female characters.
     Heroic enterprise depends on plot structure rather than gender.
     However, Dorothea Brooke exemplifies the nineteenth-century
     hypothesis that comic forms could "reconcile female demands for
     personal happiness and socially sanctioned power."

16   EMMANUEL-CHOPRA, CAROL MEERA. "Death in the Novels
     of George Eliot." Ph.D. dissertation, McGill University (Canada).
         Studies Eliot's humanitarian treatment of death and the
     inevitable consequences of the universe as reflected in her fiction. See
     Dissertations Abstracts International 45, no. 10 (1985):3135A.

17   FURST, LILIAN R. *Fictions of Romantic Irony*. Cambridge, Mass.:
     Harvard University Press, pp. 16-19, 223, 229, 230, 232, 240, 246,
     passim.
         Explores the philosophical and literary features of romantic
     irony and the uses of irony in narration. Discusses theories of
     traditional irony and romantic irony in *Middlemarch*.

1984

18 GEMMETTE, ELIZABETH VILLIERS. "George Eliot's *The Mill on the Floss* and Hardy's *Jude the Obscure*." *Explicator* 42, no. 3 (Spring):28-30.

Analyisis of the heroines Maggie Tulliver and Sue Bridehead suggests their similar sexual needs and motives. Implicit Oedipal overtones in both novels suggest the heroines' inability to enter into mature sexual relationships because of conflicts in their family relationships.

19 GNUTTI, CELESTE ANN. "'Natural History': The Pastoral Intention in the Early Fictions of George Eliot." Ph.D. dissertation, Cornell University, 235 pp.

Examines the problem of narrative organization, structure, chronology, entry and transition, and violations of pastoral norms in *Scenes of Clerical Life, Adam Bede,* and "The Lifted Veil." See *Dissertations Abstracts International* 45, no. 5 (1984):1407A.

20 GRAVER, SUZANNE [L.]. *George Eliot and Community: A Study in Social Theory and Fictional Form.* Berkeley: University of California Press, 340 pp.

Study of Victorian concerns over the loss of traditional social values and forms as depicted in Eliot's novels. Relates Eliot's novels to social thought of the nineteenth century.

21 GREENE, MILDRED SARAH. "George Eliot's *Middlemarch. Explicator* 42, no. 3 (Spring):26-28.

Describes chapters XIX and XX of *Middlemarch* as being "seminal chapters in Dorothea's emotional history. . . ." Examines the latent dream sequence and the relationship between feeling and seeing.

22 HANDLEY, GRAHAM. Introduction to *Daniel Deronda.* Oxford: Clarendon Press, pp. xiii-xxxvi.

Perceives the writing of *Daniel Deronda* as Eliot's final, overall statement of her idealism, in which she overcame her fear of disapproval and expressed her sympathy for the Jews. Description of the manuscript, expansions, interpolations, contractions, changes in sequence, and publication information.

23 HEIN, DEBORAH ANN. "To Hear Her Voice: Artifice in George Eliot's Novels." Ph.D. dissertation, University of California, Santa Barbara, 342 pp.

1984

Outlines methods of reading Eliot that are outside traditional critical analyses. Explores Eliot's direct and indirect self-references so that the reader can better understand Eliot's self-concept as an artist. See *Dissertations Abstracts International* 45, no. 9 (1985):2885A.

24 JACOBS, ROBERT L. "The Role of Music in George Eliot's Novels." *Music Review* 45, no. 3-4 (August-November):277-82.

Cites examples of music and the role it plays in *Adam Bede*, *The Mill on the Floss*, and *Daniel Deronda*.

25 JONES, VIRGINIA LOUISE. "Heroism and the Heroine in the Novels of George Eliot." Ph.D. dissertation, University of Kansas, 259 pp.

Traces the development of Eliot's "concept of the heroine and her theme of hidden heroism." Compares recurring traits and image patterns in all of her fiction. Discusses the role of male mentors and Eliot's use of foils to measure the heroines' growth. See *Dissertations Abstracts International* 46, no. 4 (1985):989A.

26 KNOEPFLMACHER, U.C. "Genre and the Integration of Gender: From Wordsworth to George Eliot to Virginia Woolf." In *Victorian Literature and Society*. Edited by James R. Kincaid and Albert J. Kuhn. Columbus: Ohio State University Press, pp. 94-118.

Analyzes Eliot's perception of Wordsworth's expression of the feminine facet of his imagination. Examines *The Mill on the Floss* for evidence of dual narratives and dual narrators. Shows how Virginia Woolf reformulated both Eliot's and Wordsworth's "myths of unity."

27 _____. "On Exile and Fiction: The Lewes and the Shelleys." In *Mothering the Mind: Twelve Studies of Writers and Their Silent Partners*. Edited by Ruth Perry and Martine Watson Brownley. New York and London: Holmes & Meier, pp. 103-21.

Study of the intellectual and sexual relationship between George Henry Lewes and George Eliot.

28 KOVALEVSKAIA, SOPHÍA V. "A Memoir of George Eliot." Translated by Miriam Haskell Berlin. *Yale Review* 73 (Summer):533-50.

Commentary on and translation of Kovalevskaia's *Vospominaniia i Pis'ma* (Izd. Akademii Nauk SSSR, 1951). Kovalevskaia's memoirs of Eliot are based in part on three visits to the

1984

author. Similarities are drawn between Eliot and Kovalevskaia and the way they dealt with women's issues and the relation of the individual to society.

29   KUBITSCHEK, MISSY DEHN. "Eliot as Activist: Marriage and Politics in *Daniel Deronda*." *CLA Journal* 28, no. 2 (December):176-89.

Finds the artistic failure of *Daniel Deronda* to be "Eliot's inability to construct an alternative to the unacceptable marriages which mirror the political context. . . . Most of the marriages in the novel center on a struggle for absolute power."

30   LANGLAND, ELIZABETH. "Society and Self in George Eliot, Hardy, and Lawrence." In *Society in the Novel*. Chapel Hill and London: University of North Carolina Press, pp. 80-123.

Discusses the novelists' need "to create a society consonant with the formal ends of the work itself." In the novel, the function of society is to define the various formal roles. In *Middlemarch*, "the tension between society as constructive community and society as destructive milieu" is Eliot's vehicle for expressing the fact that people cannot separate themselves from society and still be whole. Eliot maintains that the society provides for individual growth and encourages betterment of the whole community through the improvement of the self.

31   LAVIZZARI-RAEUBER, ALEXANDRA. "Künstliche Grenzen. Henry James als Kritiker von George Eliot." *Neue Zürcher Zeitung* (27-28 October):67.

32   LISLE, BONNIE J[EAN]. "Art and Egoism in George Eliot's Poetry." *Victorian Poetry* 22, no. 3 (Autumn):263-78

"George Eliot's poetry can help us answer questions raised by her fiction. One such question is why, in the narrow range of possibilities open to her heroines, she never allows them to become artists like herself. George Eliot's poems, which deal with the issue of art more explicitly than her fiction, reveal a series of unresolved tensions between a selfless–even self-annihilating–ideal of artistic vocation and a realistic assessment of the artist's innate egoism. Biographical evidence underscores the depth and persistence of this conflict. George Eliot's heroines cannot become artists because their creator remained self-divided."

1984

33 LONG, JOANNE THIELEN. "Work and Marriage in George
Eliot's Late Novels." Ph.D. dissertation, Rutgers University, 183 pp.
  Review of Eliot's double theme of work and marriage as they
are individually dealt with in her novels. Although her novels support
the idea of integrating work and marriage, her female characters "rarely
achieve satisfaction in work except through marriage." See *Dissertations
Abstracts International* 46, no. 2 (1985):430A.

34 McCOBB, E.A. "Of Women and Doctors: *Middlemarch* and
Wilhelmine von Hillern's *Ein Arzt de Seele*." *Neophilologus* 68, no. 4
(October):571-86.
  Draws parallels between Von Hillern's *Ein Arzt der Seele* and
Middlemarch. Both novels treat the themes of tension between
women's nature and social conditions and tie this theme to science and
medicine. Finds Von Hillern's book to be an influence on Eliot's
structure, theme, and some motifs in *Middlemarch*.

35 McKENZIE, P. "George Eliot's Nightmare, Proust's Realism."
Modern Language Review 79 (October): 810-16.
  Eliot's "The Lifted Veil" greatly influenced Marcel Proust.
Proust reworked ideas, themes, and details of Eliot's work into his *à la
recherche du temps perdu* and especially *Du côté de chez Swann*. How
Eliot's handling of metaphysics led her into writing fantasy and how
Proust writes realistically of the metaphysical.

36 McSWEENEY, KERRY. *Middlemarch*. Unwin Critical Library.
London: George Allen & Unwin, 167pp.
  Critical analysis of *Middlemarch* examines connections between
the text and Eliot's life, the role of the artist, Eliot's aesthetic, the
influence of Positivism, the historical re-creation, the omniscient
narrator, character and characterization, the development of Dorothea,
and a critical history of the novel.

37 MARTIN, CAROL A. "Pastoral and Romance in George Eliot's
The Mill on the Floss." *CLA Journal* 28, no. 1 (September):78-101.
  Traces how the "genres of pastoral and romance contain and
control the action of Books V and VI, and reinforce Eliot's emphasis
on the importance of discerning the real. . . . Book V uses the pastoral
genre and Book VI, the romance, to dichotomize illusion and reality in
the love triangles of Maggie Tulliver's adolescent and adult life. Both

have image patterns and allusions that establish the genres and both use operas as foci for the paradigms the characters envision."

38 MYERS, WILLIAM. *The Teaching of George Eliot*. N.p.: Leicester University Press, 264 pp.

    Attempts to elucidate Eliot's intellectual perspectives by studying her readings and their impact on her work, particularly Comte's influence. Discusses Eliot's place in nineteenth-century literary humanism; her fascination with animistic fantasy; and her interest in history. Suggests that the drama of writing "manifests itself on two levels, on the immediately intuitive or experiential level, the level of the feeling and the felt personality, and on the level of cognitive activity, the level of criticism."

39 NEWEY, VINCENT. "Dorothea's Awakening: The Recall of Bunyan in *Middlemarch*." *Notes and Queries* 31 (December):497-99.

    Analyzes Eliot's references to Bunyan's *The Pilgrim's Progress* in *Middlemarch*. When Dorothea is released from the confines of selfhood, she refers to illuminations and guidance from Bunyan's opening line, "What shall I do?"

40 PARKER, DAVID. "'Bound in Charity': George Eliot, Dorothea, and Casaubon." *Critical Review*, no. 26: 69-83.

    Analysis of the motto of chapter 42 of *Middlemarch*, which mocks the moral constraints of the novel and allows Eliot to satirize herself and her bound, compassionate feelings toward Casaubon.

41 PAXTON, NANCY L. "George Eliot and the City: The Imprisonment of Culture." In *Women Writers and the City: Essays in Feminist Literary Criticism*. Edited by Susan Merrill Squier. Knoxville: University of Tennessee Press, pp. 71-96.

    Study of the role of the city in the works and life of Eliot. Explores the soul-searching Eliot underwent in Florence, Italy, when researching *Romola*. In *Romola*, Eliot presents a woman's moral and physical confinement.

42 POSTLETHWAITE, DIANA [LYNN]. "'The Many in the One, the One in the Many': George Eliot's *Middlemarch* (1871-1872) as Victorian Cosmology." In *Making It Whole: A Victorian Circle and the Shape of Their World*. Columbus: Ohio State University Press, pp. 232-66.

1984

Traces methodological assumptions central to Victorian themes in the natural sciences and theories on philosophy and religion in *Middlemarch*. Influenced by Samuel Taylor Coleridge's "Theory of Life," Eliot's essay, "Notes on Form in Art," defines literary forms in terms of biological metaphors. Finds *Middlemarch* to be the fictional representation of Coleridge's cosmology.

43 ROSS, DANIEL WILLIAM. "The Evolution of Nineteenth-Century Tragic Literature." Ph.D. dissertation, Purdue University, 307 pp.
    Studies *The Mill on the Floss* as a tragic novel. Maggie Tulliver dramatizes and confronts problems from Wordsworth's poetry–adapting to an industrial world and man's separation from the natural world. Discusses how Eliot uses the narrator's role to add commentary on the tragedy of Maggie's life. See *Dissertations Abstracts International* 46, no. 2 (1985):433A.

44 RUBINSON, JILL LINDA. "Stages of Maturity: Transitions of Life in the Victorian Novel." Ph.D. dissertation, Harvard University, 186 pp.
    Examines *David Copperfield, Villette, The Mayor of Casterbridge*, and *Middlemarch* for elements of human development and maturity. The patterns of each novel emphasize the periods of self-assessment and stages of maturity as put forth in the theories of Erik Erikson. The processes of transition involve reviewing one's past and discovering elements of one's personal identity. See *Dissertations Abstracts International* 44, no. 12 (1984):3699A.

45 SALE, ROGER. "Henry James." In *Literary Inheritance*. Amherst: University of Massachusetts Press, pp. 155-201.
    Traces Eliot's influence on Henry James. Includes James's comments on *Middlemarch* and *Daniel Deronda*. Examines James's commentary on his relationship with Eliot.

46 SCHLEIFER, RONALD. "Irony and the Literary Past: On *The Concept of Irony* and *The Mill on the Floss*." In *Kierkegaard and Literature: Irony, Repetition, and Criticism*. Edited by Ronald Schleifer and Robert Markley. Norman: University of Oklahoma Press, pp. 183-216.
    Demonstrates the relationship between Sören Kierkegaard's analysis of irony in *The Concept of Irony* (Indiana University Press, 1965) and *The Mill on the Floss*.

1984

47 SHAHZADE, SUSAN ADRIAN. "Narrative Rhetoric in Nineteenth-Century British Fiction." Ph.D. dissertation, University of California at Berkeley, 253 pp.

Traces strategies of nineteenth-century narratives to "convince readers that the story is both emotionally and intellectually satisfying." Details an examination of narrative persuasion – intertext and intratext. Examines Eliot's *The Mill on the Floss* to explain textual strategies on the ideological tension regarding the role of nineteenth-century women. See *Dissertations Abstracts International* 45, no. 9 (1985): 2888A.

48 SHUTTLEWORTH, SALLY [A.]. *George Eliot and Nineteenth-Century Science: The Make-Believe of a Beginning*. Cambridge: Cambridge University Press, 265 pp.

Examines the role of science – organic theory – and its influence on the development of Eliot's fiction. Considers the theme of natural history in *Adam Bede*; studies psychological development in *The Mill on the Floss*; explains inner conflict and social evolution in *Silas Marner*. Explains Comtean theory and its social implications in *Romola*. Studies political and sexual facets of organicism in *Felix Holt, the Radical*. Discusses social and political issues of organic theory with relation to *Middlemarch* and *Daniel Deronda*. Reprinted in part: 1985.49.

49 SMITH, GRAHAME. "*Daniel Deronda*." In *The Novel and Society: DeFoe to George Eliot*. Totowa, N.J.: Barnes & Noble, pp. 193-211.

Finds *Daniel Deronda* to be the beginning of a movement away from the English social novel. Eliot questions facets of English life and provides answers that undermine the social and psychological fabric of English society.

50 STEWART, GARRETT. "Transitions." In *Death Sentences: Styles of Dying in British Fiction*. Cambridge, Mass., and London: Harvard University Press, pp. 99-138.

Analyzes the death by drowning of Maggie and Tom Tulliver in *The Mill on the Floss*. Interprets the anticipation of death through vocabulary and metaphor.

51 SZIROTNY, J.S. "Two Confectioners the Reverse of Sweet: The Role of Metaphor in Determining George Eliot's Use of Experience." *Studies in Short Fiction* 21 (Spring):127-44.

Analysis of "Brother Jacob" for the metaphorical uses of the imagery of sweets and confections. "Sweets can suggest the reality of

1984

every species of evil, falseness, inferiority, or triviality, as opposed to their seemingly attractive appearance; they can suggest verbal irony or irony of situation."

52 TAMKIN, LINDA ELLEN. "Heroines in Italy: Studies in the Novels of Ann Radcliffe, George Eliot, Henry James, E.M. Forster, and D.H. Lawrence." Ph.D. dissertation, University of California, Los Angeles, 238 pp.
    A study of six heroines who are influenced by their travels to Italy. For all, Italy becomes a place of moral crisis that tests the concepts they learned at home. How the Italian landscapes, art, and people influenced the heroines' transformations. See *Dissertations Abstracts International* 45, no. 8 (1985): 2536A.

53 VALK, ALLEN MICHAEL. "The 'Finer Medium' in Selected Novels of George ELiot." Ph.D. dissertation, University of Kansas, 218 pp.
    Demonstrates Eliot's pattern of frustration with and rebellion against the form of the conventional novel. Discusses Eliot's concern with language and her attempt to display meanings in the "word/world dynamic." See *Dissertations Abstracts International* 46, no. 4 (1985):991A.

54 VIERA, CARROLL. "'The Lifted Veil' and George Eliot's Early Aesthetic." *Studies in English Literature, 1500-1900* 24, no. 4 (Autumn):749-67.
    Eliot's aesthetic is the central issue in "The Lifted Veil" and her essays published in the *Coventry Herald* and *Observer*. In "The Lifted Veil" Eliot attempted to "synthesize her evolving critical precepts by transmuting them into fictional form." The story contains the only "artist-protagonist in the fiction of an author who, throughout her career, remained intensely concerned with the function of art and who created many artists and artist figures."

55 WARING, NANCY WINGATE. "Narrative Desire and Narrative Anxiety: The Early Novels of George Eliot." Ph.D. dissertation, Cornell University, 185 pp.
    Describes Eliot's self-conscious relation to her anonymous positions as a woman narrator in "The Lifted Veil," *Silas Marner*, and *The Mill on the Floss*. Explores her theory that "egoism is inherent in narrative itself." Considers three narrative questions: is it legitimate or

1984

self-indulgent to tell stories?; is it safe or self-exposing to give others access to one's own way of shaping experience?; and, given the unreliability of language, narrators and readers, is it possible to tell stories? See *Dissertations Abstracts International* 44, no. 12 (1984):3700A.

56 WEINSTEIN, PHILIP M. "George Eliot and the Idolatries of the Superego." In *The Semantics of Desire: Changing Models of Identity from Dickens to Joyce*. Princeton, N.J.: Princeton University Press, pp. 73-103.

 "Explores the changing relation between desire and value, as they affect the protagonists' identity. . . ." Discusses themes of the rational results of consequence and the idea of passionate generosity in *The Mill on the Floss*. Examines "in *Daniel Deronda*, the implications of an auctorial treatment of Gwendolen conducted under the novel's motto: 'Let thy chief terror be of thine own soul.'"

57 WELSH, DONNA LEVERETT. "'In the Stead of God': Male-Female Relationships and Moral Values in Selected Novels of Charles Dickens and George Eliot." Ph.D. dissertation, University of Rochester, 409 pp.

 Compares the use of male-female relationships to portray moral values in *Hard Times* and *The Mill on the Floss*, and *Dombey and Son* and *Daniel Deronda*. Discusses how gender and philosophic differences caused Dickens and Eliot to use the relationships differently, but to express the same values. Dickens's "sense of possibility is contrasted with Eliot's focus on the limitations of the other-centeredness." See *Dissertations Abstracts International* 45, no. 4 (1984): 1125A.

58 WILLIAMS, MERRYN. "George Eliot." In *Women in the English Novel, 1800-1900*. New York: St. Martin's Press, pp. 138-55.

 Traces attitudes toward women in Eliot's novels. Studies women and marriage, work, and education, as well as Eliot's perceptions on women writers.

59 WILLIAMS, RAYMOND. "George Eliot." In *The English Novel from Dickens to Lawrence*. London: Hogarth Press, pp. 75-94.

 Examines "the relation in George Eliot's development between the intense feeling which is so often in practice separating and isolating, and the practical extension in observation and sympathy of the ordinary community of the novel." Analyzes *The Mill on the Floss, Felix Holt, the*

1984

Radical, and *Middlemarch* in an attempt to elucidate the defining consciousness and the importance of history as a social and moral process.

60 WOOLF, VIRGINIA. "George Eliot." In *The Common Reader I*. Edited by Andrew McNeillie. San Diego, New York, and London: Harcourt Brace Jovanovich, pp. 162-72. Orig. pub. New York: Harcourt Brace Jovanovich, 1925.

Traces Eliot's liberation from her early familial ties through her writings and relationship with Lewes. Examines Eliot's humor and heroines.

61 WRIGHT, T.R. "*Middlemarch* as a Religious Novel, or Life without God." In *Images of Belief in Literature*. Edited by David Jasper. New York: St. Martin's Press, pp. 138-52.

Perceives *Middlemarch* to be a "religious novel in the broad sense that it is concerned with religious need, the desire to find unity, meaning and purpose in life, in a world in which God ... is a 'blank'. ... It recognises the inevitability of a certain 'epistemological egoism' and the need for an imaginative construction of hypothetical systems by which to interpret individual experience. But it tends to deplore those who make no attempt to modify their understanding of the world in accordance with ascertained facts."

1985

1 AUERBACH, NINA. "The Power of Hunger: Demonism and Maggie Tulliver." In *Romantic Imprisonment: Women and Other Glorified Outcasts*. Gender and Culture Series, edited by Carolyn G. Heilbrun and Nancy K. Miller. New York: Columbia University Press, pp. 230-49.

Examines *The Mill on the Floss* for its allusions to water, for the experience of perspectivelessness, and as a novel with qualities of Gothic romance steeped in sensations. Applies the imagery of hunger to Maggie's voracious reading, her hunger for love, and the novel's suggestions of demonism. Reprint of 1975.4.

2 _____. "Secret Performances: George Eliot and the Art of Acting." In *Romantic Imprisonment: Women and Other Glorified Outcasts*.

1985

Gender and Culture Series, edited by Carolyn G. Heilbrun and Nancy K. Miller. New York: Columbia University Press, pp. 254-67.

Considers the freedom of imposed identities Eliot created for herself in her novels, as an author, and in her publicly acknowledged relationship with Lewes.

3 BLAKE, PATRICIA. "Pride and Power." *Time* 125 (April 22):70.

Review of Haight's *Selections from George Eliot's Letters*. Finds that the letters read like an autobiography. See also 1985.14.

4 BRIGGS, ASA. "*Middlemarch* and the Doctors." In *The Collected Essays of Asa Briggs: Images, Problems, Standpoints, Forecasts*. Vol. 2. Urbana and Chicago: University of Illinois Press, pp. 49-67.

Historical analysis of Lydgate's role as physician and researcher of medical reforms of the 1860s as reflected in *Middlemarch*.

5 BROWN, JULIA PREWITT. *A Reader's Guide to the Nineteenth-Century English Novel*. New York: Macmillan Publishing; London: Collier Macmillan Publishers, pp. 26, 39, 41-42, 52, 67, 72, 82, 94, 106, passim.

Social history of Victorian England gives perspective on nineteenth-century values concerning professions, law and courts, governmental reforms, marriage, and religion in *Middlemarch* and *Daniel Deronda*.

6 CHASE, KAREN. "The Modern Family and the Ancient Image in *Romola*." In *Dickens Studies Annual: Essays on Victorian Fiction*. Vol. 14. Edited by Michael Timko, Fred Kaplan, and Edward Guiliano. New York: AMS Press, pp. 303-26.

Examines the metaphor of the family, wherein "deeds are children" and history establishes the structure of the family. "Through the series of metaphoric displacements, the novel creates an imaginative solidarity among three regions of experience: the relation of a self to its past resembles the relation of a child to its parents, which in turn resembles the relation of a community to its traditions." Also discusses the pictorial elements and the importance of sight and seeing.

7 CIVELLO, CATHERINE ANN. "A Study of Ambivalence in Modern British Female Authors." Ph.D. dissertation, University of Texas at Dallas, 202 pp.

1985

Analyzes, with regard to the theories of R.D. Laing, female ambivalence in the characters of Dorothea Brooke, Gwendolen Harleth, and Maggie Tulliver, and their passive response to male influence. Laing's observations of the behaviors of engulfment, implosion, and petrification are used as literary devices by Eliot. See *Dissertations Abstracts International* 46, no. 6 (1985):1632A.

8   COLLINS, ROWLAND L. "George Eliot." In *Dictionary of Literary Biography: Victorian Poets After 1850*. Vol. 35. Edited by William E. Fredeman and Ira B. [Bruce] Nadel. Detroit: Gale Research Co., pp. 63-71.
    Discusses Eliot's two volumes of poetry, "'The Legend of Jubal' and Other Poems" and "The Spanish Gypsy: A Poem."

9   COSTABILE, RITA MARY. "Moral Authority: George Eliot's Politics." Ph.D. dissertation, Columbia University, 239 pp.
    Discusses Eliot's conservative stand on issues of social reform in her essays and novels. Eliot believed social institutions change as a result of natural laws of evolution, not by political action. Historical experience "creates the scientific perspective and moral consciousness that can resolve social injustices and unify the human community." See *Dissertations Abstracts International* 46, no. 8 (1986):2298A.

10 DALE, PETER ALLAN. "George Eliot's 'Brother Jacob': Fables and the Physiology of Common Life." *Philological Quarterly* 64, no. 1 (Winter):17-35.
    How Eliot uses the genre of the fable and an epigraph from La Fontaine to resolve the philosophical problems in "Brother Jacob." "Brother Jacob" is written from the ironist's perception but sheds light on other parallel perceptions. Eliot's focus is on the protagonist, David Faux, the cause of capitalist corruption for which there is no redeemer.

11 DALESKI, H.M. "D.H. Lawrence and George Eliot: The Genesis of *The White Peacock*." In *Unities: Studies in the English Novel*. Athens: University of Georgia Press, pp. 83-98. Reprinted *in D.H. Lawrence and Tradition*, ed. Jeffrey Myers (Amherst: University of Massachusetts Press, 1985) pp. 51-68.
    Examines the similar narratives in *The Mill on the Floss* and Lawrence's *The White Peacock*. Eliot was a major influence on Lawrence, as is evident in their patterns involving divided heroines.

1985

12 ____. "Owning and Disowning: The Unity of *Daniel Deronda*." In *Unities: Studies in the English Novel*. Athens: University of Georgia Press, pp. 27-38.

Discusses the use of the recurrent motif of the forsaken child as a device that unifies the plot of *Daniel Deronda*.

13 DIEDRICK, JAMES. "George Eliot's Experiments in Fiction, 'Brother Jacob,' and the German Novelle." *Studies in Short Fiction* 22, no. 4 (Fall):461-68.

Analyzes the relation of the German *Novelle* theory and "Brother Jacob." "The presence in 'Brother Jacob' of the double, of disguise, of ritual unmasking, and of what M.M. Bakhtin calls 'grotesques realism' is best understood in the context of the *Novelle* form." Eliot's style is ironic and unlike her other fiction in that there is no sympathy for the characters in the narrative. "Brother Jacob" bridged the gap between the *bildungsroman* realism of *The Mill on the Floss* and the "poetic economy of *Silas Marner*."

14 ELIOT, GEORGE. *Selections from George Eliot's Letters*. Edited by Gordon S. Haight. New Haven and London: Yale University Press, 567 pp.

A one-volume condensation of the nine-volume *The George Eliot Letters* (Yale University Press, 1954-78). Eleven letters are published for the first time. Arranged chronologically; includes a name index. See also 1985.3.

15 ERMARTH, ELIZABETH DEEDS. *George Eliot*. Twayne's English Authors Series. Edited by Herbert Sussman. Boston: Twayne Publishers, 163 pp.

Addresses Eliot's works as a whole—the translations, essays, and novels. Studies the "links in her work between moral and aesthetic value, between thought and reflex, between formal and social conventions." Describes the way in which Eliot's novels demonstrate the relevance of aesthetic perceptions for moral life. Discusses issues of determinism and feminism in relation to Feuerbach's and Spinoza's influence on Eliot's concept of human freedom.

16 ____. "George Eliot's Conception of Sympathy." *Nineteenth-Century Fiction* 40, no. 1 (June):23-42.

Analysis of Eliot's concern with sympathy in the fiction of her mid-career (*Romola, Silas Marner*, and *Felix Holt, the Radical*). In these

1985

works, her "concern about sympathy begins to transform her entire treatment of social and moral problems." Sympathy depends upon a division in the psyche. This mental division is the material of conscience. Early novels treat sympathy mainly in terms of the relations between well-acquainted individuals. Eliot's mid-career fiction is concerned with sympathy between people who are not so closely related – either in the family or in the community.

17   FERRARI, MARGARET BURNS. "What the Heroines Want: Self-Discovery in *Emma, Persuasion, Jane Eyre, Villette, The Mill on the Floss, Mrs. Dalloway,* and *To the Lighthouse.*" Ph.D. dissertation, Tufts University, 351 pp.

Examines the heroines' search for what it is they want and how the role of relationships – particularly in marriage – in the self-discovery process changes as a result of changes in the nineteenth century. See *Dissertations Abstracts International* 46, no. 3 (1985):705A.

18   FERRIS, DAVID SAMUEL. "Transfigurations." Ph.D. dissertation, State University of New York at Buffalo, 262 pp.

Eliot's *Middlemarch,* DeQuincey's *Suspiria de Profundis,* and Coleridge's *Biographia Literaria* form a sequence that defines the slow development of critical reflection and the problem of the joining of discourse. "Through this sequence, the conditions of continuance and continuity in narrative are analyzed thematically by focusing upon the activity of weaving. . . . This activity involves a dissembling which serves to ensnare what would threaten the very existence of discourse and therefore deny the possibility of joining or interlacing particular discourses such as philosophy and criticism." See *Dissertations Abstracts International* 46, no. 7 (1986):1947A.

19   FOSTER, SHIRLEY. "George Eliot: Conservative Unorthodoxy." In *Victorian Women's Fiction: Marriage, Freedom, and the Individual.* Totowa, N.J.: Barnes & Noble Books, pp. 185-225.

Examines how Eliot handles the conflicting pressures of the ideology of marriage and the alternative life as a writer. Studies the dualities of Eliot's life – her stance on the woman question, reform, traditional female roles, and her relationship with Lewes. Expounds on the theme of courtship and marriage in Eliot's fiction as studies in human behavior.

1985

20   FRIEDMAN, BETTY McCLANAHAN. "The Princess in Exile: The Alienation of the Female Artist in Charlotte Brontë, George Eliot, and Virginia Woolf." Ph.D. dissertation, Ohio State University, 261 pp.

Notes the literary and historical absence of women and the failure of the woman writer to re-create herself in her fiction. Summarizes the obstacles to feminine creativity and presents the issue of alienation. Discusses *The Mill on the Floss* and the issue of feminine creative renunciation. See *Dissertations Abstracts International* 46, no. 3 (1985):705A.

21   GALLAGHER, CATHERINE. "The Politics of Culture and the Debate Over Representation in the 1860s." In *The Industrial Reformation of English Fiction: Social Discourse and Narrative Form, 1832-1867*. Chicago and London: University of Chicago Press, pp. 219-67.

Uses *Felix Holt, the Radical* as an example of the industrial novel and argues that "the Arnoldian theory of culture superseded and invalidated the Condition of England Debate. The debate over political representation impinged on the theory and practice of literary representation. . . ."

22   GATELY, PATRICIA ANN. "'A Transmutation of Self': George Eliot and the Music of Narrative." Ph.D. dissertation, University of Notre Dame, 203 pp.

Analysis of Eliot's references to music, her characters' response to music, and how she uses art and music to inspire moral sympathy. The musical metaphor can be likened to Eliot's use of narrative form, which enables the reader to perceive Eliot's vision of the unity of human experience. See *Dissertations Abstracts International* 46, no. 3 (1985):706A.

23   GILBERT, SANDRA M. "Life's Empty Pack: Notes toward a Literary Daughteronomy." *Critical Inquiry* 11, no. 3 (March):355-84.

"Juxtaposes the accounts of female maturation and obligation that are offered by theorists like Sigmund Freud and Claude Lévi-Strauss" with *Silas Marner* to reveal an aspect of female psychosexual development. Compares *Silas Marner* with Edith Wharton's *Summer* and finds the force of the novels lies in the "fatality provided by the mother's complicity in her daughter's destiny."

1985

24 GORDON, JAN B. "Affiliation as (Dis)semination: Gossip and Family in George Eliot's European Novel." *Journal of European Studies* 15, no. 59 (September):155-89.

Examines *Romola* as a "novel about the necessary interdependence of politics and scholarship and the 'crisis of succession' that afflicts both in similar ways." Discusses the discoursive role gossip has on the novel.

25 GRAY, BERYL. Afterword to "The Lifted Veil." London: Virago Press, pp. 69-91.

Finds that "The Lifted Veil" is a moral journey, like Eliot's other work, but has received little recognition because of its supernatural subject matter. The clairvoyant first-person narrator, Lattimer, is in spiritual quandry because he is unable to reconcile his clairvoyant discovery with his desire for what is not his.

26 HARDY, BARBARA. "George Eliot: 1) Allegory and Analysis; 2) Narrators, Actors, and Readers." In *Forms of Feeling in Victorian Fiction*. London: Peter Owen, pp. 131-57.

Attempts to clarify elements of the inexpressibility of personification in Eliot's narrators and characters who "recognize the limits of emotional clarity and comprehension."

27 HERRICK, JIM. "John Stuart Mill and George Eliot: A Religion of Humanity." In *Against the Faith: Essays on Deists, Skeptics, and Atheists*. Buffalo, N.Y.: Prometheus Books, pp. 170-81.

Traces elements of atheism, skepticism, and deism in the religion of humanity shared by Mill and Eliot. Examines Eliot's serious but skeptical attitude to religion. Both believed that man "needed large aspirations and high ideals."

28 HERTZ, NEIL. "Recognizing Casaubon." In *The End of the Line: Essays on Psychoanalysis and the Sublime*. New York: Columbia University Press, pp. 75-96.

Reprint of 1979.30.

29 JOHNSON, PATRICIA ELLEN. "The Role of the Middle-Class Woman in the Mid-Nineteenth-Century British Industrial Novel." Ph.D. dissertation, University of Minnesota, 225 pp.

Examines two aspects of women's place in the overall industrial social structure of the mid-nineteenth-century British novel: their place in the family and their social status within the working class. In Eliot's *Felix Holt, the Radical*, Dickens's *Hard Times*, Gaskell's *North and South*, and Charlotte Brontë's *Shirley*, each female protagonist tries to evaluate social alternatives to her life, examines her relationship with parent figures, and marries a man who is representative of industrial changes in English life. See *Dissertations Abstracts International* 46, no. 10 (1986):3041A.

30   KELLY, MARGUERITE ANNE. "George Eliot and Philanthropy." Ph.D. dissertation, University of Pittsburgh, 441 pp.

Eliot regarded herself as a literary philanthropist who sought to contribute to the improvement of society by invoking her readers' sympathies. However, Eliot's literary effectiveness is limited by her reluctance to depict the needy; her idealization of philanthropic characters; and her emphasis on self-forgetfulness. See *Dissertations Abstracts International* 46, no. 8 (1986):2301A.

31   KIDD, MILLIE MARIE. "George Eliot's Use of Irony." Ph.D. dissertation, University of Illinois at Urbana-Champaign, 350 pp.

The development of irony in Eliot's fiction begins as a verbal, corrective device in the early novels and becomes thematic irony in later works. The pattern of development is nonlinear and reflects Eliot's personal conflicts. In her fiction, Eliot used irony to reflect the turmoil of the times and her need to depict human values against the turmoil. See *Dissertations Abstracts International* 46, no. 7 (1986):1950A.

32   LANGBAUER, LAURIE. "Empty Constructions: Women and Romance in the English Novel." Ph.D. dissertation, Cornell University, 214 pp.

"Examines how novelists try to make their constructions of novels (and men) seem stable, meaningful, even real, by scapegoating the more open fictionality of women and romance." Without romance, the novel cannot be constructed. "George Eliot uses romance to indict representation by associating women and romance with what cannot be seen, with what is opposed to and subverts realism's supposedly transparent presentation." See *Dissertations Abstracts International* 46, no. 9 (1986):2700A.

1985

33   McCOBB, E.A. "*Daniel Deronda* as Will and Representation: George Eliot and Schopenhauer." *Modern Language Review* 80 (July):533-49.

"Empirical evidence suggests that Schopenhauer's works, *Weltanschauung* and *Die Welt als Wille und Vorstellung*, exerted influence during Eliot's transition from optimistic realism to the pessimistic non-realism of *Daniel Deronda*." The ideas of Schopenhauer and his imagery concerning the psychological nexus of individual identity, will power and the perception of reality are integrated into questions of guilt and redemption in *Daniel Deronda*. This is demonstrated in Eliot's use of gaming scenes and her "appreciation of causality's limited use in elucidating the human psyche."

34   MILLER, J. HILLIS. "The Two Rhetorics: George Eliot's Bestiary." In *Writing and Reading Differently: Deconstruction and the Teaching of Composition and Literature*. Edited by G. Douglas Atkins and Michael L. Johnson. Lawrence: University Press of Kansas, pp. 101-14.

Analyzes and identifies passages from Plato's *Phaedrus* and Eliot's *The Mill on the Floss* as examples of deconstructionist methods of reading the texts.

35   NESTOR, PAULINE. "George Eliot's Fiction." In *Female Friendships and Communities: Charlotte Brontë, George Eliot, Elizabeth Gaskell*. Oxford: Oxford University Press, pp. 167-204.

In her fiction, "Eliot values acquiescence more highly than assertion in her women and her ideal heterosexual relationships are not struggles for equality ... women are dependent on men in a most fundamental way. ... Eliot's view of the nature of women's relations is deeply ambivalent, recognizing at once the positive, sustaining role and the divisive, destructive element in women's various and inevitable interactions."

36   _____. "George Eliot, Surpassing Her Sex." In *Female Friendships and Communities: Charlotte Brontë, George Eliot, Elizabeth Gaskell*. Oxford: Oxford University Press, pp. 141-66.

"Biographical context sheds light on the literary depictions of female friendships and communities, ... the aloof severity of George Eliot's male-centered life is mirrored in her creation of male-dependent heroines."

1985

37 NOBLE, THOMAS A., ed. Introduction to *Scenes of Clerical Life*. Oxford: Clarendon Press, pp. xv-xl.
    Description of Eliot's writing of *Scenes of Clerical Life* and her life during its conception. Includes publication information, Eliot's choice of text, emendations, and a descriptive list of editions between 1858 and 1878.

38 OLSON, CHRISTOPHER PETER. "Narrational and Temporal Form in the Nineteenth- and Twentieth-Century Novel." Ph.D. dissertation, Northwestern University, 269 pp.
    Eliot's development as a novelist from *Adam Bede* to *The Mill on the Floss* demonstrates an attempt to make narrative structure the "recording of impressions in time on the individual consciousness and their subsequent recall in memory." Because of this, the standard first-person situation changes in that it does not report on past events, but rather focuses on the experience of recalling past events in the narrational present. See *Dissertations Abstracts International* 46, no. 8 (1986):2290A.

39 PRITCHETT, V.S. "George Eliot: Warwickshire." In *A Man of Letters: Selected Essays*. New York: Random House, pp. 74-85.
    Analyzes Eliot's ethics and moral judgement in *Adam Bede* and *Middlemarch*.

40 PUGH, JANE RICHMOND. "Woman as Other: Feminine Portraiture and Role in Hardy, Charlotte Brontë, and Eliot." Ph.D. dissertation, Case Western Reserve University, 502 pp.
    Uses de Beauvoir's terminology to designate role and analyze the correlation between the novelists' portrayal of women and their own independence. Eliot's portrait of Dorothea Brooke in *Middlemarch* moves from an inferior self-image to one that is strong and independent. Eliot uses religious, mythological, and historical associations to add heroic dimension to Dorothea. See *Dissertations Abstracts International* 46, no. 3 (1985):709A.

41 PURKIS, JOHN. *A Preface to George Eliot*. London and New York: Longman Group, 207 pp.
    Study of Eliot's background, religious crisis, doctrine of realism, and growth as a writer. Includes critical survey of all novels, with an emphasis on *Middlemarch*.

1985

42   al-RAHEB, HANI. "The Zionist Discoverer of Self and Nation." In
      The Zionist Character in the English Novel. London: Zed Books, pp.
      62-96.
         Study of Eliot's Zionist sympathy and character in *Daniel
      Deronda*. Traces Eliot's developing interest in Jewish nationalism, the
      Jew in an English environment, and the failure of the characterization
      of Deronda.

43   RAINA, BADRI. "*Daniel Deronda*: A View of Grandcourt." *Studies
      in the Novel* 17, no. 4 (Winter):371-82.
         Examines the "conceptual underpinnings and the magnitude of
      Henleigh Grandcourt as presentation." The interaction between
      Grandcourt and Gwendolen dramatizes Eliot's conception of
      Schopenhauer's determinism. Eliot's philosophy of willfulness is
      presented in Grandcourt, who is a "created presence," whereas
      Deronda is a "philosophical postulate."

44   RALPH, PHYLLIS C. "Transformations: Fairy Tales, Adolescence,
      and the Novel of Female Development in Victorian Fiction." Ph.D.
      dissertation, University of Kansas, 240 pp.
         "Explores the psychological implications of fairy tales of
      transformation as motifs used by nineteenth-century novelists in the
      development of their female protagonists." George Eliot, Jane Austen,
      and Charlotte and Emily Brontë created female characters who grow
      and change by their own initiative. Eliot uses the "animal groom pattern
      in *The Mill on the Floss* and *Middlemarch* to provide theme and
      structure, having moved beyond the simple Cinderella story." See
      Dissertations Abstracts International 46, no. 10 (1986):3042A.

45   REED, JOHN R., and HERRON, JERRY [SIM]. "George Eliot's
      Illegitimate Children." *Nineteenth-Century Fiction* 40, no. 2
      (September):175-86.
         Discusses Eliot's amicable treatment of illegitimate children.
      Eliot does not allow them to suffer humiliation but allows children of
      sin to find favor in their communities. The presence of bastard children
      is Eliot's ironic humor and "commentary on the sowing of wild oats."
      Refers to images of germination in *Romola, Adam Bede, Felix Holt, the
      Radical*, and *The Mill on the Floss*.

1985

46 ROGERS, PHILIP. "Lessons for Fine Ladies: Tolstoj and George Eliot's *Felix Holt, the Radical.*" *Slavic and East European Journal* 29, no. 4 (Winter):379-92.

Discusses Eliot's influence on Tolstoy following his reading of *Felix Holt, the Radical*. Tolstoy was particularly interested in Eliot's "criticism of the coquetry and materialism of middle-class women."

47 SCHÄFER, WERNER. "Komik in den Romanen George Eliot". *Bochum Studies in English.* Vol. 19. Amsterdam: Verlag B.R. Grüner, 239 pp.

In Dutch with English abstract following: examines Eliot's biographical and artistic background in comedy; the function and subjects of her comedy; use of implicit and explicit comedy.

48 SEDGWICK, EVE KOSOFSKY. "*Adam Bede* and *Henry Esmond*: Homosocial Desire and Historicity of the Female." In *Between Men: English Literature and Male Homosocial Desire.* New York: Columbia University Press, pp. 134-60.

Adam Bede and *Henry Esmond* are employed to embody "a dialectic between Marxist-feminist and radical-feminist views of the historicity of women's status in relation to male homosocial desire."

49 SHUTTLEWORTH, SALLY A. "The Language of Science and Psychology in George Eliot's *Daniel Deronda*." In *Victorian Science and Victorian Values: Literary Perspectives.* Edited by James Paradis and Thomas Postlewait. New Brunswick, N.J.: Rutgers University Press, pp. 269-98. Orig. pub. in *Annals of the New York Academy of Sciences,* vol. 360 (New York: New York Academy of Sciences, 1981).

"Demonstrates that contemporary scientific ideas and theories of method provided a basis not only for the psychological theory, but also for the social and moral vision, and narrative methodology of *Daniel Deronda*." Studies scientific and social theories of organicism. "Through Mordecai, George Eliot questions atomistic and inductive science, and theories of linear causality; through Gwendolen, she questions social and psychological atomism, the opposition between self and other, conscious and the unconscious." Reprinted from 1984.48.

50 SMITH, JOHANNA MARY. "Domestic Passion: Sister-Brother Incest in Four Nineteenth-Century Novels." Ph.D. dissertation, Claremont Graduate School, 518 pp.

Examines the concept of sister-brother incest in *The Mill on the Floss*, Emily Brontë's *Wuthering Heights*, Herman Melville's *Pierre; or The Ambiguities*, and Jane Austen's *Mansfield Park*. These novels present incest as the domestic affection that inhibits positive emotional relationships outside the family and causes the inescapability of the family. "As they demonstrate familial inescapability, incestuous constrictions in these novels both attest to and challenge the constraints of narrative form." See *Dissertations Abstracts International* 46, no. 9 (1986):2702A.

51 SPENCE, MARTIN C. "Charlotte Brontë's *Jane Eyre* and George Eliot's *Middlemarch*." *Explicator* 43, no. 3 (Spring):10-11.
     Discusses the influence of *Jane Eyre* on the Dorothea-Casaubon proposal scene of *Middlemarch*. Critical analysis of Eliot's imitation of Brontë's work in terms of setting, imagery, and use of vocabulary.

52 STASSIJNS, MACHTELD LUCIA. "'By Force of Art': The Place of Melodrama in George Eliot's Early Fiction." Ph.D. dissertation, Queen's University at Kingston (Canada).
     Examines the influence of the English theater and melodrama on George Eliot's early fiction. Discusses the relationship of melodrama to the artistic forms of expression of pastoral, tragedy, and realism. See *Dissertations Abstracts International* 46, no. 11 (1986):3349A.

53 STOKES, EDWARD. "Hawthorne and George Eliot." In *Hawthorne's Influence on Dickens and George Eliot*. St. Lucia, Queensland, Australia: University of Queensland Press, pp. 87-209.
     Illustrates Eliot's knowledge of Nathaniel Hawthorne's works; offers critical comparisons of the authors; compares their theories of fiction; examines in detail Hawthorne's influence on each of Eliot's novels.

54 SWINDELLS, JULIA. "The Gentleman's Club, Literature." In *Victorian Writing and Working Women: The Other Side of Silence*. Minneapolis: University of Minnesota Press, pp. 91-113.
     Deals with "polemical and autobiographical utterances about literary professionalism." Compares different kinds of novelists – Eliot, Gaskell, and Thackeray – and nineteenth-century attitudes regarding class and gender that led to the authors' varied careers and writings.

Discusses gender prejudices that led to the use of pseudonyms by women writers of the 1840s and 1850s.

55 _____. "George Eliot: Man at Work and the Masculine Professional." In *Victorian Writing and Working Women: The Other Side of Silence.* Minneapolis: University of Minnesota Press, pp. 45-64.
   Discusses Eliot's representation and presentation of the division of labor by class and gender and the significance of the artisan. Analyzes Eliot's treatment of "mental" and "manual" work. Deals with Eliot as a woman and with the pressures on women who enter the masculine traditions of the literary production process.

56 THOMAS, JEANIE GAYLE. "Reading *Middlemarch*: Re-claiming the Middle Distance." Ph.D. dissertation, University of Washington, 228 pp.
   In *Middlemarch*, Eliot accepts a Godless world, denies simple answers, and acknowledges life's ambiguities. Argues for the positive conditions of a "psychological midland" by discussing the issues of sympathy, feminism, comic spirit, and narrative authority. See *Dissertations Abstracts International* 46, no. 7 (1986):1953A. See also 1987.34.

57 THURIN, SUSAN SCHOENBAUER. "The Madonna and the Child Wife in *Romola*." *Tulsa Studies in Women's Literature* 4, no. 2 (Fall):217-33.
   Compares parallel figures of Romola and Dora, of Dickens's *David Copperfield*, who both become friends with their husbands' mistress or friend. "In Dickens's novel the madonna becomes a mother, while in Eliot's novel the child wife does, and in both works the madonna develops a protective concern for the child wife." Eliot's novel demonstrates how "patriarchal values confine women."

58 VANN, J. DON. "George Eliot." In *Victorian Novels in Serial*. New York: Modern Language Association of America, pp. 76-77.
   Cites serial publication information about *Romola*, *Middlemarch*, and *Daniel Deronda*.

59 VARGISH, THOMAS. "George Eliot: Providence as Metaphor." In *The Providential Aesthetic in Victorian Fiction*. Charlottesville: University Press of Virginia, pp. 163-243.

1985

"George Eliot demonstrates the power of the narrative conventions generic to the providential aesthetic as she redirects them to the representation of an entirely human world. ... [She] took the chief thematic and structural convention of the English novel and adapted it to the representation of a reality uninformed by the premises upon which that convention was founded. In her work we can see the late tendency of Christian providentialism to diffuse and disguise itself in other moral and philosophical paradigms or systems."

60 WELSH, ALEXANDER. *George Eliot and Blackmail*. Cambridge, Mass.: Harvard University Press, 388 pp.
    Examines the theme of blackmail in *Romola, Daniel Deronda*, and *Middlemarch*. Ties the importance of the rise of information as a commodity to the blackmail theme. Correlates the blackmail theme and psychoanalysis. Reprinted. 1987.37.

61 WHEELER, MICHAEL. "Incarnate History and Unhistoric Acts: George Eliot." In *English Fiction of the Victorian Period 1830-1890*. Longman Literature in English Series, edited by David Carroll and Michael Wheeler. London and New York: Longman Group, pp. 119-38.
    Studies *Silas Marner, Romola*, and *Middlemarch* as histories.

62 YEAZELL, RUTH BERNARD. "Why Political Novels Have Heroines: *Sybil, Mary Barton*, and *Felix Holt*." *Novel* 18, no. 2 (Winter):126-44.
    Examines the novelists' reliance on the courtship plot in Disraeli's *Sybil*, Gaskell's *Mary Barton*, and *Felix Holt, the Radical*. "Each of these novels entertains the possibility of violence ... only to take refuge at critical moments in the representation of female innocence, exchanging a politically dangerous man for a sexually unaggressive young woman, and a narrative that threatens drastic for one that proves reassuringly static."

63 ZEMEL, CAROL. "The 'Spook' in the Machine: Van Gogh's Pictures of Weavers in Brabant." *Art Bulletin* 67, no. 1 (March):123-37.
    Applies Eliot's recurrent theme and use of the individual artisan and rural community set against the intrusion of modern industry to Vincent Van Gogh's paintings of the weavers. Weavers appear in both

1986

Silas Marner and *Felix Holt, the Radical* as symbols of the simpler and more harmonious society that preceeded the advent of industrialization.

1986

1   ALLEN, WALTER. "*The Mill on the Floss*." In *George Eliot*. Edited by Harold Bloom. Modern Critical Views. New York: Chelsea House Publishers, pp. 55-63. Orig. pub. in Allen, Walter, *George Eliot* (New York: Macmillan Co.; London: Weidenfed & Nicholson, 1964).

Commentary on *The Mill on the Floss* focuses on Eliot's identification with the heroine, Maggie Tulliver, and Eliot's understanding of the property basis of Victorian society. Comments on the resolution of the novel's tragedy and the dissatisfaction readers and critics have had with it. Defends the resolution as being a product of Eliot's age and date of the writing.

2   BENNETT, BRUCE. "Catherine Spence, George Eliot, and the Contexts of Literary Possibility." *Journal of Commonwealth Literature* 21, no. 1:202-10.

Examines Eliot's influence on her Australian contemporary, Catherine Helen Spence. Compares their literary careers.

3   BLESSINGTON, FRANCIS C. "The Portrait in the Spoon: George Eliot's Casaubon and John Milton." *Milton Quarterly* 20, no. 1 (March):29-31.

Cites how poet John Milton could have served as the model for the character of Casaubon of *Middlemarch*.

4   BLOOM, HAROLD, ed. Introduction to *George Eliot*. Modern Critical Views. New York: Chelsea House Publishers, pp. 1-8.

Discusses Eliot's moral stance as it is revealed in her personal letters and in *Daniel Deronda*. Describes Eliot as a moralist, "precisely delineating our discomfort with culture and remorselessly weighing the economics of the psyche's civil wars." Sees Eliot's greatest power as the ability to represent the falling away of a solipsism into the void of sublime solitude, as represented by Gwendolen Harleth in *Daniel Deronda*.

1986

5   BOOTH, ALISON. "*Little Dorrit* and Dorothea Brooke: Interpreting the Heroines of History." *Nineteenth-Century Literature* 41, no. 2 (September):190-216.
    Compares how Eliot and Dickens interpret historical heroes as women as well as men. Both describe heroes who are neither "preeminent nor manly, who yet redeem the common experience of a burdensome past." A comparison of *Little Dorrit* and *Middlemarch* heroines.

6   CARPENTER, MARY WILSON. *George Eliot and the Landscape of Time: Narrative Form and Protestant Apocalyptic History.* Studies in Religion, edited by Charles H. Long. Chapel Hill and London: University of North Carolina Press, 257 pp.
    Examines Eliot's interest in the "intricacies of apocalyptic continuous historical interpretation centering on the Books of Daniel and Revelation" to better understand Eliot as an historian. Considers the effects of Eliot's break from her church and the hypothesis that her "narratives construct multiple fictions of history through reference to various formal and symbolic systems of codification."

7   CARROL, DAVID, ed. Introduction to *Middlemarch*. Oxford: Clarendon Press, pp. xiii-lxxxv.
    Discusses Eliot's research and thoughts on preparing the text of *Middlemarch*. Details publishing arrangements, choice and treatment of text, emendations, treatment of accidentals, and a descriptive list of editions between 1871 and 1878.

8   CASERIO, ROBERT [LAWRENCE, Jr.]. "*Felix Holt* and *Bleak House*." In *George Eliot.* Edited by Harold Bloom. Modern Critical Views. New York: Chelsea House Publishers, pp. 127-50.
    Reprinted from 1979.12.

9   CAVELL, RICHARD ANTHONY. "Sub Voce: Voice and the Poetics of Indirection in Flaubert, George Eliot, and Verga." Ph.D. dissertation, University of Toronto (Canada).
    "Explores the phenomenon of voice in nineteenth-century fiction through a consideration of the modality known as Free Indirect Discourse (FID), seeking to identify the formal implications of the indeterminacy of FID." An examination of the methodologies of FID – stylistic, mimetic, linguistic, dialogical. Summarizes the doubling

of narrative voices in *Middlemarch*. See *Dissertations Abstracts International* 47, no. 6 (1986):2150A.

10 CHASE, CYNTHIA. "The Decomposition of the Elephants: Double Reading *Daniel Deronda*." In *Decomposing Figures: Rhetorical Readings in the Romantic Tradition*. Baltimore, Md.: Johns Hopkins University Press, pp. 157-74.
Reprint of 1978.8. See also 1978.50.

11 COHAN, STEVEN. "*The Mill on the Floss* and *Middlemarch*: 'An Intimate Penetration.'" In *Violation and Repair in the English Novel: The Paradigm of Experience from Richardson to Woolf*. Detroit, Mich.: Wayne State University Press, pp. 131-69.
"*Middlemarch* constructs experience to demonstrate that adulthood is not the horrific violation of an innocent self. ... *The Mill on the Floss* complicates its paradigmatic toward direction by raising a dread of maturity through Maggie Tulliver's regressive longing for childhood."

12 DENTITH, SIMON. *George Eliot*. Atlantic Highlands, N.J.: Humanities Press International, 150 pp.
Discusses Eliot as a realist writer who "attempts to understand and make sense of social history of her time and the possibilities for individual fulfilment made available by that history." Examines issues regarding class, gender, and human sympathy.

13 ELLMANN, RICHARD. "Dorothea's Husbands." In *George Eliot*. Edited by Harold Bloom. Modern Critical Views. New York: Chelsea House Publishers, pp. 65-80.
Reprint of 1973.18.

14 FELTES, N.N. "One Round of a Long Ladder: Gender, Profession and the Production of *Middlemarch*." In *Modes of Production in Victorian Novels*. Chicago and London: University of Chicago Press, pp. 36-56.
Examines the details of the publishing of *Middlemarch* and how the novel reflects Eliot's struggle between "her vocation, her will to be a professional, and the dominant, patriarchal structures of professional authorship and publishing."

1986

15   FRASER, HILARY S. "St. Theresa, St. Dorothea and Miss Brooke in *Middlemarch*." *Nineteenth-Century Fiction* 40, no. 4 (March):400-11.

Discusses the analogy between Dorothea and St.Theresa and Dorothea's idealization. Examines how Eliot's "moral idealization of Dorothea is bound up with her romantic idealization of Dorothea's love for Ladislaw through the analogy of the dialectic between self-sacrifice and sexuality in the myth of St. Theresa."

16   FREADMAN, RICHARD. "Character, Narration, and the Novel." In *Eliot, James and the Fictional Self: A Study in Character and Narration*. New York: St. Martin's Press, pp. 3-22.

"Comparative reading of George Eliot and Henry James centres on their concepts of characters and narration, and on the interplay between character and narrative structure in their novels." Discusses the linguistic analogy, the self, social fictions, and character and self.

17   _____. "Choice: *Daniel Deronda* and *The Portrait of a Lady*." In *Eliot, James and The Fictional Self: A Study in Character and Narration*. New York: St. Martin's Press, pp. 48-122.

Examines the centrality of the theme of choice in *Daniel Deronda* and *The Portrait of a Lady*. In *Daniel Deronda*, "George Eliot has apparently ranged before the reader a spectrum of choices and choosers in an effort to unravel the mysteries of volition and consequence. "*The Portrait of a Lady* is seen as an extension of *Daniel Deronda*. "*The Portrait of a Lady* subjectivises and so problematicises individual choice further than does *Daniel Deronda*."

18   _____. "Knowledge: *Middlemarch* and *The Golden Bowl*." In *Eliot, James and the Fictional Self: A Study in Character and Narration*. New York: St. Martin's Press, pp. 123-211.

Middlemarch is about "*how* knowledge is constituted and with what authority. ... *Middlemarch* and *The Golden Bowl* are creative inquiries into what the philosophers call the problem of other minds." Discusses Eliot's perception on "other minds" as she related them in her letters, novels and in "The Lifted Veil." Finds that "*The Golden Bowl* acknowledges a more radical process of fictionalising in intersubjective relationships than does *Middlemarch*."

1986

19 _____. "Morality: *Romola* and *The Wings of the Dove*." In *Eliot, James and the Fictional Self: A Study in Character and Narration*. New York: St. Martin's Press, pp. 212-51.
   Romola's "moral argument tries to counter cynicism by reopening two central problems in Western ethics. It asks how far and in what way other persons can be conceived as individual, and how great a part in their formation is played by nature and culture." Examines James's response to *Romola* and morality in fiction. Compares *Romola* with *The Wings of the Dove* and finds that *The Wings of the Dove* "concedes more to the isolated moral sovereignty of the individual than does *Romola*."

20 _____. "Two Views of the Novel: Eliot and James on the Novel, James on George Eliot." In *Eliot, James and the Fictional Self: A Study in Character and Narration*. New York: St. Martin's Press, pp. 23-47.
   Compares Eliot's and James's theories of the novel. Discusses James's indebtedness to Eliot.

21 GALLAGHER, CATHERINE. "George Eliot and *Daniel Deronda*: The Prostitute and the Jewish Question." In *Sex, Politics, and Science in the Nineteenth-Century Novel*. Edited by Ruth Bernard Yeazell. Baltimore and London: Johns Hopkins University Press, pp. 39-62.
   Distinguishes "the metaphor of the author as whore" to interpret the ending of Eliot's career and to understand *Daniel Deronda*. Cites by examples in Eliot's essays, her references to authorship, usury, and writing as social and economic acts. In *Daniel Deronda*, usury, prostitution, and art become interchangeable activities of loss and gain.

22 GILMOUR, ROBIN. "Continuity and Change in the Later Victorian Novel: George Eliot, Meredith, James and Stevenson." In *The Novel in the Victorian Age: A Modern Introduction*. London: Edward Arnold Publishers, pp. 146-79.
   Surveys the transitional phase of English fiction and society during the 1870s and 1880s. Discusses Eliot's influence on Henry James and Thomas Hardy.

23 _____. "The Novel in the Age of Equipoise: Wilkie Collins, Trollope and George Eliot." In *The Novel in the Victorian Age: A Modern Introduction*. London: Edward Arnold Publishers, pp. 107-45.

1986

Evaluates changes in opinion during the years 1850-1865, as reflected in the literature of that period. Analysis of Eliot's novels attempts "to balance the tragic stress with a hope for 'the growing good of the world.'"

24 GOLDFARB, RUSSELL M. "Rosamond Vincy of *Middlemarch*." *CLA Journal* 30, no. 1 (September):83-99.
Disputes critics who find Rosamond Vincy hateful and empty-headed. Finds her to be a character worthy of sympathy. "The character George Eliot has given us is one of life's winners, though Rosamond's victories are middle-class victories."

25 HARDY, BARBARA. "The Moment of Disenchantment." In *George Eliot*. Edited by Harold Bloom. Modern Critical Views. New York: Chelsea House Publishers, pp. 45-53. Orig. pub. in *Review of English Studies*, n.s. 19, vol. 5 (July):256-64. Oxford: Clarendon Press, 1954.
Description of the crisis of disenchantment that occurs in nearly all of Eliot's novels. Eliot's characteristic negation and use of antithetical images of space and light provide symbolic contrast between reality and glory. The disenchantment is a prelude to change and character metamorphosis.

26 HARDY, BARBARA; MILLER, J. HILLIS; and POIRIER, RICHARD. "*Middlemarch*, Chapter 85: Three Commentaries." In *George Eliot*. Edited by Harold Bloom. Modern Critical Views. New York: Chelsea House Publishers, pp. 167-85.
Reprint of 1980.33.

27 HAYLES, N. KATHERINE. "Anger in Different Voices: Carol Gilligan and *The Mill on the Floss*." *Signs* 12, no. 1 (Autumn):23-39.
Compares narrative strategies of Gilligan's *In a Different Voice* with *The Mill on the Floss*. Both are about misunderstanding, conflict, and reconciliation. "Where Gilligan counsels understanding, Eliot presents the effects of suppressed anger; where Gilligan sees a future in which men and women learn from each other, Eliot creates an ending that joins revenge and reconciliation into a single gesture. Together, Gilligan's and Eliot's texts present a fuller statement about female development than either does alone."

1986

28 HERTZ, NEIL. "Recognizing Casaubon." In *George Eliot*. Edited by
    Harold Bloom. Modern Critical Views. New York: Chelsea House
    Publishers, pp. 151-66.
        Reprint of 1979.30.

29 HOLLOWAY, JOHN. "*Silas Marner* and the System of Nature." In
    George Eliot. Edited by Harold Bloom. Modern Critical Views. New
    York: Chelsea House Publishers, pp. 37-44. Reprinted from *The
    Victorian Sage: Studies in Argument* (New York: Macmillan & Co.,
    1953).
        Presents *Silas Marner* as a vision of human life and poetic
    justice. Examines the general features of Eliot's novels as
    representations of a vision of life and historical change. "The sense of a
    deterministic world where everything happens of necessity is increased
    by the novel's stress on kinship." *Silas Marner, The Mill on the Floss*,
    and *Felix Holt, the Radical* represent kinship as an aspect of the system
    of nature.

30 HOMANS, MARGARET. "Eliot, Wordsworth, and the Scenes of
    the Sisters' Instruction." In *Bearing the Word: Language and Female
    Experience in Nineteenth-Century Women's Writing*. Women in
    Culture and Society Series, edited by Catherine R. Stimpson.
    Chicago and London: University of Chicago Press, pp. 120-52.
        Examines Eliot's divergence from Wordworth's prototypes in
    The Mill on the Floss and *Middlemarch*. Eliot deals with female
    education and the brother-sister relationship in *The Mill on the Floss*
    and deals with the "determining difference between children who grow
    up in male-female pairs in *Middlemarch*." See also 1981.26.

31 _____. "Figuring the Mother: Madonna Romola's Incarnation." In
    *Bearing the Word: Language and Female Experience in Nineteenth-
    Century Women's Writing*. Women in Culture and Society Series,
    edited by Catherine R. Stimpson. Chicago and London: University of
    Chicago Press, pp. 189-222.
        Analyzes Eliot's treatment of the ideology of motherhood in
    Romola. "Romola is a figure for the Madonna. . . . Romola's bearing of
    language and of the child is never more than figurative. She is a foster
    mother, a figurative mother. . . . Like Eliot herself, she is a mother
    without ever bearing children of her own."

1986

32 JACOBUS, MARY. "Hysterics Suffer Mainly from Reminiscences." In *Reading Woman: Essays in Feminist Criticism*. Gender and Culture Series. New York: Columbia University Press, pp. 249-74.

Feminist critique of readings and interpretations of "The Lifted Veil." Includes reaction to Eliot's works and letters by Alice James and commentary on writing and the self-conscious.

33 _____. "Men of Maxims and *The Mill on the Floss*." In *Reading Woman: Essays in Feminist Criticism*. Gender and Culture Series. New York: Columbia University Press, pp. 62-79.

Reprint of 1981.29.

34 KNAPP, SHOSHANA. "George Eliot and W.S. Gilbert: *Silas Marner* into *Dan'l Druce*." *Nineteenth-Century Fiction* 40, no. 4 (March):438-59.

Criticism of W.S. Gilbert's attempt at a dramatic adaption of *Silas Marner*, in his *Dan'l Druce, Blacksmith*. Explains why Gilbert selected *Silas Marner* for adaptation and the difficulties in reproducing the structure and characterizations of the novel.

35 LEAVIS, F.R. "The Early Phase." In *George Eliot*. Edited by Harold Bloom. Modern Critical Views. New York: Chelsea House Publishers, pp. 9-25. Orig. pub. in Leavis, F.R., *The Great Tradition* (Conrad, N.Y.:New York University Press, 1964).

Analysis of Eliot's early phase, *Scenes of Clerical Life*, and *Adam Bede*.

36 LEAVIS, L.R. "George Eliot's Creative Mind: *Felix Holt* as the Turning Point of Her Art." *English Studies* 67, no. 4 (August):311-26.

Outlines Eliot's progress as a novelist and the changes in her work following the publication of *Felix Holt, the Radical*. Illustrates how *Felix Holt, the Radical* is central to Eliot's development as a novelist because of its failures and how these failures are rectified in *Middlemarch*.

37 LENIHAN, PATRICIA DIANE. "Regionalism in the Fictional Debuts of Trollope, Gaskell, and Eliot." Ph.D. dissertation, Catholic University of America, 166 pp.

Examines the period 1847-57 as the beginning of regionalism as a genre for Trollope, Gaskell, and Eliot. Eliot's *Scenes of Clerical Life* emphasizes her use of regionalism as an "early version of psychological realism." Discusses the connection between regionalism and literary debut. See *Dissertations Abstracts International* 47, no. 4 (1986):1334A.

38 LEVINE, GEORGE [L.]. "The Lifted Veil." *New York Times Book Review*, 13 April, p. 12.
    Review of "The Lifted Veil" (Penguin Books/Virago Press, 1986). Cites how different the story is from Eliot's other works and finds Eliot's personal division of self within the story.

39 ____. "The Scientific Texture of *Middlemarch*." In *George Eliot*. Edited by Harold Bloom. Modern Critical Views. New York: Chelsea House Publishers, pp. 187-202.
    Middlemarch is an illustration of man's moral need for scientific vision. Discusses how science made sense of life in the Victorian debate over evolution and consciousness in nature. "By virtue of rigorous secularity Eliot attempts, in a way comparable to that of Feuerbach, to resacralize a world from which God has been dismissed." Discusses the widespread fragmentation in the beginning of *Middlemarch* and its later attempt to find order in reality and epistemology. Reprint of 1981.38.

40 LUNDBERG, PATRICIA LORIMER. "George Eliot: Mary Ann Evan's Subversive Tool in *Middlemarch*?" *Studies in the Novel* 18, no. 3 (Fall):270-82.
    Defines the two personae within *Middlemarch* that are the two personalities of George Eliot/Mary Ann Evans. Mary Ann Evans as Dorothea rejects the social order of Victorian England; George Eliot as Dorothea creates havoc among the male characters in an attempt to show society a better world than the one she was a part of.

41 McCORMACK, KATHLEEN. "George Eliot and Victorian Science Fiction: *Daniel Deronda* as Alternative History." *Extrapolation* 27, no.3 (Fall):185-96.
    Argues for the placement of *Daniel Deronda* in the science fiction subgenre of the alternate history. Analyzes the theme of utopia, Eliot's attack on Victorian social institutions, the novel's geographical scope, and the pivotal role women play "in the politics of the alternate society."

42 McGOWAN, JOHN P. "The Development of George Eliot's Realism." In *Representation and Revelation: Victorian Realism from Carlyle to Yeats*. Columbia: University of Missouri Press, pp. 132-57.

1986

Finds that Eliot's novels have reference to a reality that transcends the self. "Her realism is preoccupied with establishing the literary work's relation to the world and its power to denote, describe, and represent things and events in the world. . . ." Argues that Eliot moves from a "simple realism of matching words to world in *The Mill on the Floss* to a more complex realism, one that envisions a world and converts readers to that world's reality in her last two novels, *Middlemarch* and *Daniel Deronda*."

43   McKEE, PATRICIA. "George Eliot's Redemption of Meaning: *Daniel Deronda*." In *Heroic Commitment in Richardson, Eliot, and James*. Princeton, N.J.: Princeton University Press, pp. 208-69.
     "The redemption of the meaning of both Deronda and Gwendolen entails a discovery that precludes their own emptiness and enables them to see both self and others in terms of reflective fullness rather than reflected lack. The redemption of meaning, then, maintains the reflective relation of self and world."

44   _____. "Power as Partiality in *Middlemarch*." In *Heroic Commitment in Richardson, Eliot, and James*. Princeton, N.J.: Princeton University Press, pp. 150-207.
     Studies the possibilities of meaning in *Middlemarch*. Analyzes Dorothea's power and authority as having an excess of meaning. "The power of Dorothea's interpretations lies in her refusal to distinguish the boundaries between herself and others." Reprinted: 1987.24.

45   MARSHALL, DAVID. "*Daniel Deronda* and the Wisest Beholder." In *The Figure of Theater: Shaftesbury, Defoe, Adam Smith and George Eliot*. New York: Columbia University Press, pp. 193-240.
     Traces the role of the theater in *Daniel Deronda* and how "Eliot displays the correspondences between sympathy and theater." Suggests "that as it explores the theatrical conditions of its own characters and world, the novel acts as a dramatization of Adam Smith's *Theory of Moral Sentiments*.

46   MASSARDIER-KENNEY, FRANCOISE. "A Study of Women in Four Realist Writers: Sand, Flaubert, Eliot, and James." Ph.D. dissertation, Kent State University, 185 pp.
     Examines the authors' physical and psychological descriptions of characters and studies the notion of "function" and "actant" narrative development of women protagonists. Finds that authorial gender has

little bearing on the specificity of the female literary experience. See *Dissertations Abstracts International* 47, no. 5 (1986):1721A.

47 MILLER, JANE. *Women Writing About Men*. New York: Pantheon Books; London: Virago Press, pp. 20-26, 121-33, 139-41, 152-59, passim.

Discusses "the novel as a form which women writers have used to question and challenge men's appropriation of women's experience." Examines women's perceptions of men, male/female relationships, and how the form of women's writing conveys their perceptions of men. Examines Eliot's conflicts with her dual sexual voice; her depiction of mothers and sons; and her portrayal of women and male heroes.

48 MILLER, J. HILLIS. "Optic and and Semiotic in *Middlemarch*." In *George Eliot*. Edited by Harold Bloom. Modern Critical Views. New York: Chelsea House Publishers, pp. 99-110.

Reprint of 1975.62.

49 PETERSON, CARLA L. "*The Mill on the Floss* and *Jude the Obscure*: The Return of the Pagan." In *The Determined Reader: Gender and Culture in the Novel From Napoleon to Victoria*. Brunswick, N.J.: Rutgers University Press, pp. 180-226.

Analysis of "the motif of the reader-protagonist and his or her reading activity. . . ." Using a "method of radical comparativism," the similarities between male and female experiences are juxtaposed. "Although both *The Mill on the Floss* and *Jude the Obscure* have been considered Bildungsromane, they are novels of education in which the protagonists' quests and goals have become problematical. . . ." In *The Mill on the Floss*, Maggie discovers that the spiritual quest is not an adequate method of experience.

50 PRICE, MARTIN. "The Nature of Decision." In *George Eliot*. Edited by Harold Bloom. Modern Critical Views. New York: Chelsea House Publishers, pp. 223-41.

Discusses Eliot's reflections on moral freedom, man's free acceptance of duty and free recognition of obligation. The moment of decision and how it reveals man's complex nature is illustrated by passages from *Felix Holt, the Radical*, *Daniel Deronda*, and *Middlemarch*. Comments on moral decisions, the emergence of self, moral realism, and literary realism. Eliot's characters make decisions that are the result of egoism or sympathy. "The moment of decision is

one in which we reveal most clearly the complexity of our nature."
Eliot's insistence upon inevitable cost implicates man's virtues and
errors; she is concerned with how choice is limited by circumstance or
the structure of situation. Reprint of 1983.53.

51   QUALLS, BARRY V. "Speaking through Parable: *Daniel Deronda*."
In *George Eliot*. Edited by Harold Bloom. Modern Critical Views.
New York: Chelsea House Publishers, pp. 203-21.
        Analysis of *Daniel Deronda* as biblical romance and parable.
Daniel Deronda questions the place of art, fiction, and music in man's
life. In the novel, Eliot proposes that the source of art is in the religious
myths that make up people's consciousness. The novel's characters,
save for Grandcourt, seek historic and symbolic situations to shed
understanding on their lives.

52   ROBICHEAU, JOAN MARGARET. "George Henry Lewes,
George Eliot, and Anthony Trollope: Experiments in Realism."
Ph.D. dissertation, University of Toronto (Canada).
        Compares *Daniel Deronda* and Trollope's *Nina Balatka* and the
influence of George Henry Lewes's theory of Reasoned Realism upon
the two novels. Asseses both novels with reference to the balance of
realism/idealism and Lewes's Twofold Aspect of a Complete Reality,
wherein there is no actual distinction between the real and the ideal.
See *Dissertations Abstracts International* 47, no. 6 (1986):2171A.

53   ROSS, ALEXANDER M. "George Eliot." In *The Imprint of the
Picturesque on Nineteenth-Century British Fiction*. Waterloo, Ontario:
Wilfred Laurier University Press, pp. 113-32.
        Illustrates Eliot's use of the picturesque to describe setting,
architecture, and character.

54   SHUTTLEWORTH, SALLY [A]. "Fairy Tale or Science?
Physiological Psychology in *Silas Marner*." In *Languages of Nature:
Critical Essays on Science and Literature*. Edited by L.J. Jordanova.
New Brunswick, N.J.: Rutgers University Press, pp. 244-88.
        Identifies the interrelatedness of the psychological and social
premises of *Silas Marner* and how it relates to the debates concerning
evolution during the 1860s. Discusses the importance of memory and
personal identity within the vast social environment. Outlines Eliot's
concern with the integration of psychological continuity and
community.

1986

55 VAN GHENT, DOROTHY. "*Adam Bede*." In *George Eliot*. Edited by Harold Bloom. Modern Critical Views. New York: Chelsea House Publishers, pp. 27-36. Orig. pub. Van Ghent, Dorothy. *The English Novel: Form and Function*. New York: Rinehart, 1953, pp. 171-81.

Discusses the slow movement of *Adam Bede* and the use of mirrors and reflections. Examines the use of time, clocks, and rhythms and their significance in rural life.

56 WARHOL, ROBYN R. "Toward a Theory of the Engaging Narrator: Earnest Interventions in Gaskell, Stowe and Eliot." *PMLA* 101, no. 5 (October):811-18.

The engaging narrators of Stowe, Eliot, and Gaskell encourage the reader to identify with the "you" in narrative interventions. The novelists hope to stir the readers' sympathies and move them to action.

57 WEED, ELIZABETH. "The Liquidation of Maggie Tulliver." In *George Eliot*. Edited by Harold Bloom. Modern Critical Views. New York: Chelsea House Publishers, pp. 111-26.

Reprint of 1978.48.

58 WEISS, BARBARA. "Bankruptcy as a Metaphor: The Threatened Self." In *The Hell of the English: Bankruptcy and the Victorian Novel*. Lewisburg, Pa.: Bucknell University Press, pp. 88-109.

Analysis of bankruptcy as a "metaphor for the vulnerability of the individual." Links the loss of economic, social, sexual, and religious identity to the issues of bankruptcy in *The Mill on the Floss*.

59 WILLIAMS, RAYMOND. "Knowable Communities." In *George Eliot*. Edited by Harold Bloom. Modern Critical Views. New York: Chelsea House Publishers, pp. 81-97.

Presents reflections on the traditions of English country workers as represented in *Adam Bede* and *The Mill on the Floss*. Eliot presents social and economic relationships as elements that determine conduct. Eliot uses speech and language to connect her characters' upbringing and education. The author's development of a "knowable community" reflects on the values, both past and present, of that society. Reprint of 1973.70; see also 1977.51.

60 WOODFIELD, MALCOLM. "George Eliot and the Novel." In *R.H. Hutton, Critic and Theologian*. Oxford: Clarendon Press, pp. 152-84.

1986

Discusses R.H. Hutton's writings on George Eliot and George Henry Lewes; the importance of narrative and ethical fiction; Eliot and spiritual irony; her aesthetic and moral laws.

61 ZIM, RIVKAH. "Awakened Perceptions in *Daniel Deronda*." *Essays in Criticism* 36, no. 3 (July):210-34.
Studies the character Mirah as Eliot's attempt to assess the capacity of both emotion and thought. Parallels are drawn between the Judaic themes of *Daniel Deronda* and Eliot's essay "The Modern Hep! Hep! Hep!" (1879). Associates Eliot's use of the metaphors of light and vision with perception and understanding.

1987

1 AMALRIC, JEAN-CLAUDE. "The Opening of *Daniel Deronda*." *Cahiers victoriens & edouardiens* (Montpellier) 26 (October):111-19.
"In *Daniel Deronda*, George Eliot, setting off *in medias res*, offers a fascinating beginning, by showing the heroes of the two parts of the novel and by introducing some major themes which will be developed in the course of the narrative. In addition, some of the novelist's intentions concerning the type and technique of the novel, its rhythm and structure, can be inferred from the opening pages."

2 BEER, GILLIAN. "Circulatory Systems: Money and Gossip in *Middlemarch*." *Cahiers victoriens & edouardiens* (Montpellier) 26 (October):47-62.
"In *Middlemarch* the interconnections of money and gossip impel the plot and focus questions concerning value. Money and gossip are shown as systems of circulation. . . ."

3 BLAKE, KATHLEEN. "*Middlemarch* and the Woman Question." In *George Eliot's Middlemarch*. Modern Critical Interpretations, edited by Harold Bloom. New York, New Haven, and Edgemont, Pa.: Chelsea House Publishers, pp. 49-70.
Reprint of 1976.9.

4 BLOOM, HAROLD. Introduction to *George Eliot's Middlemarch*. Modern Critical Interpretations, edited by Harold Bloom. New York, New Haven, and Edgemont, Pa.: Chelsea House Publishers, pp. 1-7.

"Centers upon George Eliot as a prophet of the Moral Sublime and upon Dorothea Brooke as a heroine of the Protestant Will." Articles cited separately.

5   BOUMELHA, PENNY. "George Eliot and the End of Realism." In *Women Reading Women's Writing*. Edited by Sue Roe. New York: St. Martin's Press, pp. 15-35.

Discusses Eliot's use of a pseudonym and why the choice reflects on the relation between text and writer. Eliot's ambivalence regarding her choice of names has bearing on her double perspective endings. "The tension between the centrality of women in her fiction and her desire to stake a claim within the recognisable and respectable literary traditions and practices of her time will show the form of the novels under a pressure most clearly translated in their endings."

6   BRODY, SELMA B. "Physics in *Middlemarch*: Gas Molecules and Ethereal Atoms." *Modern Philology* 85, no. 1 (August):42-53.

Examines Eliot's method of presenting physical theories as metaphor. Includes a discussion of the kinetic theory of gases as a metaphor for society. Allusions to biology and geometry are also traced.

7   CARAES, COLETTE. "Du comique dans *Middlemarch*." *Cahiers victoriens & edouardiens* (Montpellier) 26 (October):63-76.

Chapters 6 and 84 of *Middlemarch* are examined in detail for the nature and role of comedy in the novel.

8   COCKS, NANCY M. "Illuminating the Vision of Ordinary Life: A Tribute to *Middlemarch*." *English Journal* 76, no. 3 (March):78-81.

Perceptions of the author's participation in a *Middlemarch* seminar at Drake University. Teaching methods for the novel are examined; themes from the novel include reform movements, nineteenth-century art and music, economic theory, theology, science, and politics.

9   COLLINS, K[ENNY] K[AYLE]. "Reading George Eliot Reading Lewes's Obituaries." *Modern Philology* 85, no. 2 (November):153-69.

A reading of Eliot's reading of Lewes's obituaries includes her commentaries. Essay argues that Eliot's comments explore the concepts of sincerity, sympathy, and self-reflection.

1987

10   COTTOM, DANIEL. *Social Figures: George Eliot, Social History and Literary Representation*. Vol. 44. Theory and History of Literature, edited by Wlad Godzich and Jochen Schulte-Sasse. Minneapolis: University of Minnesota Press, 259 pp.
     Examines the "uses of language in relation to those structurings of social life for which these uses constitute reality." Discourse is understood to be a construction of society. Discusses Eliot's role as author; education and Eliot's realism; the rhetoric of experience and its politics as it concerns the individual; how Eliot meant her work to be representative of moral example; the relation between "Eliot's conception of aesthetics . . . and of the liberal intellectual"; the concept of realism and the romance genre; "how Eliot's rhetoric is always utopian in nature, although tragic in tone and dramatic effect"; public/private duality; and Eliot's language of sympathy.

11   ESCURET, ANNIE. "The Lifted Veil," ou le scandale de la mémoire trouée." *Cahiers victoriens & edouardiens* (Montpellier) 26 (October):21-35.
     Examines fantastic and macabre elements of "The Lifted Veil" and the theme of moral progress. Categorizes Eliot as an agnostic positivist.

12   FENVES, PETER. "Exiling the Encyclopedia: The Individual in 'Janet's Repentence.'" *Nineteenth-Century Literature* 41, no. 4 (March):419-44.
     "Janet's Repentence" from *Scenes of Clerical Life*, and its movement "[demand] the suppression of the possibility of an encyclopedia as the public reservoir of information and universal history." Examines how this suppression will centralize the lawyer, Dempster, as the one who describes "social stratification as a prelude to victimization." The story "moves toward the elimination of history through its interiorization."

13   GORDON, JAN B. "Origins, *Middlemarch*, Endings: George Eliot's Crisis of the Antecedent." In *George Eliot's Middlemarch*. Modern Critical Interpretations, edited by Harold Bloom. New York, New Haven, and Edgemont, Pa.: Chelsea House Publishers, pp. 91-112.
     Reprint of 1980.30.

14   HARDY, BARBARA. "*Middlemarch*: Public and Private Worlds." In *George Eliot's Middlemarch*. Modern Critical Interpretations,

edited by Harold Bloom. New York, New Haven, and Edgemont, Pa.: Chelsea House Publishers, pp. 27-47.
Reprint of 1976.28.

15 _____. "The Relationship of Beginning and End in George Eliot's Fiction." *Cahiers victoriens & edouardiens* (Montpellier) 26 (October):7-19.
Discusses "beginning" and "ending" with reference to narrative mode, language, and thematic concept in all of Eliot's fiction.

16 HERTZ, NEIL. "Recognizing Casaubon." In *George Eliot's Middlemarch*. Modern Critical Interpretations, edited by Harold Bloom. New York, New Haven, and Edgemont, Pa.: Chelsea House Publishers, pp. 71-89.
Reprint of 1979.30.

17 HILL, JAMES. "George Eliot's *Middlemarch*." *Explicator* 45, no. 2 (Winter):26-27.
Analysis of the surgeon Tertius Lydgate, who is symbolic of the reforms in medicine in the nineteenth century. The conflicts between the medical doctors of the novel demonstrate Eliot's awareness of the traditional and innovative approaches to treatment in the history of medicine.

18 JUMEAU, ALAIN. "Le gentleman anglais dans *Daniel Deronda*: Critique d'un modèle artificiel." *Cahiers victoriens & edouardiens* (Montpellier) 26 (October):89-99.
Analysis of Eliot's criticism of the English upper class in her characterizations of Grandcourt and of Deronda.

19 KEARNS, MICHAEL S. "Toward the Life of the Mind: James and Eliot Discover Sentience." In *Metaphors of Mind in Fiction and Psychology*. Lexington: University Press of Kentucky, pp. 178-226.
"Eliot and James used new metaphors and renewed old metaphors to present the mental history of sentient beings. Eliot and James portrayed the operation of all identifiable forces – those external to the individual, those related to the association of ideas, and those which remain ultimately mysterious – within the field of sentient awareness. Their metaphors show that all forces have an immediate influence on that awareness and a longer-term, formative influence on the sense of self."

1987

20   KUCICH, JOHN. "George Eliot." In *Repression in Victorian Fiction: Charlotte Brontë, George Eliot, and Charles Dickens*. Berkeley: University of California Press, pp. 114-200.

Examines Eliot's "attempts to make her recommendations for social improvement incarnate in the desires and decisions of her central characters, particularly in their commitment to repression, and their replacement of selfish desires with a more impersonal 'sympathy.'" Discusses the religion of humanity, altruism, and love as self-negating desires, personal compensation in *Middlemarch*, and egotism as submission.

21   LACAPRA, DOMINICK. "In Quest of Casaubon: George Eliot's *Middlemarch*." In *History, Politics and the Novel*. Ithaca, N.Y., and London: Cornell University Press, pp. 56-82.

Appraises contemporary searches for the model for the character Casaubon of *Middlemarch*. Attempts to trace historical contexts for the character by citing references to Mark Pattison's biography *Isaac Casaubon, 1559-1614* (Oxford, 1892).

22   LEFKOVITZ, LORI HOPE. *The Character of Beauty in the Victorian Novel*. Nineteenth-Century Studies Series, edited by Juliet McMaster. Ann Arbor, Mich.: UMI Research Press, pp. 62-67, 101-8, 160-64, 167-69, 175-86.

Considers the element of beauty in characterizations in *Middlemarch*. Eliot begins the novel by setting up an opposition between nature and art. The symbolism of jewelry is examined. In *Adam Bede*, the images of beauty and delicacy are examined.

23   _____. "Delicate Beauty Goes Out: *Adam Bede*'s Transgressive Heroines." *Kenyon Review* 9, n.s. no. 3 (Summer):84-96.

This reading of *Adam Bede*'s characterization through its descriptions, traces Eliot's allusions to her heroine's beauty. Finds that the "neglect of language's power to negate woman through ambiguous idealizations of her image has resulted in critical failures to understand the meaning of woman's delicate health in the nineteenth century." In *Adam Bede*, Eliot presents both the aspect of delicate health and that of healthy delicacy.

24   McKEE, PATRICIA. "Power as Partiality in *Middlemarch*." In *George Eliot's Middlemarch*. Modern Critical Interpretations, edited

by Harold Bloom. New York, New Haven, and Edgemont, Pa.: Chelsea House Publishers, pp. 141-49.

Reprint of 1986.44.

25 MALCOLM, DAVID. "*The Mill on the Floss* and Contemporary Social Values: Tom Tulliver and Samuel Smiles." *Cahiers victoriens & edouardiens* (Montpellier) 26 (October):37-45.

Samuel Smiles's concepts of individualism and material success are examined in the character Tom Tulliver and the society of St. Ogg's.

26 MECKIER, JEROME. "'That Arduous Invention': *Middlemarch*." In *Hidden Rivalries in Victorian Fiction: Dickens, Realism, and Revaluation*. Lexington: University Press of Kentucky, pp. 201-42.

"*Middlemarch* reaffirmed Eliot's parodic treatment of *Bleak House*. . . ." *Middlemarch* makes a statement against social criticism that is not motivated by improvement. See also 1978.36.

27 _____. "The Victorian 'Multiverse': *Bleak House/Felix Holt*." In *Hidden Rivalries in Victorian Fiction: Dickens, Realism, and Revaluation*. Lexington: University Press of Kentucky, pp. 1-26.

Examines the authors' double purpose and rivalry in Dickens's *Bleak House* and Eliot's *Felix Holt, the Radical*. "George Eliot rewrites Dickens in order, she hopes, to erase him entirely." Eliot hoped to present a valid depiction of change in a changing social system. *Felix Holt, the Radical* confirms "the efficacy of parodic revaluation as a major factor in Victorian realism." See also 1983.47.

28 MILLER, J. HILLIS. "Optic and Semiotic in *Middlemarch*." In *George Eliot's Middlemarch*. Modern Critical Interpretations, edited by Harold Bloom. New York, New Haven, and Edgemont, Pa.: Chelsea House Publishers, pp. 9-25.

Reprint of 1975.62.

29 PATRICK, ANNE E. "Rosamond Rescued: George Eliot's Critique of Sexism in *Middlemarch*." *Journal of Religion* 67, no. 2 (April):220-38.

Argues that "*Middlemarch* contains a systematic critique of gender stereotyping, one that is integral to the action of the novel and central to its chief thematic concern. . . . Lydgate's tragedy is much more closely linked with his flawed perspective on women than most readers recognize and the narrator does not share the common opinion that the failure of the idealistic young doctor is due chiefly to the selfishness of his wife Rosamond Vincy."

30 PONS, XAVIER. *"Daniel Deronda*: A 'Silly Novel by a Lady Novelist'?" *Cahiers victoriens & edouardiens* (Montpellier) 26 (October):101-09.
    Finds elements of artificiality in the Jewish half of *Daniel Deronda* regarding characters, plot, themes, and language. Finds that the book resembles those Eliot criticized in her essay "Silly Novels by Lady Novelists."

31 SABISTON, ELIZABETH JEAN. "Dorothea Brooke: The Reluctant Aesthete." In *The Prison of Womanhood: Four Provincial Heroines in Nineteenth-Century Fiction*. New York: St. Martin's Press, pp. 81-113.
    Study of the characterization of *Middlemarch*'s Dorothea Brooke as an "example of the interaction of micro- and macrocosm, individual and society. . . . Dorothea's destiny is the structural, as well a spiritual, centre of the novel."

32 SAINT VICTOR, CAROLE de. "Acting and Action: Sexual Distinctions in *Daniel Deronda*." *Cahiers victoriens & edouardiens* (Montpellier) 26 (October):77-88.
    Focuses on Eliot's use of performance to explore male/female relationships. Scenes involving acting are the basis of the novel's theme–"the implications of make-believe in a relationship, the necessity of dissimulation, and the aesthetic and moral distinctions implicit in gender distinctions."

33 STOVEL, BRUCE. "Subjective to Objective: A Career Pattern in Jane Austen, George Eliot, and Contemporary Women Novelists." *Ariel* 18, no. 1 (January):53-61.
    Survey of the careers of Eliot, Jane Austen, Doris Lessing, Barbara Pym, and Margaret Drabble to demonstrate their change from subjective to objective fiction.

34 THOMAS, JEANIE [GAYLE]. *Reading Middlemarch: Reclaiming the Middle Distance*. Nineteenth-Century Studies Series, edited by Juliet McMaster. Ann Arbor, Mich.: UMI Research Press, 114 pp.
    Revision of author's thesis. See 1985.56.

1987

35 UGLOW, JENNIFER. *George Eliot.* New York: Pantheon Books; London: Virago Press, 273 pp.
    Feminist biography that explores Eliot's views on women and feminism. Examines Eliot's childhood and reflects on the conflicts in her life and novels.

36 WEISSMAN, JUDITH. "George Eliot: Women and World History." In *Half Savage and Hardy and Free: Women and Rural Radicalism in the Nineteenth-Century Novel.* Middletown, Conn.: Wesleyan University Press, pp. 164-88.
    "Emphasizes the meanings of the radical tradition of resistance for rural women." Examines Eliot's schemes of historical fiction and how she used "false radicalism to turn her back on rural England, on contemporary historical fact, and on women." Applies Eliot's theory of historical decay to *Middlemarch* and finds within the novel "biological pessimism and spiritual optimism, and her pervasive antifeminism."

37 WELSH, ALEXANDER. "Knowledge In *Middlemarch*." In *George Eliot's Middlemarch.* Modern Critical Interpretations, edited by Harold Bloom. New York, New Haven, and Edgemont, Pa.: Chelsea House Publishers, pp. 113-39.
    Reprint of 1985.60.

38 WILT, JUDITH. "'He Would Come Back': The Fathers of Daughters in *Daniel Deronda*." *Nineteenth-Century Literature* 42, no. 3 (December):313-38.
    Examines the theme of the search for origins and original sin in *Daniel Deronda* by following the lives of the female characters and their fathers. Correlates the uses of memory and fantasy to identity-originating.

Index of Primary Titles

Adam Bede, 1976.42; 1977.50;
    1978.16, 39; 1979.44; 1981.20
characterization in, 1972.13, 23,
    49, 52, 57; 1973.25, 45;
    1974.1, 15, 31, 54; 1975.16,
    37-38, 54; 1977.7, 9; 1978.26;
    1979.9, 20; 1981.3, 44;
    1982.4, 21; 1983.28, 30;
    1987.23
comparisons and influences of,
    1972.2, 21, 39; 1973.34, 42;
    1974.15, 68; 1975.56, 66;
    1977.24, 34; 1978.12;
    1979.25; 1980.38; 1981.7, 50;
    1983.28, 34; 1985.48
criticisms and reviews of,
    1972.19, 30, 56, 70; 1973.2, 7,
    51, 55; 1974.71, 75; 1975.1,
    85; 1976.38; 1978.23;
    1979.13; 1983.49; 1985.38;
    1986.35
plot structure of, 1984.19
themes of, 1972.12, 15, 18, 29;
    1973.6, 23, 31, 56, 59, 65, 70;
    1974.26, 30, 46, 52, 58, 61;
    1975.23, 52, 69; 1976.33-35,
    43; 1977.1, 7, 9, 19, 51, 57;
    1978.25, 30; 1979.2, 12, 19,

33-34, 43; 1984.19, 24, 48;
    1985.39, 45; 1986.55, 59;
    1987.22-23
"Armgart," 1973.44; 1980.11. *See
    also* Poetry

"Brother Jacob," 1972.58; 1981.22;
    1984.51; 1985.10, 13

Daniel Deronda, 1972.2; 1978.17;
    1979.21-22, 44; 1981.20;
    1982.10; 1985.58
characterization in, 1972.1, 13,
    38, 40, 43, 51, 57, 66; 1973.3,
    22, 25, 27, 47, 69; 1974.5, 15,
    54, 65-66, 73; 1975.16, 26, 51,
    54, 70, 78; 1976.12, 29, 41,
    54, 62; 1977.7, 9, 53; 1978.1,
    8, 50; 1979.2, 9, 20, 39-40,
    55; 1980.44, 53, 74; 1981.13,
    15, 52; 1982.43, 60, 63;
    1983.3, 22, 48; 1985.7, 42-43,
    49; 1986.10, 43; 1987.18, 30
comparisons and influences of,
    1972.27, 38; 1973.38, 62, 68-
    69; 1974.15, 44; 1975.14, 20,
    22, 40, 56, 66, 77; 1976.45,
    48, 54, 59; 1978.20, 31;

1979.25, 39-40, 59; 1981.15-
16; 1982.15, 70; 1983.4, 16,
48; 1984.45, 57; 1985.33;
1986.17, 45, 52
criticisms and reviews of,
1972.56; 1973.14, 51, 64;
1974.8, 17, 75; 1975.5-6, 55;
1976.53; 1978.23; 1981.8, 14;
1982.7; 1983.59
plot structure of, 1972.31;
1973.71; 1976.29; 1977.12;
1980.25; 1981.5; 1983.54;
1984.10; 1985.12; 1987.1, 30
themes of, 1972.11, 29, 40;
1973.13, 23, 29; 1974.26, 30,
49, 61, 63, 65-66, 73; 1975.12,
20, 69-70, 81; 1976.12, 17,
29-30, 39, 63; 1977.7, 9, 13,
32, 57; 1978.3, 18, 30, 37;
1979.23, 25, 32, 53, 57;
1980.29, 52, 72; 1981.10, 12,
19, 28, 46, 52, 63; 1982.15,
46, 60, 63, 73; 1983.2, 4, 9-
10, 13, 16, 25, 52; 1984.10,
22, 24, 29, 48-49, 56; 1985.5,
33, 42, 49, 60; 1986.4, 17, 21,
41-43, 45, 50-52, 61; 1987.1,
30, 32, 38

Essays, 1972.55; 1973.52; 1974.13,
40, 45; 1975.6, 42; 1976.8;
1977.40; 1978.15, 34; 1980.4,
7, 19, 64-65, 69; 1981.24, 42,
54; 1982.4, 26, 61, 65;
1984.42, 54; 1985.9, 15;
1986.21, 61; 1987.30

Felix Holt, the Radical, 1978.16;
1979.44; 1981.20
characterizations in, 1972.69;
1974.54; 1975.54, 70;
1976.58; 1977.9, 53; 1978.29;
1979.20; 1982.68; 1985.62

comparisons and influences of,
1973.11, 62; 1974.67-68;
1976.55; 1977.45; 1978.31;
1979.11-12; 1983.47; 1985.29,
46, 62; 1986.8, 36; 1987.27
criticisms and reviews of,
1972.17, 19; 1973.51;
1974.17; 1975.5, 25; 1980.24,
34
plot structure of, 1972.44;
1978.13; 1980.24; 1981.5;
1986.8
themes, 1972.7; 1974.13, 46, 49,
61; 1975.10, 23, 39, 70, 73;
1976.21; 1977.9, 27, 45;
1978.3, 29, 47; 1979.18, 43,
47, 62; 1980.13, 52, 66-67;
1981.10, 19; 1982.59, 67-69;
1983.13, 35, 47; 1984.48, 59;
1985.16, 21, 29, 45, 63;
1986.29, 50

"The Impressions of Theophrastus
Such," 1978.17, 46; 1980.64.
See also Essays

"Janet's Repentence," 1972.32, 58;
1973.51; 1974.52; 1976.33;
1980.13, 15; 1981.57;
1987.12. *See also Scenes of
Clerical Life*
Journals, 1974.27, 45; 1978.43. *See
also* Letters; Notebooks

"The Legend of Jubal," 1980.46;
1983.10; 1985.8. *See also*
Poetry
Letters, 1972.34; 1974.27; 1975.8-
9, 16, 42; 1976.15-16, 23, 26,
50; 1977.8, 10, 13; 1978.16-
17, 32, 43; 1979.33; 1980.20;
1981.10; 1982.26, 65;
1983.35; 1984.13; 1985.3, 14;

characterizations in, 1972.33,
51, 57; 1973.25, 43, 61;
1974.14-15, 20, 50, 55;
1975.4, 16, 26, 29-30, 51, 53-
54, 71, 78, 83; 1976.58;
1977.7, 9, 15; 1978.9, 48;
1979.1, 9-10, 39, 56; 1980.61;
1981.43, 51; 1983.27-28, 32,
40, 50; 1984.9, 12, 37, 43, 50;
1985.7, 17; 1986.1, 57;
1987.25
comparisons and influences of,
1972.21, 27; 1973.9, 61, 68;
1974.10, 14-15, 22, 34, 68;
1975.29, 66; 1976.47, 64;
1977.25; 1978.31; 1979.25,
39, 42, 51; 1980.31, 57;
1981.26, 29, 49, 60; 1982.40,
42; 1983.16, 24, 27-28, 32;
1984.18, 26, 46, 57; 1985.11,
17, 20, 23, 34, 44, 50;
1986.27, 33, 49; 1987.25
criticisms and reviews of,
1972.19, 30, 54, 56, 58;
1973.16, 30, 51, 55; 1974.71,
75; 1977.11; 1978.23;
1980.22, 45, 47; 1985.38
plot structure of, 1981.5
themes of, 1972.12, 15, 18, 29,
48; 1973.5, 9, 23, 59, 65;
1974.4, 6, 26, 59, 61, 64;
1975.35, 57, 83; 1976.13, 21,
34, 60; 1977.7, 9, 13, 51;
1978.25, 30, 38, 42, 47;
1979.10, 23, 25, 35, 37, 54,
56; 1980.36, 40; 1981.2, 6, 19,
26, 28-29; 1982.1, 18, 30, 40,
49, 72; 1983.2, 12, 16, 24-25,
36, 50; 1984.18, 24, 26, 37,
47-48, 50, 55-56, 59; 1985.1,
13, 20, 23, 44-45, 50; 1986.1,
11, 29, 30, 33, 58-59

"The Modern Hep! Hep! Hep!,"
1975.6; 1986.61. *See also*
Essays
"Mr.Gilfil's Love Story," 1972.32,
58; 1973.51; 1976.13. *See
also Scenes of Clerical Life*

"The Natural History of German
Life," 1972.55. *See also*
Essays
Notebooks, 1975.7; 1976.5;
1979.19; 1980.8; 1981.10, 18,
61; 1982.66; 1984.10. *See
also* Journals; Letters

"O May I Join the Choir
Invisible," 1982.71. *See also*
Poetry

Poetry, 1973.44; 1974.60; 1975.72;
1976.8; 1977.49; 1978.16;
1980.11, 46; 1981.39, 61;
1982.26, 61, 71; 1983.10, 45,
51; 1984.32; 1985.8. *See also*
"Armgart"; "The Legend of
Jubal"; "O May I Join the
Choir Invisible"; "The
Spanish Gypsy"

Romola, 1977.39; 1978.16; 1979.8,
44, 60; 1981.20; 1982.2;
1985.58
characterization in, 1972.64;
1973.20, 47; 1975.19, 70;
1977.53; 1978.6; 1979.9;
1980.55; 1983.51; 1985.57;
1986.31
comparisons and influences of,
1973.36, 38, 66; 1974.68;
1975.14; 1976.10; 1978.40;
1982.47; 1983.63; 1985.57;
1986.19

criticisms and reviews of,
1972.19, 30, 59; 1973.14, 38;
1974.17; 1975.5, 61; 1980.34
themes of, 1972.18; 1973.23, 51;
1974.26, 61, 69; 1975.70, 73;
1976.13, 21, 33; 1980.13, 17,
26, 52, 72; 1981.10, 23, 28;
1982.59, 67, 73; 1983.10, 25;
1984.2, 41, 48; 1985.6, 16, 24,
45, 60-61; 1986.19

"The Sad Fortunes of the Rev.
Amos Barton," 1972.32, 58;
1973.51; 1974.52; 1982.67.
*See also Scenes of Clerical
Life*
Scenes of Clerical Life, 1980.39;
1985.37
characterization in, 1973.20, 25,
45; 1974.54; 1976.58; 1977.52
comparisons and influences of,
1974.68; 1981.57; 1986.37
criticisms and reviews of,
1972.19, 32, 48, 58; 1973.41,
51, 55; 1981.9; 1986.35
plot structure of, 1984.19
themes of, 1972.48; 1973.23, 41;
1974.11, 13, 52; 1975.59;
1976.13, 33, 35; 1977.1;
1979.25, 37; 1980.13, 15;
1981.22; 1983.12; 1984.19;
1987.12. *See also* "Janet's
Repentence"; "Mr.Gilfil's
Love Story"; "The Sad
Fortunes of the Rev. Amos
Barton"
Silas Marner, 1978.16; 1979.44;
1983.39

autobiographical elements of,
1979.17
characterization in, 1972.50;
1973.20; 1974.51; 1975.3, 30,
78; 1981.43; 1983.14, 18, 28,
56
comparisons and influences of,
1972.21; 1973.34, 68;
1974.51, 68; 1976.20;
1977.25; 1983.28, 56;
1985.23; 1986.34
criticisms and reviews of,
1972.48, 56, 58; 1973.55;
1976.53; 1977.11; 1980.34
plot structure of, 1978.13;
1981.5
themes of, 1972.12, 15, 29;
1973.65; 1974.4, 33; 1975.35;
1976.21, 34; 1977.21;
1978.42; 1980.58, 72;
1981.46; 1982.36, 67; 1983.2,
12, 33, 38; 1984.48, 55;
1985.13, 16, 23, 61, 63;
1986.29, 54
"Silly Novels by Lady Novelists,"
1977.40; 1981.42; 1982.4;
1987.30. *See also* Essays
"The Spanish Gypsy," 1973.44;
1978.16, 31; 1980.55;
1981.20, 54; 1983.45, 51;
1985.8. *See also* Poetry

Translations, 1972.63; 1974.60;
1976.7; 1978.3; 1980.5-6;
1981.24; 1982.16; 1985.15

Index of Authors

Abel, Elizabeth, 1982.21, 40;
    1983.32, 58
Adam, Ian, 1975.1-2, 13, 21, 33,
    34, 47; 1982.1
Adams, Harriet Farwell, 1984.1
Adams, Kathleen, 1972.28; 1976.1;
    1980.1
Aiken, Ralph, 1980.2
Allen, Walter, 1986.1
Alley, Henry, 1972.1; 1978.1;
    1979.1-3; 1984.2
Altholz, Josef, 1976.38
Altick, Richard D., 1973.1; 1978.2
Amalric, Jean-Claude, 1987.1
Anderson, Roland F., 1973.2;
    1982.2
Androne, Mary Jane Petersen,
    1977.1
apRoberts, Ruth, 1982.3
Arac, Jonathan, 1979.4
Argyle, Gisela, 1976.1; 1977.2
Ashton, Rosemary D., 1979.5;
    1980.3-7; 1983.1-2
Atkins, Dorothy J., 1977.3; 1978.3
Atkins, G. Douglas, 1985.34
Auerbach, Emily, 1983.3
Auerbach, Nina, 1975.3, 4; 1978.4,
    5; 1982.4; 1985.1-2

Austen, Zelda, 1976.3
Auster, Henry, 1975.5

Baker, Tracey Alison, 1984.3
Baker, William, 1972.2; 1973.3;
    1975.6-9; 1976.4; 1976.5;
    1980.8; 1981.1; 1982.6-7
Bamber, Linda, 1975.10
Barker, Francis, 1977.45
Barolini, Helen, 1972.3
Barrett, Michèle, 1979.61
Barton, Robert E., 1973.4
Basch, Françoise, 1974.1
Bates, Richard, 1984.4
Baumgarten, Murray, 1975.11
Beaty, Jerome, 1974.2; 1976.6;
    1980.9
Bedick, David R., 1975.12
Bedient, Calvin, 1972.4-8
Beer, Gillian, 1975.13; 1979.6;
    1980.10; 1983.4; 1987.2
Beer, Patricia, 1974.3
Beeton, D.R., 1976.7-8; 1977.4
Beeton, Ridley, 1975.14
Belcher, Susan, 1972.47
Bell, Brenda Joyce Harrison,
    1974.4
Bellringer, Alan W., 1979.7

Index of Secondary Titles

"Empty Constructions: Women and Romance in the English Novel," 1985.32

The End of the Line: Essays on Psychoanalysis and the Sublime, 1985.28

"The Engaging Narrator: Gaskell, Stowe, Eliot, and 'You,'" 1982.38

Der Englische Roman im 19, Jahrhunudert: Interpretationen zu Ehren von Horst Oppel, 1973.7

"English and Italian Portraiture in *Daniel Deronda*," 1976.62

English Fiction of the Victorian Period, 1830-1890, 1985.61

The English Middle-Class Novel, 1976.54-56

The English Novel: Defoe to the Victorians, 1977.41

The English Novel from Dickens to Lawrence, 1984.59

The English Novel in the Nineteenth-Century: Essays on the Literary Mediation of Human Values, 1972.15, 31

The English Novel: Select Bibliographical Guides, 1974.2

"English Novels of the Eighteen-Seventies," 1975.55

"English Realism: George Eliot and the Pre-Raphaelites," 1974.47

English Romanticism and the French Tradition, 1976.49

"Eric and Janet: Two Studies in Repentence," 1977.52

Eros and Psyche: The Representation of Personality in Charlotte Brontë, Charles Dickens, and George Eliot, 1984.11

Essays and Studies, 1975.50; 1984.5

"The Ethos of Work in Nineteenth Century Literature," 1974.46

Everywhere Spoken Against: Dissent in the Victorian Novel, 1975.23

"Evil and Eliot's Religion of Humanity: Grandcourt in *Daniel Deronda*," 1980.44

"Evolution and Revolution: Politics and Form in *Felix Holt* and *The Revolution in Tanner's Lane*," 1977.45

"Evolution and the Mother in the Novels of George Eliot," 1982.59

"The Evolution of Nineteenth-Century Tragic Literature," 1984.43

The Evolving Consciousness: An Hegelian Reading of the Novels of George Eliot, 1982.62

"Exiling the Encyclopedia: The Individual in 'Janet's Repentence,'" 1987.12

"Experimental Method and the Epistemology of *Middlemarch*," 1976.14

"Failure of Design in *The Mill on the Floss*," 1973.30

"The Failure of Realism: *Felix Holt*," 1980.24

"Fairy Tale or Science? Physiological Psychology in *Silas Marner*," 1986.54

Time and English Fiction,
1977.19
"Time and Typology in George
Eliot's Early Fiction,"
1976.35
"To Hear Her Voice: Artifice
in George Eliot's Novels,"
1984.23
"Tolstoj's Reading of George
Eliot: Visions and
Revisions," 1983.35
*Toward a Recognition of
Androgyny,* 1973.29
"Toward a Theory of the
Engaging Narrator: Earnest
Interventions in Gaskell,
Stowe, and Eliot," 1986.56
"Toward *Middlemarch*: The
Heroine's Search for
Guidance as Motif in the
Earlier Novels of George
Eliot," 1974.69
Towards a Poetics of Fiction,
1977.51
"Toward the Life of the Mind:
James and Eliot Discover
Sentience," 1987.19
"Tragedy and Parable in
George Eliot's Novels,"
1981.5
"Tragedy in George Eliot and
Thomas Hardy," 1972.27
*Tragedy in the Victorian Novel:
Theory and Practice in the
Novels of George Eliot,
Thomas Hardy, and Henry
James,* 1978.31
"Transfigurations," 1985.18
"Transformation: Deliverance
or Death, Structure and
Theme of George Eliot's
Daniel Deronda,"* 1976.17

"Transformations: Fairy Tales,
Adolescence, and the Novel
of Female Development in
Victorian Fiction," 1985.44
"Transitions," 1984.50
"'A Transmutation of Self':
George Eliot and the Music
of Narrative," 1985.22
"The Treatment of Community
in the Novels of George
Eliot," 1972.68
*The Triptych and the Cross: The
Central Myths of George
Eliot's Poetic Imagination,*
1979.8
*The Triumph of Wit: A Study in
Victorian Comic Theory,*
1974.40
"The Truer Message: Setting in
Emma, Middlemarch, and
Howard's End," 1977.23
*True Story of George Eliot in
Relation to Adam Bede,
Giving the Real Life History
of the More Prominent
Characters,* 1972.52
"The Turn of George Eliot's
Realism," 1980.45
"Two Confectioners the
Reverse of Sweet: The Role
of Metaphor in Determining
George Eliot's Use of
Experience," 1984.51
"Two Crises of Decision in
Jane Eyre," 1976.64
"The Two Georges," 1977.46
"The Two Rhetorics: George
Eliot's Bestiary," 1985.34
"Two Staunch Walkers: Tom
Thurnall and Tom Tulliver,"
1978.25
"Two Velvet Peaches," 1983.2

Index of Subjects

Aeschylus, myth of, 1980.37
after-history, use of, 1981.59
Agee, James, 1974.12
Alice; or, The Mysteries (Bulwer-
　　Lytton) 1981.50
allegory, use of, 1982.46
allusion, use of, 1979.58; 1983.52;
　　1985.1
The Ambassadors (James),
　　1976.37
An American Tragedy (Dreiser),
　　1976.59
Anatomy of Criticism (Frye),
　　1978.12
Anna Karenina (Tolstoy), 1977.14
Antigone (Euripides), 1981.32
*Antique Gems: Their Origin, Uses
　　and Values as Interpreters of
　　Ancient History* (King),
　　1982.73
Ariadne, myth of, 1973.60; 1982.75
Aristotle, 1983.56
Arnold, Matthew, 1973.4; 1981.32;
　　1982.17; 1985.21
art and artists, 1972.18, 64-65;
　　1973.1, 22; 1974.37, 47;
　　1975.51; 1976.62; 1977.39;
　　1978.19-20; 1979.15, 34, 60;

1980.11, 19, 49, 57; 1982.21,
　　26, 75; 1983.43, 45; 1984.7,
　　32, 54; 1985.22, 63; 1986.51,
　　53; 1987.22
Austen, Jane, 1972.24, 36; 1973.35,
　　41, 53; 1974.3, 16; 1975.29,
　　60; 1976.24, 46; 1977.22-23,
　　33, 54; 1978.4; 1980.72;
　　1981.48; 1982.42; 1983.7-8;
　　1984.3; 1985.50; 1987.33
autobiographical elements,
　　1972.54; 1978.33; 1979.17;
　　1980.75; 1983.20; 1985.54;
　　1986.1, 38, 40
"Autobiography of a Shirt-Maker"
　　(Simcox), 1978.35
The Awakening (Chopin), 1983.58

Bakhtin, M.M., 1985.14
Balzac, Honoré de, 1976.32
Bennett, Agnes Maria, 1980.23
Bentham, Jeremy, 1972.37
Bernstein, Aaron David, 1976.41
bibliographies, 1974.2; 1977.4, 16;
　　1978.32; 1979.44; 1980.9, 35;
　　1981.1
bildungsroman, 1973.5, 17, 43;
　　1974.6, 12; 1980.34; 1981.2,

Little Dorrit (Dickens), 1974.22;
  1979.27; 1983.37; 1986.5
Locke, John, 1981.18
Lord Jim (Conrad), 1975.14, 20;
  1987.57

Mackay, Robert William, 1973.18
Madame Bovary (Flaubert),
  1972.35; 1974.56; 1976.49;
  1977.17; 1980.57; 1983.58
Mahfūz, Najīb, 1979.28
male-female relationship, 1972.26;
  1973.27; 1974.25, 74;
  1976.54; 1978.14; 1979.25;
  1982.54-55; 1983.34; 1984.57;
  1985.62; 1986.27, 30, 47, 49;
  1987.32
Mansfield, Katherine, 1980.62
Mansfield Park (Austen), 1976.24;
  1985.50
Marcella (Ward), 1983.16
marriage, 1972.41-42, 49; 1974.15;
  1975.60; 1976.9, 12; 1977.6,
  55; 1978.47; 1979.2, 23, 48,
  55; 1980.52; 1982.54, 75;
  1983.6; 1984.1, 29, 33, 58;
  1985.5, 17, 19, 29
Martineau, Harriet, 1974.7
Mary Barton (Gaskell), 1974.67;
  1976.55; 1985.62
Maslow, Abraham, 1974.50
The Master of Ballantrae
  (Stevenson), 1975.22
The Mayor of Casterbridge
  (Hardy), 1975.56; 1981.30,
  36; 1983.34; 1984.44
Medea, myth of, 1972.38; 1973.69
meditation, 1972.36; 1973.27;
  1977.43; 1982.64
melodrama, elements of, 1979.21;
  1980.36; 1985.52
Melville, Herman, 1985.50

memory, 1972.1, 15, 21; 1974.41;
  1975.35; 1977.15; 1979.15;
  1980.31, 40; 1981.53;
  1982.41, 64; 1983.17, 19;
  1985.38; 1986.54; 1987.38
Mendel Gibbor (Bernstein),
  1976.41
Meredith, George, 1972.36;
  1974.14, 36, 40; 1975.84;
  1976.22; 1977.2; 1979.46;
  1982.15; 1986.22
mesmerism, 1982.20
metaphor, use of, 1973.66;
  1974.57; 1975.45, 56; 1977.6-
  7, 43, 57; 1978.21, 44;
  1980.10, 15, 46; 1981.15, 46;
  1982.13, 51, 56, 60; 1983.8,
  48, 56; 1984.8, 42, 50-51;
  1985.6, 59; 1986.48, 61;
  1987.6, 19
Methodism, 1983.43. *See also*
  religion
"Michael" (Wordsworth), 1977.25
Midrash, 1977.32
Mill, John Stuart, 1972.37;
  1975.40; 1985.27
Milton, John, 1986.3
Miss Marjoribanks (Oliphant),
  1974.7
modernism, 1972.43; 1973.14;
  1975.5; 1979.28
Modern Painters (Ruskin), 1981.17
moral issues, 1972.7, 21, 45;
  1973.10; 1974.38; 1975.17,
  35; 1976.59; 1977.3, 26, 28,
  38; 1978.11, 38, 47; 1980.29,
  52, 59, 64; 1981.16, 21;
  1982.18, 62, 77; 1983.12, 53,
  59; 1984.57, 59; 1985.15, 39;
  1986.4, 19, 50, 60; 1987.10-11
motherhood, 1978.4; 1979.49;
  1980.11, 60, 75; 1982.59;
  1983.33, 46; 1985.23; 1986.47

The Physical Basis of the Mind
(Lewes), 1975.81
physiological psychology, 1978.25;
1986.54
Pierre; or The Ambiguities
(Melville), 1985.50
Pilgrim's Progress (Bunyan),
1980.33; 1984.39
plot structure, 1972.31, 40;
1973.11, 30, 71; 1974.35, 59;
1976.29; 1977.12, 14, 51;
1978.8, 13; 1979.6, 51;
1980.25, 50; 1981.5, 49;
1982.37, 42; 1983.18, 44;
1984.15, 19; 1985.12; 1986.8;
1987.1, 30
poetic justice, use of, 1972.45, 48;
1986.29
Pomis, David de, 1982.76
The Portrait of a Lady (James),
1973.38; 1975.24; 1977.20;
1983.37; 1986.17
Positivism, 1972.60; 1975.19;
1980.68; 1981.63; 1984.36;
1987.11. *See also* Comte,
Auguste
Pride and Prejudice (Austen),
1973.35
La Princesse de Clèves
(Lafayette), 1981.49
Problems of Life and Mind
(Lewes), 1978.11
Proust, Marcel, 1974.41; 1984.35
provincialism, 1974.7; 1979.7, 10;
1981.6; 1983.1, 28
pseudonym, use of a, 1974.25;
1975.74; 1977.44; 1980.28;
1981.62; 1985.54; 1987.5
psychological novel, 1972.56;
1977.24; 1978.44; 1979.9;
1982.41; 1983.59
psychology, 1975.5, 69, 81;
1976.34; 1977.6; 1985.49

publication information, 1972.34;
1973.2; 1974.27; 1975.55, 80;
1976.8, 52; 1979.14, 19;
1980.8, 32, 66, 71; 1981.18,
20, 58; 1982.2; 1983.15, 60-
61; 1984.22; 1985.37, 58;
1986.7, 14
Pym, Barbara, 1987.33

Quarles, Francis, 1972.39

Radcliffe, Ann, 1984.52
reader, 1977.42-43; 1978.23, 44
character as, 1981.41; 1980.57;
1982.69; 1986.49
created, 1974.68; 1975.30
role of the, 1981.9, 59
realism, 1972.6, 12, 40-41, 55, 67,
70; 1973.14, 19, 51, 62;
1974.11, 37, 47, 59, 70-71;
1975.1, 5, 11, 47, 76, 86;
1976.32, 38, 44; 1977.21, 24,
27; 1978.14, 26, 31, 39, 41,
45; 1979.4, 16, 21, 46;
1980.14, 24, 36, 42, 45;
1981.16-17, 27, 33, 36;
1982.14, 31, 44, 46, 51;
1983.1, 13, 53; 1984.6, 11;
1985.13, 33, 41, 52; 1986.42,
50, 52; 1987.10
à la recherche du temps perdu
(Proust), 1984.35
regionalism, as genre, 1986.37, 59
religion, 1972.37; 1973.1, 4, 6, 41,
65; 1974.26, 66; 1975.23, 41;
1976.33, 53; 1977.6, 28, 52,
55; 1979.33, 43; 1980.13, 16,
67; 1981.6, 24, 33; 1982.30;
1983.32, 43; 1984.43, 61;
1985.5, 27, 40-41, 59; 1986.6
religion of humanity, 1976.22, 40;
1980.6, 44, 68; 1982.3;

social reform, 1973.13, 64;
1975.10, 39, 64; 1976.51;
1980.19, 66-67; 1983.8;
1984.20; 1985.5, 9, 19;
1987.8, 20
society, 1972.8-9, 42, 69; 1974.61;
1976.56; 1979.28; 1980.58;
1983.8, 39; 1984.30, 49;
1985.63. *See also* community
Sons and Lovers (Lawrence),
1975.56; 1983.8, 34
The Sound and the Fury
(Faulkner), 1973.9
speech-act theory, 1983.49
Spence, Catherine, 1986.2
Spencer, Herbert, 1972.47;
1973.18, 51; 1975.8-9;
1976.50; 1978.16-17; 1980.1,
18; 1982.59; 1983.41
Spinoza, Benedict de, 1975.6;
1976.34; 1977.3; 1978.3;
1979.5; 1980.6; 1982.16;
1985.15
Staël, Madame de, 1975.66;
1976.45
Stafford, Jean, 1981.60
Stendhal, 1977.33; 1981.48
Stephen, Leslie, 1974.40
Stevenson, Robert Louis, 1975.22;
1986.22
La Storia di Girolamo Savonarola
(Villari), 1972.59
Stowe, Harriet Beecher, 1974.39;
1979.25; 1982.38; 1986.56
Strauss, David Friedrich, 1975.6;
1976.7; 1979.5, 57; 1980.5;
1981.24, 33
The Study of Sociology (Spencer),
1980.18
Summer (Wharton), 1985.23
The Summer Before the Dark
(Lessing), 1979.39

Suspiria de Profundis (De
Quincey), 1985.18
Sybil (Disraeli), 1974.67; 1976.55;
1984.13; 1985.62
symbolism, 1972.16; 1973.32, 47;
1974.11; 1975.53; 1978.31;
1979.8, 27; 1981.3, 12, 60;
1982.35, 42; 1983.36-37;
1984.2; 1985.63
of bankruptcy, 1986.58
of the Bible, 1975.41; 1982.69
of bibliomancy, 1973.31
characters as, 1972.67
of the child, 1974.4
of dance, 1972.24
of enclosure, 1973.35
of the flood, 1975.57
German, 1977.2
of the harvest, 1972.51
of hunger, 1975.4
of jewelry, 1977.57; 1987.22
of nature, 1975.36-37
of science, 1975.31
of sortilège, 1974.33
of the theatre, 1974.8; 1986.45;
1987.32
of time, 1977.19
of vision, 1972.30. *See also*
imagery; theme
sympathy, 1972.41, 51, 55; 1973.9,
40; 1974.11, 32, 36; 1975.13,
15; 1977.56; 1978.33;
1979.47; 1980.4, 67; 1981.19,
27, 33; 1982.33; 1985.16, 56;
1986.12, 45, 50; 1987.9-10, 20

A Tale of Two Cities (Dickens),
1982.47
Talmud, 1977.32
Tennyson, Alfred, Lord, 1974.36
Thackeray, William Makepeace,
1972.45; 1973.5, 10; 1974.68;